Sunset

BEST HOME PLANS

Vacation Homes

Weekend hideaway turns a scant 535 square feet of living space into a cozy, highly functional retreat. See plan H-968-1A on page 53.

Sunset Publishing Corporation ■ **Menlo Park, California**

SUNSET BOOKS

Vice President, Sales & Marketing:
Richard A. Smeby

Editorial Director:
Bob Doyle

Production Director:
Lory Day

Contributing Editor:
Don Vandervort

Photographers: Karl Bischoff: 4 bottom; Mark Englund: 5 bottom; Philip Harvey: 10 top, back cover; HomeStyles Publishing: 5 top left; Stephen Marley: 11 top left and right; Pam Nobles: 5 top right; Russ Widstrand: 10 bottom; Tom Wyatt: 11 bottom.

Fifth printing June 1998

A Dream Come True

Planning and building a house is one of life's most creative and rewarding challenges. Whether you're seriously considering building a new home or you're just dreaming about it, this book offers a wealth of inspiration and information to help you get started.

On the following pages, you'll learn how to plan and manage a home-building project—and how to ensure its success. Then you'll discover more than 200 proven home plans, designed for families just like yours by architects and professional designers. Peruse the pages and study the floor plans; you're sure to find a home that's just right for you. When you're ready to order blueprints, you can simply call or mail in your order, and you'll receive the plans within days.

Enjoy the adventure!

Focused on a view, this open-plan home features vaulted ceilings, a 5-foot-wide fireplace, and a generous wraparound deck. See plans H-855-1 and -1A on page 49.

Contents

The Great Escape

Escape—that's what vacation homes offer. Whether nestled in a stand of pines, edging a mountain lake, or basking in the desert sun, a vacation home provides a retreat from hectic city life. For many people, nature's attraction is so great that they spend nearly as much time in their vacation home as in their city home. For some, it eventually becomes a permanent residence.

Most of today's vacation homes are not very different from primary residences. Although they may be smaller in scale and highly space efficient, they usually offer the same construction and many of the same amenities. Perhaps the biggest difference is in appearance—vacation homes often look more rustic, blending into natural settings. And many are designed to cope with harsh weather, unusual sites, difficult access during construction, and fewer available conventional utilities.

The two keys to success in building a vacation home are capable project management and good design. The next few pages will walk you through some of the most important aspects of project management: you'll find an overview of the building process, directions for selecting the right plan and getting the most from it, and methods for successfully working with a builder and other professionals.

The balance of the book presents professionally designed stock plans for vacation homes in a wide range of styles and configurations. Even if you're just dreaming about building a vacation home, you'll enjoy browsing through the hundreds of wonderful choices. Once you find a plan that will work for you—perhaps with a few modifications made later to personalize it for your family—you can order construction blueprints for a fraction of the cost of a custom design, a savings of many thousands of dollars (see pages 12–15 for information on how to order).

Octagonal plan favors every bedroom and living space with a spectacular view. See plans H-942-1/1A and -2/2A on page 52.

Compact vacation home features a simple rectangular plan and an open living/dining area with a glazed solar-collection corner. See plans H-951-1A and -1B on page 26.

Although it contains only 1,188 square feet of living space, this recreation home is built on three levels—a basement and garage at the bottom, living areas and bedrooms above, and a master bedroom on the top floor. See plan H-863-2 on page 80.

For vacations or full-time living, this four-bedroom contemporary has all the amenities of home and more! See plans P-7627-4A and -4D on page 216.

The Art of Building

As you embark on your home-building project, think of it as a trip—clearly not a vacation but rather an interesting, adventurous, at times difficult expedition. Meticulous planning will make your journey not only far more enjoyable but also much more successful. By careful planning, you can avoid—or at least minimize—some of the pitfalls along the way.

Start with realistic expectations of the road ahead. To do this, you'll want to gain an understanding of the basic house-building process, settle on a design that will work for you and your family, and make sure your project is actually doable. By taking those initial steps, you can gain a clear idea of how much time, money, and energy you'll need to invest to make your dream come true.

The Building Process

Your role in planning and managing a house-building project can be divided into two parts: prebuilding preparation and construction management.

■ **Prebuilding preparation.** This is where you should focus most of your attention. In the hands of a qualified contractor whose expertise you can rely on, the actual building process should go fairly smoothly. But during most of the prebuilding stage, you're generally on your own. Your job will be to launch the project and develop a talented team that can help you bring your new home to fruition.

When you work with stock plans, the prebuilding process usually goes as follows:

First, you research the general area where you want to build, selecting one or more possible home sites (unless you already own a suitable lot). Then you choose a basic house design, with the idea that it may require some modification. Finally, you analyze the site, the design, and your budget to determine if the project is actually attainable.

If you decide that it is, you purchase the land and order blueprints. If you want to modify them, you consult an architect, designer, or contractor. Once the plans are finalized, you request bids from contractors and arrange any necessary construction financing.

After selecting a builder and signing a contract, you (or your contractor) then file the plans with the building department. When the plans are approved, often several weeks—or even months—later, you're ready to begin construction.

■ **Construction management.** Unless you intend to act as your own contractor, your role during the building process is mostly one of quality control and time management. Even so, it's important to know the sequence of events and something about construction methods so you can discuss progress with your builder and prepare for any important decisions you may need to make along the way.

Decision-making is critical. Once construction begins, the builder must usually plunge ahead, keeping his carpenters and subcontractors progressing steadily. If you haven't made a key decision—which model bathtub or sink to install, for example—it can bring construction to a frustrating and expensive halt.

Usually, you'll make such decisions before the onset of building, but, inevitably, some issue or another will arise during construction. Being knowledgeable about the building process will help you anticipate and circumvent potential logjams.

Selecting a House Plan

Searching for the right plan can be a fun, interactive family experience—one of the most exciting parts of a house-building project. Gather the family around as you peruse the home plans in this book. Study the size, location, and configuration of each room; traffic patterns both inside the house and to the outdoors; exterior style; and how you'll use the available space. Discuss the pros and cons of the various plans.

Look at pictures of homes in magazines to stimulate ideas. Clip photos you like so you can think about your favorite options. When you visit the homes of friends, note special features that appeal to you. Also, look carefully at the homes in your neighborhood, noting their style and how they fit the site.

Mark those plans that most closely suit your ideals. Then, to narrow down your choices, critique each plan, using the following information as a guide.

■ **Overall size and budget.** How large a house do you want? Will the house you're considering fit your family's requirements? Look at the overall square footage and room sizes. If you have a hard time visualizing room sizes, measure some of the rooms in your present home and compare.

It's often better for the house to be a little too big than a little too small, but remember that every extra square foot will cost more money to build and maintain.

■ **Number and type of rooms.** Beyond thinking about the number of bedrooms and baths in a house, consider your family's life-style and how you use space. Do you want individual bedrooms or a large, dormitory-style room? Will one large great room suffice or do you want a separate living room, dining room, and kitchen? Would you like lots of windows to capture nature's beauty?

■ **Room placement and traffic patterns.** What are your preferences for locations of master bedroom and children's rooms? Do you prefer a kitchen that's open to family areas or private and out of the way? Is it important to have easy access to the outdoors?

Once you make those determinations, look carefully at the floor plan of the house you're considering to see if it meets your needs and if the traffic flow will be convenient for your family.

■ **Architectural style.** With a vacation home, especially one that's tucked away in a picturesque spot, it's particularly important that the style of the home be in harmony with its surroundings. Moreover, climatic conditions may make certain demands on style, such as a roof designed for snow in a heavy snowfall area. Be sure to choose a style that's appropriate for the location.

■ **Site considerations.** Most people choose a site before selecting a plan—or at least they've zeroed in on the type of land where they'll situate their house. It sounds elementary, but choose a house that will fit the site. Survey the site to clarify boundaries, if needed.

When figuring the "footprint" of a house, you must know about any restrictions that will affect your home's height or proximity to the property lines. Call the local building department (look under county listings in the phone book) and get a description of any restrictions, such as setbacks, height limits, and lot coverage, that will affect what you can build (see "Working with City Hall," at right).

When you visit potential sites, note trees, rock outcroppings, slopes, views, prevailing winds, direction of sun, and other similar factors. All will have an impact on how your house works on a particular site. Also, check for available utilities.

Once you've narrowed down the choice of sites, consult an architect or building designer (see page 8) to help you evaluate how some potential houses will work on the sites you have in mind.

Is Your Project Doable?

Before you purchase land, make sure your project is doable. Although it's too early at this stage to pinpoint costs, making a few phone calls will help you determine whether your project is realistic. You'll be able to learn if you can afford to build the house, how long it will take, and what obstacles may stand in your way.

To get a ballpark estimate of cost, multiply a house's total

Working with City Hall

For any building project, even a minor one, it's essential to be familiar with building codes and other restrictions that can affect your project.

■ **Building codes,** generally implemented by the city or county building department, set the standards for safe, lasting construction. Codes specify minimum construction techniques and materials for foundations, framing, electrical wiring, plumbing, insulation, and all other aspects of a building. Although codes are adopted and enforced locally, most regional codes conform to the standards set by the national Uniform Building Code, Standard Building Code, or Basic Building Code. In some cases, local codes set more restrictive standards than national ones.

■ **Building permits** are required for home-building projects nearly everywhere. If you work with a contractor, the builder's firm should handle all necessary permits.

More than one permit may be needed; for example, one will cover the foundation, another the electrical wiring, and still another the heating equipment installation. Each will probably involve a fee and require inspections by building officials before work can proceed. (Inspections benefit *you*, as they ensure that the job is being done satisfactorily.) Permit fees are generally a percentage (1 to 1.5 percent) of the project's estimated value, often calculated on square footage.

It's important to file for the necessary permits. Failure to do so can result in fines or legal action against you. You can even be forced to undo the work performed. At the very least, your negligence may come back to haunt you later when you're ready to sell your house.

■ **Zoning ordinances,** particular to your community, restrict setbacks (how near to property lines you may build), your house's allowable height, lot coverage factors (how much of your property you can cover with structures), and other factors that impact design and building. If your plans don't conform to zoning ordinances, you can try to obtain a variance, an exception to the rules. But this legal work can be expensive and time-consuming. Even if you prove that your project won't negatively affect your neighbors, the building department can still refuse to grant the variance.

■ **Deeds and covenants** attach to the lot. Deeds set out property lines and easements; covenants may establish architectural standards in a neighborhood. Since both can seriously impact your project, make sure you have complete information on any deeds or covenants before you turn over a spadeful of soil.

square footage (of livable space) by the local average cost per square foot for new construction. (To obtain local averages, call a contractor, an architect, a realtor, or the local chapter of the National Association of Home Builders.) Some contractors may even be willing to give you a prelim inary bid. Once you know approximate costs, speak to your lender to explore financing.

It's a good idea to discuss your project with several contractors (see page 8). They may be aware of problems in your area that could limit your options—bedrock that makes digging basements difficult, for example. These conversations are actually the first step in developing a list of contractors from which you'll choose the one who will build your home.

Recruiting Your Home Team

A home-building project will inject you and your family into the building business, an area that may be unfamiliar territory. Among the people you'll be working with are architects, designers, landscapers, contractors, and subcontractors.

Design Help

A qualified architect or designer can help you modify and personalize your home plan, taking into account your family's needs and budget and the house's style. In fact, you may want to consider consulting such a person while you're selecting a plan to help you articulate your needs.

Design professionals are capable of handling any or all aspects of the design process. For example, they can review your house plans, suggest options, and then provide rough sketches of the options on tracing paper. Many architects will even secure needed permits and negotiate with contractors or subcontractors, as well as oversee the quality of the work.

Of course, you don't necessarily need an architect or designer to implement minor changes in a plan; although most contractors aren't trained in design, some can help you with modifications.

An open-ended, hourly-fee arrangement that you work out with your architect or designer allows for flexibility, but it often turns out to be more costly than working on a flat-fee basis. On a flat fee, you agree to pay a specific amount of money for a certain amount of work.

To find architects and designers, contact such trade associations as the American Institute of Architects (AIA), American Institute of Building Designers (AIBD), American Society of Landscape Architects (ASLA), and American Society of Interior Designers (ASID). Although many professionals choose not to belong to trade associations, those who do have met the standards of their respective associations. For phone numbers of local branches, check the Yellow Pages.

■ **Architects** are licensed by the state and have degrees. They're trained in all facets of building design and construction. Although some can handle interior design and structural engineering, others hire specialists for those tasks.

■ **Building designers** are generally unlicensed but may be accredited by the American Institute of Building Designers. Their backgrounds are varied: some may be unlicensed architects in apprenticeship; others are interior designers or contractors with design skills.

■ **Draftspersons** offer an economical route to making simple changes on your drawings. Like building designers, these people may be unlicensed architect apprentices, engineers, or members of related trades. Most are accomplished at drawing up plans.

■ **Interior designers,** as their job title suggests, design interiors. They work with you to choose room finishes, furnishings, appliances, and decorative elements. Part of their expertise is in arranging furnishings to create a workable space plan. Some interior designers are employed by architectural firms; others work independently. Financial arrangements vary, depending on the designer's preference.

Related professionals are kitchen and bathroom designers, who concentrate on fixtures, cabinetry, appliances, materials, and space planning for the kitchen and bath.

■ **Landscape architects, designers, and contractors** design outdoor areas. Landscape architects are state-licensed to practice landscape design. A landscape designer usually has a landscape architect's education and training but does not have a state license. Licensed landscape contractors specialize in garden construction, though some also have design skills and experience.

■ **Soils specialists and structural engineers** may be needed for projects where unstable soils or uncommon wind loads or seismic forces must be taken into account. Any structural changes to a house require the expertise of a structural engineer to verify that the house won't fall down.

Services of these specialists can be expensive, but they're imperative in certain conditions to ensure a safe, sturdy structure. Your building department will probably let you know if their services are required.

General Contractors

To build your house, hire a licensed general contractor. Most states require a contractor to be licensed and insured for worker's compensation in order to contract a building project and hire other subcontractors. State licensing ensures that contractors have met minimum training standards and have a specified level of experience. Licensing does not guarantee, however, that they're good at what they do.

When contractors hire subcontractors, they're responsible for overseeing the quality of work and materials of the subcontractors and for paying them.

■ **Finding a contractor.** How do you find a good contractor? Start by getting referrals from people you know who have built or remodeled their home. Nothing beats a personal recommendation. The best contractors are usually busily moving from one satisfied client to another prospect, advertised only by word of mouth.

You can also ask local real estate brokers and lenders or even your building inspector for names of qualified builders. Experienced lumber dealers are another good source of names.

In the Yellow Pages, look under "Contractors–Building, General"; or call the local chapter of the National Association of Home Builders.

■ **Choosing a contractor.** Once you have a list of names of prospective builders, call several of them. On the telephone, ask first whether they handle your type of job and can work within your schedule. If they can, arrange a meeting with each one and ask them to be prepared with references of former clients and photos of previous jobs. Better still, meet them at one of their current work sites so you can get a glimpse of the quality of their work and how organized and thorough they are.

Take your plan to the meeting and discuss it enough to request a rough estimate (some builders will comply, while others will be reluctant to offer a ballpark estimate, preferring to give you a hard bid based on complete drawings). Don't hesitate to probe for advice or suggestions that might make building your house less expensive.

Be especially aware of each contractor's personality and how well you communicate. Good chemistry between you and your builder is a key ingredient for success.

Narrow down the candidates to three or four. Ask each for a firm bid, based on the exact same set of plans and specifications. For the bids to be accurate, your plans need to be complete and the specifications as precise as possible, call-ing out particular appliances, fixtures, floorings, roofing material, and so forth. (Some of these are specified in a stock-plan set; others are not.)

Call the contractors' references and ask about the quality of their work, their relationship with their clients, their promptness, and their readiness to follow up on problems. Visit former clients to check the contractor's work firsthand.

Be sure your final candidates are licensed, bonded, and insured for worker's compensation, public liability, and property damage. Also, try to determine how financially solvent they are (you can call their bank and credit references). Avoid contractors who are operating hand-to-mouth.

Don't automatically hire the contractor with the lowest bid if you don't think you'll get along well or if you have any doubts about the quality of the person's work. Instead, look for both the most reasonable bid and the contractor with the best credentials, references, terms, and compatibility with your family.

A word about bonds: You can request a performance bond that guarantees that your job will be finished by your contractor. If the job isn't completed, the bonding company will cover the cost of hiring another contractor to finish it. Bonds cost from 2 to 6 percent of the value of the project.

Your Building Contract

A building contract (see below) binds and protects both you and your contractor. It isn't just a legal document. It's also a list of the expectations of both parties. The best way to minimize the possibility of misunderstandings and costly changes later on is to write down every possible detail. Whether the contract is a standard form or one composed by you, have an attorney look it over before both you and the contractor sign it.

The contract should clearly specify all the work that needs to be done, including particular materials and work descriptions, the time schedule, and method of payment. It should be keyed to the working drawings.

A Sample Building Contract

Project and participants. Give a general description of the project, its address, and the names and addresses of both you and the builder.

Construction materials. Identify all construction materials by brand name, quality markings (species, grades, etc.), and model numbers where applicable. Avoid the clause "or equal," which allows the builder to substitute other materials for your choices. For materials you can't specify now, set down a budget figure.

Time schedule. Include both start and completion dates and specify that work will be "continuous." Although a contractor cannot be responsible for delays caused by strikes and material shortages, your builder should assume responsibility for completing the project within a reasonable period of time.

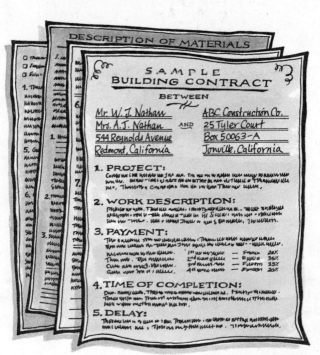

Work to be performed. State all work you expect the contractor to perform, from initial grading to finished painting.

Method and schedule of payment. Specify how and when payments are to be made. Typical agreements specify installment payments as particular phases of work are completed. Final payment is withheld until the job receives its final inspection and is cleared of all liens.

Waiver of liens. Protect yourself with a waiver of liens signed by the general contractor, the subcontractors, and all major suppliers. That way, subcontractors who are not paid for materials or services cannot place a lien on your property.

Personalizing Stock Plans

The beauty of buying stock plans for your new home is that they offer tested, well-conceived design at an affordable price. And stock plans dramatically reduce the time it takes to design a house, since the plans are ready when you are.

Because they were not created specifically for your family, stock plans may not reflect your personal taste. But it's not difficult to make revisions in stock plans that will turn your home into an expression of your family's personality. You'll surely want to add personal touches and choose your own finishes.

Ideally, the modifications you implement will be fairly minor. The more extensive the changes, the more expensive the plans. Major changes take valuable design time, and those that affect a house's structure may require a structural engineer's approval.

If you anticipate wholesale changes, such as moving a number of bearing walls or changing the roofline significantly, you may be better off selecting another plan. On the other hand, reconfiguring or changing the sizes of some rooms can probably be handled fairly easily.

Some structural changes may even be necessary to comply with local codes. Your area may have specific requirements for snow loads, energy codes, seismic or wind resistance, and so forth. Those types of modifications are likely to require the services of an architect or structural engineer.

Plan Modifications

Before you pencil in any changes, live with your plans for a while. Study them carefully—at your building site, if possible. Try to picture the finished house: how rooms will interrelate, where the sun will enter and at what angle, what the view will be from each window. Think about traffic patterns, access to rooms, room sizes, window and door locations, natural light, and kitchen and bathroom layouts.

Typical changes might involve adding windows or skylights to bring in natural light or capture a view. Or you may want to widen a hallway or doorway for roomier access, extend a room, eliminate doors, or change window and door sizes. Perhaps you'd like to shorten a room, stealing the gained space for a large closet. Look closely at the kitchen; it's not difficult to reconfigure the layout if it makes the space more convenient for you.

Above all, take your time—this is your home and it should reflect your taste and needs. Make your changes now, during the planning stage. Once construction begins, it will take crowbars, hammers, saws, new materials, and, most significantly, time to alter the plans. Because changes are not part of your building contract, you can count on them being expensive extras once construction begins.

Specifying Finishes

One way to personalize a house without changing its structure is to substitute your favorite finishes for those specified on the plan.

Would you prefer a stuccoed exterior rather than the wood siding shown on the plan? In most cases, this is a relatively easy change. Do you like the look of a wood shingle roof rather than the composition shingles shown on the plan? This, too, is easy. Perhaps you would like to change the windows from sliders to casements, or upgrade to high-efficiency glazing. No problem. Many of those kinds of changes can be worked out with your contractor.

Inside, you may want hardwood where vinyl flooring is shown. In fact, you can—and should—choose types, colors, and styles of floorings, wall coverings, tile, plumbing fixtures, door hardware, cabinetry, appliances, lighting fixtures, and other interior details, for it's these materials that will personalize your home. For help in making selections, consult an architect or interior designer (see page 8).

Each material you select should be spelled out clearly and precisely in your building contract.

Finishing touches can transform a house built from stock plans into an expression of your family's taste and style. Clockwise, from far left: Colorful tilework and custom cabinetry enliven a bathroom (Design: Osburn Design); highly organized closet system maximizes storage space (Architect: David Jeremiah Hurley); low-level deck expands living space to outdoor areas (Landscape architects: The Runa Group, Inc.); built-ins convert the corner of a guest room into a home office (Design: Lynn Williams of The French Connection); French country cabinetry lends style and old-world charm to a kitchen (Design: Garry Bishop/Showcase Kitchens).

What the Plans Include

Complete construction blueprints are available for every house shown in this book. Clear and concise, these detailed blueprints are designed by licensed architects or members of the American Institute of Building Designers (AIBD). Each plan is designed to meet standards set down by nationally recognized building codes (the Uniform Building Code, Standard Building Code, or Basic Building Code) at the time and for the area where they were drawn.

Remember, however, that every state, county, and municipality has its own codes, zoning requirements, ordinances, and building regulations. Modifications may be necessary to comply with such local requirements as snow loads, energy codes, seismic zones, and flood areas.

Although blueprint sets vary depending on the size and complexity of the house and on the individual designer's style, each set may include the elements described below and shown at right.

■ **Exterior elevations** show the front, rear, and sides of the house, including exterior materials, details, and measurements.

■ **Foundation plans** include drawings for a full, partial, or daylight basement, crawlspace, pole, pier, or slab foundation. All necessary notations and dimensions are included. (Foundation options will vary for each plan. If the plan you choose doesn't have the type of foundation you desire, a generic conversion diagram is available.)

■ **Detailed floor plans** show the placement of interior walls and the dimensions of rooms, doors, windows, stairways, and similar elements for each level of the house.

■ **Cross sections** show details of the house as though it were cut in slices from the roof to the foundation. The cross sections give the home's construction, insulation, flooring, and roofing details.

■ **Interior elevations** show the specific details of cabinets (kitchen, bathroom, and utility room), fireplaces, built-in units, and other special interior features.

■ **Roof details** give the layout of rafters, dormers, gables, and other roof elements, including clerestory windows and skylights. These details may be shown on the elevation sheet or on a separate diagram.

■ **Schematic electrical layouts** show the suggested locations for switches, fixtures, and outlets. These details may be shown on the floor plan or on a separate diagram.

■ **General specifications** provide instructions and information regarding excavation and grading, masonry and concrete work, carpentry and woodwork, thermal and moisture protection, drywall, tile, flooring, glazing, and caulking and sealants.

Other Helpful Building Aids

In addition to the construction information on every set of plans, you can buy the following guides.

■ **Reproducible blueprints** are helpful if you'll be making changes to the stock plan you've chosen. These blueprints are original line drawings produced on erasable, reproducible paper for the purpose of modification. When alterations are complete, working copies can be made.

■ **Itemized materials list** details the quantity, type, and size of materials needed to build your home. (This list is extremely helpful in obtaining an accurate construction bid. It's not intended for use to order materials.)

■ **Mirror-reverse plans** are useful if you want to build your home in the reverse of the plan that's shown. Because the lettering and dimensions read backwards, be sure to buy at least one regular-reading set of blueprints.

■ **Description of materials** gives the type and quality of materials suggested for the home. This form may be required for obtaining FHA or VA financing.

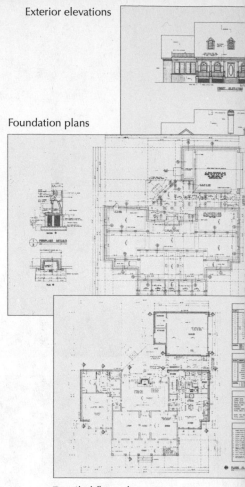

Exterior elevations

Foundation plans

Detailed floor plans

■ **How-to diagrams** for plumbing, wiring, solar heating, framing and foundation conversions show how to plumb, wire, install a solar heating system, convert plans with 2 by 4 exterior walls to 2 by 6 construction (or vice versa), and adapt a plan for a basement, crawlspace, or slab foundation. These diagrams are not specific to any one plan.

NOTE: Due to regional variations, local availability of materials, local codes, methods of installation, and individual preferences, detailed heating, plumbing, and electrical specifications are not included on plans. The duct work, venting, and other details will vary, depending on the heating and cooling system you use and the type of energy that operates it. These details and specifications are easily obtained from your builder or local supplier.

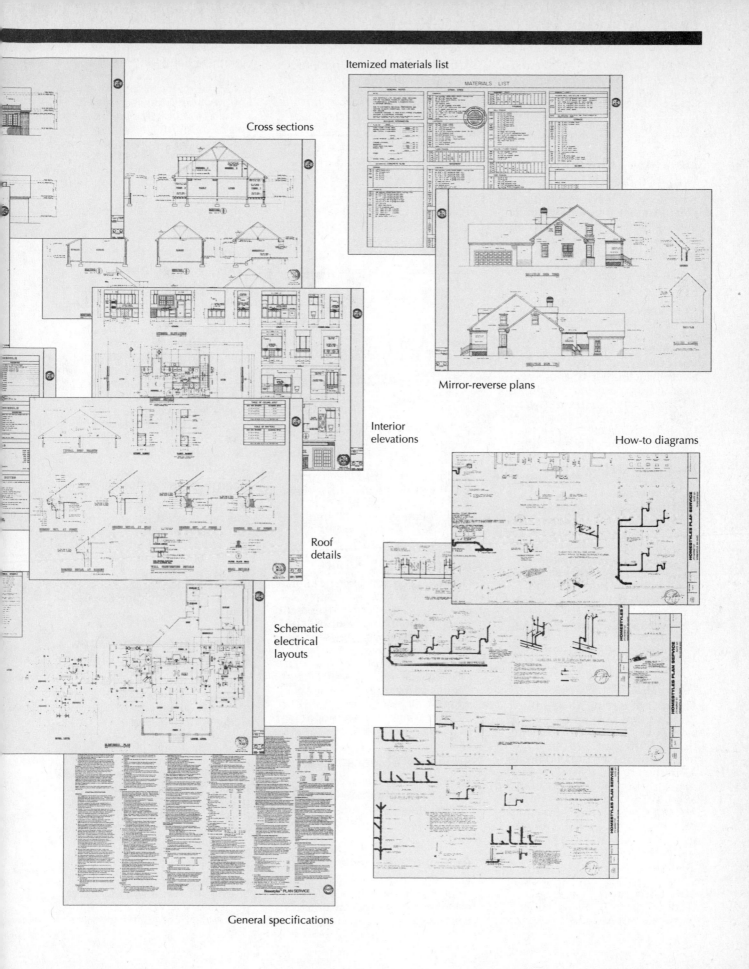

Itemized materials list

Cross sections

Mirror-reverse plans

Interior elevations

How-to diagrams

Roof details

Schematic electrical layouts

General specifications

Before You Order

Once you've chosen the one or two house plans that work best for you, you're ready to order blueprints. Before filling in the form on the facing page, note the information that follows.

How Many Blueprints Will You Need?

A single set of blueprints will allow you to study a home design in detail. You'll need more for obtaining bids and permits, as well as some to use as reference at the building site. If you'll be modifying your home plan, order a reproducible set (see page 12).

Figure you'll need at least one set each for yourself, your builder, the building department, and your lender. In addition, some subcontractors—foundation, plumber, electrician, and HVAC—may also need at least partial sets. If they do, ask them to return the sets when they're finished. The chart below can help you calculate how many sets you're likely to need.

Blueprint Checklist

____ Owner's set(s)

____ Builder usually requires at least three sets: one for legal documentation, one for inspections, and a minimum of one set for subcontractors.

____ Building department requires at least one set. Check with your local department before ordering.

____ Lending institution usually needs one set for a conventional mortgage, three sets for FHA or VA loans.

____ TOTAL SETS NEEDED

Blueprint Prices

The cost of having an architect design a new custom home typically runs from 5 to 15 percent of the building cost, or from $5,000 to $15,000 for a $100,000 home. A single set of blueprints for the plans in this book ranges from $295 to $505, depending on the house's size. Working with these drawings, you can save enough on design fees to add a deck, a swimming pool, or a luxurious kitchen.

Pricing is based on "total finished living space." Garages, porches, decks, and unfinished basements are not included.

Building Costs

Building costs vary widely, depending on a number of factors, includ-

Price Code (Size)	1 Set	4 Sets	7 Sets	Reproducible Set
AAA (under 500 sq. ft.)	$245	$295	$330	$430
AA (500-999 sq. ft.)	$285	$335	$370	$470
A (1,000-1,499 sq. ft.)	$325	$375	$410	$510
B (1,500-1,999 sq. ft.)	$365	$415	$450	$550
C (2,000-2,499 sq. ft.)	$405	$455	$490	$590
D (2,500-2,999 sq. ft.)	$445	$495	$530	$630
E (3,000-3,499 sq. ft.)	$485	$535	$570	$670
F (3,500-3,999 sq. ft.)	$525	$575	$610	$710
G (4,000-4,499 sq. ft.)	$565	$615	$650	$750
H (4,500-4,999 sq. ft.)	$605	$655	$690	$790
I (5,000 sq. ft. & above)	$645	$695	$730	$830

ing local material and labor costs and the finishing materials you select. For help estimating costs, see "Is Your Project Doable?" on page 7.

Foundation Options & Exterior Construction

Depending on your site and climate, your home will be built with a slab, pier, pole, crawlspace, or basement foundation. Exterior walls will be framed with either 2 by 4s or 2 by 6s, determined by structural and insulation standards in your area. Most contractors can easily adapt a home to meet the foundation and/or wall requirements for your area. Or ask for a conversion how-to diagram (see page 12).

Service & Blueprint Delivery

Service representatives are available to answer questions and assist you in placing your order. Every effort is made to process and ship orders within 48 hours.

Returns & Exchanges

Each set of blueprints is specially printed and shipped to you in response to your specific order; consequently, requests for refunds

cannot be honored. However, if the prints you order cannot be used, you may exchange them for another plan from any Sunset home plan book. For an exchange, you must return all sets of plans within 30 days. A nonrefundable service charge will be assessed for all exchanges; for more information, call the toll-free number on the facing page. Note: Reproducible sets cannot be exchanged.

Compliance with Local Codes & Regulations

Because of climatic, geographic, and political variations, building codes and regulations vary from one area to another. These plans are authorized for your use expressly conditioned on your obligation and agreement to comply strictly with all local building codes, ordinances, regulations, and requirements, including permits and in-spections at time of construction.

Architectural & Engineering Seals

With increased concern about energy costs and safety, many cities and states now require that an architect or engineer review and "seal" a blueprint prior to construction. To find out whether this is a requirement in your area, contact your local building department.

License Agreement, Copy Restrictions & Copyright

When you purchase your blueprints, you are granted the right to use those documents to construct a single unit. All the plans in this publication are protected under the Federal Copyright Act, Title XVII of the United States Code and Chap-ter 37 of the Code of Federal Regu-lations. Each designer retains title and ownership of the original documents. The blueprints licensed to you cannot be used by or resold to any other person, copied, or reproduced by any means. The copying restrictions do not apply to reproducible blueprints. When you buy a reproducible set, you may modify and reproduce it for your own use.

Blueprint Order Form

Complete this order form in just three easy steps. Then mail in your order or, for faster service, call toll-free.

1. Blueprints & Accessories

BLUEPRINT CHART

Price Code	1 Set	4 Sets	7 Sets	Reproducible Set*
AAA	$245	$295	$330	$430
AA	$285	$335	$370	$470
A	$325	$375	$410	$510
B	$365	$415	$450	$550
C	$405	$455	$490	$590
D	$445	$495	$530	$630
E	$485	$535	$570	$670
F	$525	$575	$610	$710
G	$565	$615	$650	$750
H	$605	$655	$690	$790
I	$645	$695	$730	$830

*A reproducible set is produced on erasable paper for the purpose of modification. It is only available for plans with prefixes A, AG, AGH, AH, AHP, APS, AX, B, C, CC, CPS, DCL, DD, DW, E, EOF, FB, GL, GML, GSA, H, HDS, HFL, J, K, KD, KLF, L, LRD, LS, M, NW, OH, PH, PI, RD, S, SDG, THD, U, UDG, V.

Prices subject to change

Mirror-Reverse Sets: $50 surcharge. From the total number of sets you ordered above, choose the number you want to be reversed. *Note: All writing on mirror-reverse plans is backwards. Order at least one regular-reading set.*

Itemized Materials List: One set $50; each additional set $15. Details the quantity, type, and size of materials needed to build your home.

Description of Materials: Sold in a set of two for $50 (for use in obtaining FHA or VA financing).

Typical How-To Diagrams: One set $20; two sets $30; three sets $40; four sets $45. General guides on plumbing, wiring, and solar heating, plus information on how to convert from one foundation or exterior framing to another. *Note: These diagrams are not specific to any one plan.*

2. Sales Tax & Shipping

Determine your subtotal and add appropriate local state sales tax, plus shipping and handling (see chart below).

SHIPPING & HANDLING

	1–3 Sets	4–6 Sets	7 or More Sets	Reproducible Set
U.S. Regular (5–6 business days)	$17.50	$20.00	$22.50	$17.50
U.S. Express (2–3 business days)	$29.50	$32.50	$35.00	$29.50
Canada Regular (2–3 weeks)	$20.00	$22.50	$25.00	$20.00
Canada Express (5–6 business days)	$35.00	$40.00	$45.00	$35.00
Overseas/Airmail (7–10 business days)	$57.50	$67.50	$77.50	$57.50

3. Customer Information

Choose the method of payment you prefer. Include check, money order, or credit card information, complete name and address portion, and mail, fax, or call using the information at the right.

SS06

REAR VIEW

Solar Flair

- Full window walls and a sun room with glass roof act as passive energy collectors in this popular floor plan.
- Expansive living room features wood stove and vaulted ceilings.
- Dining room shares a breakfast counter with the merging kitchen.
- Convenient laundry room is positioned near kitchen and garage entrance.
- Second level is devoted entirely to the private master suite, featuring vaulted ceiling and a balcony view to the living room below.

Plans H-877-5A & -5B

Bedrooms: 3-4		**Baths:** 2-3	

Space:

Upper floor:	382 sq. ft.
Main floor:	1,200 sq. ft.
Sun room:	162 sq. ft.
Total living area:	**1,744 sq. ft.**
Basement:	approx. 1,200 sq. ft.
Garage:	457 sq. ft.

Exterior Wall Framing: 2x6

Foundation options:
Daylight basement (Plan H-877-5B).
Crawlspace (Plan H-877-5A).
(Foundation & framing conversion diagram available — see order form.)

Blueprint Price Code:

Without basement:	B
With basement:	D

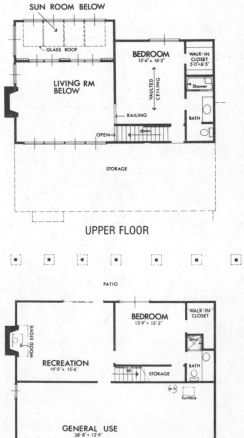

SUN ROOM BELOW
GLASS ROOF
LIVING RM BELOW
BEDROOM 13'-6" x 16'-3"
VAULTED CEILING
WALK-IN CLOSET 5'-0" x 6'-5"
Shower
BATH
RAILING
OPEN
down
STORAGE

UPPER FLOOR

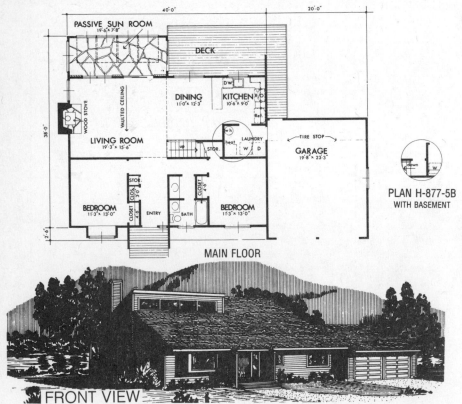

PASSIVE SUN ROOM 19'-6" x 7'-8"
40'-0"
20'-0"
DECK
WOOD STOVE
VAULTED CEILING
DINING 11'-0" x 12'-3"
KITCHEN 10'-6" x 9'-0"
DW
Ref.
LIVING ROOM 19'-3" x 15'-6"
38'-0"
w h heat
LAUNDRY W D
STOR.
TIRE STOP
GARAGE 19'-8" x 23'-3"
up
STOR.
CLOSET 4'-5" x 3'-0"
BEDROOM 11'-3" x 13'-0"
ENTRY
BATH
CLOSET 4'-6"
BEDROOM 11'-3" x 13'-0"
2'-6"

MAIN FLOOR

down
W

PLAN H-877-5B
WITH BASEMENT

PATIO
WOOD STOVE
RECREATION 19'-0" x 15'-6"
BEDROOM 13'-9" x 12'-2"
WALK-IN CLOSET
Shower
BATH
up
STORAGE
w h
furnace
GENERAL USE 38'-8" x 12'-9"

BASEMENT

FRONT VIEW

TO ORDER THIS BLUEPRINT, CALL TOLL-FREE 1-800-547-5570
16 (prices and details on pp. 12-15.)

Plans H-877-5A & -5B

Simple Passive Solar

- The beauty of this design is found in its simple but thoughtful open plan and the wise use of passive solar principles.
- The sun garden contributes light, free heat and eye appeal. Solar energy is absorbed in the tile-covered, insulated concrete floor for release after sunset.
- For summertime, the sun garden features built-in adjustable shades, and an automatic vent dispels built-up heat.
- A two-story-high entry leads to an expansive activity area with a large fireplace.
- The kitchen is well-planned and includes an informal eating area.
- The upstairs master suite features a private bath, two closets and a private balcony. Two other upstairs bedrooms share another full bath.

Plan K-524-C

Bedrooms: 3	Baths: 2½
Space:	
Upper floor	813 sq. ft.
Main floor	775 sq. ft.
Sun garden	120 sq. ft.
Total Living Area	**1,708 sq. ft.**
Partial basement	627 sq. ft.
Garage and storage	506 sq. ft.
Exterior Wall Framing	**2x4 or 2x6**
Foundation options:	

Partial Basement
Slab
(Foundation & framing conversion diagram available—see order form.)

Blueprint Price Code	**B**

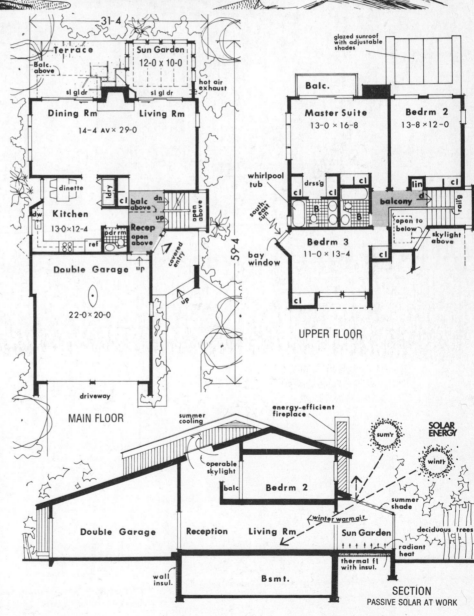

MAIN FLOOR

UPPER FLOOR

SECTION
PASSIVE SOLAR AT WORK

Plan K-524-C

**TO ORDER THIS BLUEPRINT,
CALL TOLL-FREE 1-800-547-5570**
(prices and details on pp. 12-15.)

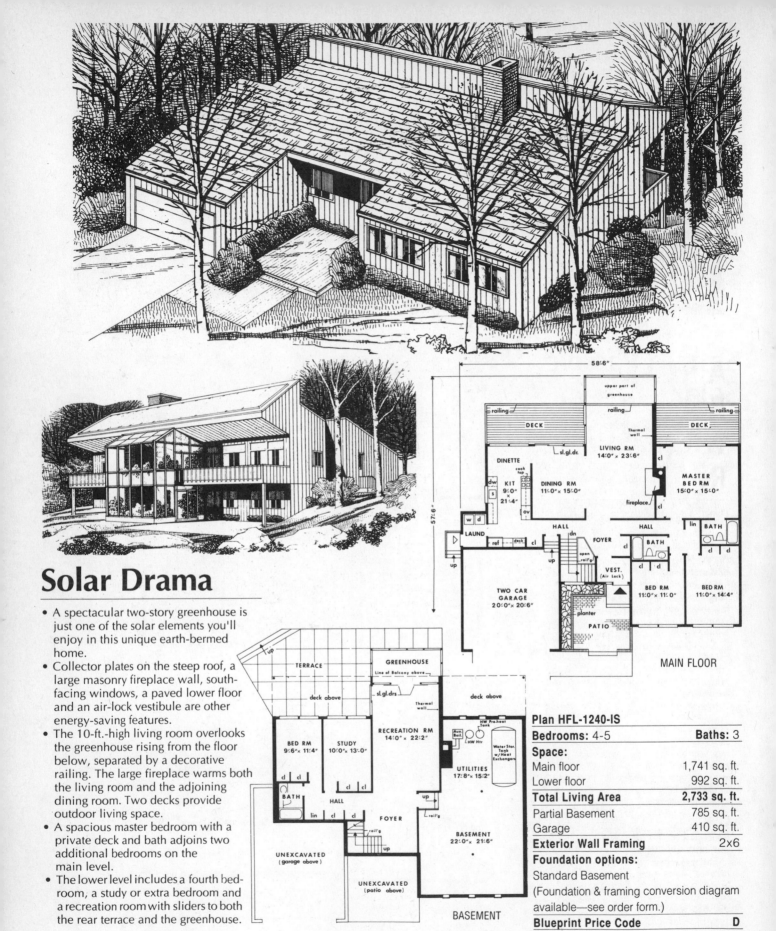

Solar Drama

- A spectacular two-story greenhouse is just one of the solar elements you'll enjoy in this unique earth-bermed home.
- Collector plates on the steep roof, a large masonry fireplace wall, south-facing windows, a paved lower floor and an air-lock vestibule are other energy-saving features.
- The 10-ft.-high living room overlooks the greenhouse rising from the floor below, separated by a decorative railing. The large fireplace warms both the living room and the adjoining dining room. Two decks provide outdoor living space.
- A spacious master bedroom with a private deck and bath adjoins two additional bedrooms on the main level.
- The lower level includes a fourth bed-room, a study or extra bedroom and a recreation room with sliders to both the rear terrace and the greenhouse.

MAIN FLOOR

BASEMENT

Plan HFL-1240-IS	
Bedrooms: 4-5	**Baths: 3**
Space:	
Main floor	1,741 sq. ft.
Lower floor	992 sq. ft.
Total Living Area	**2,733 sq. ft.**
Partial Basement	785 sq. ft.
Garage	410 sq. ft.
Exterior Wall Framing	2x6
Foundation options:	
Standard Basement (Foundation & framing conversion diagram available—see order form.)	
Blueprint Price Code	D

Plan HFL-1240-IS

A "Great-Room" Design with Sweeping Roof Lines

Dynamic exterior lines coupled with rustic natural woods make this home a real "eye stopper" in a city or suburban setting. Vertical cedar siding is specified, although the exterior looks equally good with horizontal siding.

The interior "swing-back" stair landing has as its focal point a two-piece arched top window which also acts as a counterpoint to the rectangular transom window over the entry door.

A continuation of the roof over the exterior entry area offers wide protection from the elements and provides visual continuity with the two-car garage roof overhang.

Interior planning is based on the "open-plan" concept featuring a Great Room integrated with a "super" kitchen design.

A wet bar is placed to the left of the masonry wall where an efficient wood stove is located on a raised slate hearth.

The master suite includes a walk-in closet with dressing area. The bath provides double vanities, a tub on a raised platform and a separate shower. Two additional bedrooms and another bathroom are located on the upper level.

The majority of glass in this home is located on the rear of the home to provide a real "plus" for those considering solar orientation. A sunspace may be added to the master bedroom if desired.

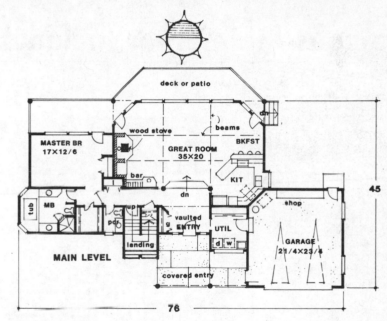

MAIN LEVEL

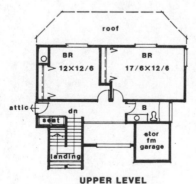

UPPER LEVEL

S-22884-HS
WITH CRAWLSPACE

S-22884-HS-B
WITH BASEMENT

Main floor:	1,686 sq. ft.
Upper floor:	674 sq. ft.
Total living area: (Not counting garage or basement)	2,360 sq. ft.

Blueprint Price Code C

Plan S-22884-HS

TO ORDER THIS BLUEPRINT, CALL TOLL-FREE 1-800-547-5570 (prices and details on pp. 12-15.)

Spacious Main Floor Includes Greenhouse

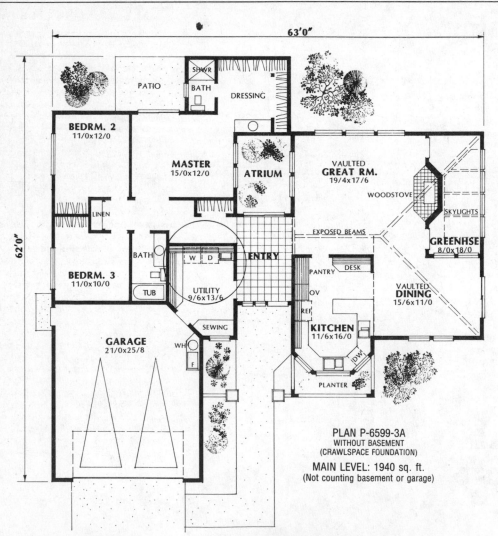

63'0"

62'0"

PATIO

SHWR
BATH

DRESSING

BEDRM. 2
11/0x12/0

MASTER
15/0x12/0

ATRIUM

VAULTED
GREAT RM.
19/4x17/6

WOODSTOVE

SKYLIGHTS

LINEN

EXPOSED BEAMS

GREENHSE
8/0x18/0

BATH

W D

ENTRY

BEDRM. 3
11/0x10/0

TUB

UTILITY
9/6x13/6

PANTRY   DESK

OV

VAULTED
DINING
15/6x11/0

REF

SEWING

KITCHEN
11/6x16/0

GARAGE
21/0x25/8

WH

F

DW

PLANTER

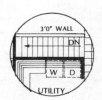

3'0" WALL

DN

W D

UTILITY

PLAN P-6599-3D
WITH DAYLIGHT BASEMENT
BASEMENT LEVEL: 1650 sq. ft.

PLAN P-6599-3A
WITHOUT BASEMENT
(CRAWLSPACE FOUNDATION)

MAIN LEVEL: 1940 sq. ft.
(Not counting basement or garage)

Blueprint Price Code B

Plans P-6599-3A & -3D

Passive Solar Design . . . from the Foundation Up

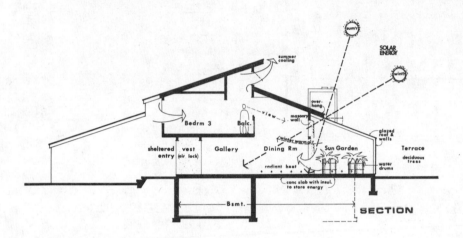

SECTION

Labels in section: summer cooling; SOLAR ENERGY; sum'r; win'tr; overhang; masonry wall; view; Bedrm 3; Balc.; glazed roof & walls; winter warmth; sheltered entry; vest (air lock); Gallery; Dining Rm; Sun Garden; Terrace; deciduous trees; radiant heat; water drums; conc slab with insul. to store energy; Bsmt.

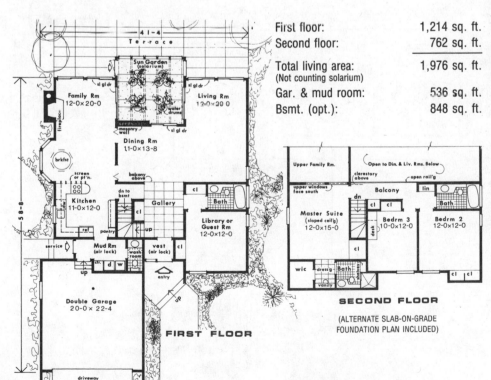

First floor labels: Terrace; 41-4; 58-8; Sun Garden (solarium); sl gl dr; Family Rm 12-0×20-0; Living Rm 12-0×20-0; water drums; masonry wall; fireplace; Dining Rm 11-0×13-8; brkfst; screen or pt'n; balcony above; cl; Bath; Kitchen 11-0×12-0; dn to bsmt; Gallery; up; ref; pantry; Library or Guest Rm 12-0×12-0; service; Mud Rm (air lock); dr; d; w; wash room; vest (air lock); entry; up; Double Garage 20-0×22-4; driveway

FIRST FLOOR

Second floor labels: Upper Family Rm.; Open to Din. & Liv. Rms. Below; clerestory above; open rail'g; lin; Balcony; Master Suite (sloped ceil'g); upper windows face south; dn; cl; desk; Bedrm 3 10-0×12-0; Bedrm 2 12-0×12-0; Bath; wic; dress'g; vanity; Bath; shelves; cl; cl

SECOND FLOOR

(ALTERNATE SLAB-ON-GRADE FOUNDATION PLAN INCLUDED)

First floor:	1,214 sq. ft.
Second floor:	762 sq. ft.
Total living area: (Not counting solarium)	1,976 sq. ft.
Gar. & mud room:	536 sq. ft.
Bsmt. (opt.):	848 sq. ft.

Designed to embrace the warming sun, this two-story passive solar house is constructed of standard lumber, and its dramatic exterior is finished in vertical wood siding and roof shingles. Focal point of the concept is a glass-enclosed, south-facing sun garden that is visible from the entrance gallery and is wrapped by the living, dining and family rooms. The open plan provides for a cheerful well-organized kitchen, situated to serve the dining room and family room. A library (or guest room) and bath are located off the entrance gallery.

Isolated on the second floor are three bedrooms and two baths with a balcony that overlooks the living and dining rooms. Solar energy is absorbed and stored in the masonry wall and dense floor for heating. The sun garden generates heat to the adjacent areas by opening the sliding doors. Direct heat gain is maintained through glazed walls that face south. For summer cooling, eave overhang keeps out unwanted sun. Operable vents in the clerestory draw air out of the house by convection to provide natural ventilation. Many other energy saving features are planned into the house to assure a high retention of heat, and a back-up heating system is provided for use as needed. Total living area, excluding the sun garden, is 1,214 sq. ft. on the first floor and 762 sq. ft. on the second; garage and mudroom, 536 sq. ft.; optional basement, 848 sq. ft.

Blueprint Price Code B

Plan K-279-T

*TO ORDER THIS BLUEPRINT,
CALL TOLL-FREE 1-800-547-5570*
(prices and details on pp. 12-15.)

Impressive Contemporary

- A wide, sweeping facade introduces this striking contemporary design.
- Inside, the good impression continues, with the sight of a huge Great Room with a large masonry fireplace.
- The large passive sun room can serve as a breakfast room, family room or arboretum, while at the same time collecting and redistributing the sun's heat throughout the house.
- The bedroom adjoining the sun room features a luxurious private bath and huge walk-in closet. Another downstairs bedroom is next to a second full bath.
- The upstairs offers enormous potential as a special retreat for kids or adults, a studio, office, exercise area, additional bedroom or "dormitory" for kids' overnighters.
- Also note the large utility area and the abundance of storage space throughout the home.

UPPER FLOOR

CLERESTORY WINDOWS
OVER GREAT ROOM

Plans H-958-1A & -1B	
Bedrooms: 2-3	Baths: 3
Space:	
Upper floor	511 sq. ft.
Main floor	1,568 sq. ft.
Sun room	194 sq. ft.
Total Living Area	**2,273 sq. ft.**
Basement (approx)	1,560 sq. ft.
Garage	484 sq. ft.
Exterior Wall Framing	2x6
Foundation options:	**Plan #**
Daylight Basement	H-958-1B
Crawlspace	H-958-1A
(Foundation & framing conversion diagram available—see order form.)	
Blueprint Price Code	C

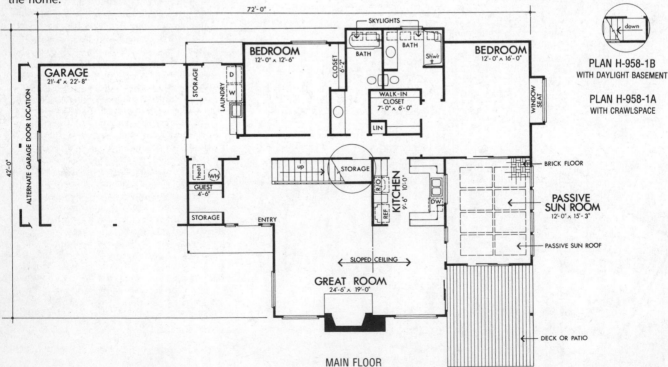

PLAN H-958-1B
WITH DAYLIGHT BASEMENT

PLAN H-958-1A
WITH CRAWLSPACE

MAIN FLOOR

TO ORDER THIS BLUEPRINT, CALL TOLL-FREE 1-800-547-5570 (prices and details on pp. 12-15.)

Plans H-958-1A & -1B

summer
cooling

sum'r
vent

operable
clerestory
window

Entry | vest | Lounge

SOLAR
ENERGY

sum'r   wint'r

glazed
roof

Sun Rm / Den

water
drums

wd. const.

insulation

Bsmt.

deciduous trees for
summer shade

heat from winter sun
stored in thermal floor

SECTION
PASSIVE SOLAR AT WORK

71-8

Terrace

water
drums

service

Sun Rm / Den

Master Bedrm
12-8 x 15-4

wic

Bath

Kitchen / Dining
12-0 x 17-4

Mud
Rm

sl gl dr   sl gl dr

sl gl dr

hall

Bath

Double Garage
20-0 x 20-4

up
dn

Living Lounge
15-0 x 22-0

clerestory
above

Vest

lin

cl

Bedrm 3
10-0 x 11-0

Bedrm 2
10-4 x 11-0

hi-efficiency
fireplace

cl

covered
entry

up

44-8

driveway

FLOOR PLAN

Dramatic Angles

Dramatically angled to maximize the benefits of passive solar technology, this compact one-story home can be adapted to many sites and orientations. South-facing rooms, including sun room/den, absorb and store heat energy in thermal floors for night time radiation. Heavy insulation in exterior walls and ceilings, plus double glazing in windows, keep heat loss to a minimum. During the summer, heat is expelled through an operable clerestory window and through an automatic vent in the sun room.

Inside, entrance vestibule overlooks a breathtaking view of the sun room and the outdoors beyond; kitchen/dining area opens to a large rear terrace. Three bedrooms are isolated for total privacy. Living area, excluding sun room, is 1,223 sq. ft.; garage, mud room, etc. 504 sq. ft.; partial basement, 1,030 sq. ft.

Living Area:	1,223 sq. ft.
Garage and Mud Room:	504 sq. ft.
Basement (Opt.):	1,030 sq. ft.

(Alternate slab-on-grade foundation plan included.)

Blueprint Price Code A

Plan K-505-R

TO ORDER THIS BLUEPRINT,
CALL TOLL-FREE 1-800-547-5570
(prices and details on pp. 12-15.)

REAR ELEVATION

A Crisp Contemporary With Solar Options

Clean geometric lines coupled with a generous usage of windows lend a crisp image to this bright contemporary. This home is literally flooded with outdoor light from the top floor to the lower level.

The "open concept" floor plan allows good distribution of heated or cooled air to all parts of the interior spaces.

The sunspace is designed as an integral part of this home, but can be eliminated if not required at this time. For those of you desiring the sunspace as illustrated, the addition of a spa or hot tub affords easy access from the family room or the master bedroom suite.

Room sizes are generous with emphasis on a super kitchen design.

Den can perform double duty as a guest bedroom or as a fourth bedroom when needed.

Total square footage of this spacious home is 2,702 not including the 160 sq. ft. sunspace.

Home as illustrated may be constructed as a three-car garage version with the simple expansion of the two-car bay as plans indicate. The width of this home is 54', depth is 56'. A basement version is also available — please specify that version if desired.

Main level:	1,514 sq. ft.
Upper level:	1,188 sq. ft.
(Not incl. optional sauna & storage rm.)	
Sunspace:	160 sq. ft.
Total living area:	2,862 sq. ft.
(Not counting basement or garage)	

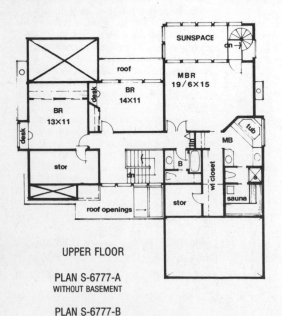

UPPER FLOOR

PLAN S-6777-A
WITHOUT BASEMENT

PLAN S-6777-B
BASEMENT VERSION

MAIN FLOOR

Blueprint Price Code D

Plans S-6777-A & S-6777-B

FRONT VIEW

Sun Chaser

A passive sun room with two fully glazed walls and an all-glass roof offers leeway when siting this comfortable, contemporary leisure home. Orientation is towards the south to capture maximum solar warmth. The window wall in the living room and a bank of clerestory windows high on the master bedroom wall soak up the winter rays for direct heat gain, yet are shaded with overhangs to block out the higher sun in the summer.

The 165 sq. ft. sun room is a focal point from the living and family rooms, through windows and sliding glass doors between these rooms. A dining table in the family room would command a sweeping view, or meals could be enjoyed in the sun room.

Sloping ceilings in the living and sun rooms allow balcony railings to open the master bedroom partially for a view down to these rooms, and let warm air flow up from the masonry storage floor of the sun room.

Accent walls of solid board paneling add visual warmth and texture to the rooms. Western cedar bevel siding adds beauty and individuality to the exterior. Exterior walls are of 2x6 construction.

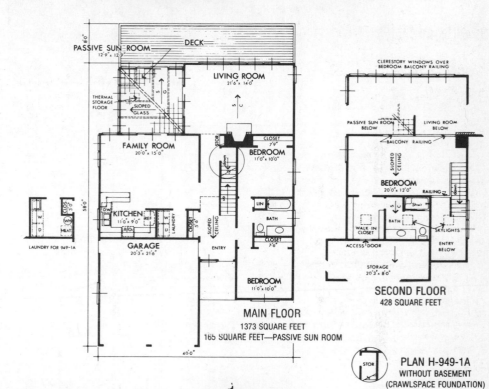

MAIN FLOOR
1373 SQUARE FEET
165 SQUARE FEET—PASSIVE SUN ROOM

LAUNDRY FOR 949-1A

SECOND FLOOR
428 SQUARE FEET

PLAN H-949-1A
WITHOUT BASEMENT
(CRAWLSPACE FOUNDATION)

PLAN H-949-1B
DAYLIGHT BASEMENT

PLAN H-949-1
STANDARD BASEMENT

First floor:	1,373 sq. ft.
Passive sun room:	165 sq. ft.
Second floor:	428 sq. ft.
Total living area:	1,966 sq. ft.

(Not counting basement or garage)

Blueprint Price Code B

Plans H-949-1, -1A & -1B

TO ORDER THIS BLUEPRINT,
CALL TOLL-FREE 1-800-547-5570
(prices and details on pp. 12-15.)

Floating Sunspace

- Designed to take advantage of narrow or 'left-over' lots, this compact home is intended for the economy-minded small family. Even so, it still includes an entry hall and a spacious sun room, features not often found in plans of this size.
- Both the living and dining rooms are spacious and flow together to create a great space for parties or family gatherings.
- The optional daylight basement provides an additional bedroom as well as a garage and storage space.

Plans H-951-1A & -1B

Bedrooms: 2-3	Baths: 1-2
Space:	
Main floor	1,075 sq. ft.
Sun room	100 sq. ft.
Total Living Area	**1,175 sq. ft.**
Basement	662 sq. ft.
Garage	311 sq. ft.
Exterior Wall Framing	**2x6**

Foundation options:
Daylight Basement
Crawlspace
(Foundation & framing conversion diagram available—see order form.)

Blueprint Price Code:	
Without Basement	**A**
With Basement	**B**

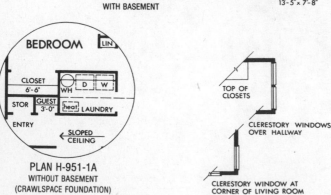

PLAN H-951-1B
WITH BASEMENT

PASSIVE SUN ROOM
13'-5" x 7'-8"

PLAN H-951-1A
WITHOUT BASEMENT
(CRAWLSPACE FOUNDATION)

CLERESTORY WINDOWS
OVER HALLWAY

CLERESTORY WINDOW AT
CORNER OF LIVING ROOM

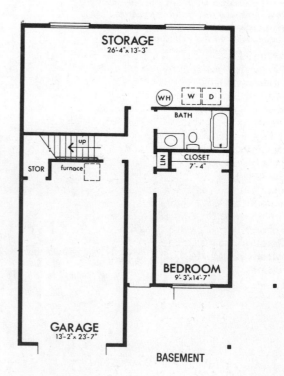

BASEMENT

Plans H-951-1A & -1B

Plans H-946-1A & -1B (Two Bedrooms)

Bedrooms: 2	Baths: 2

Space:	
Upper floor:	381 sq. ft.
Main floor:	814 sq. ft.

Total living area:	1,195 sq. ft.
Basement	approx. 814 sq. ft.
Garage:	315 sq. ft.

Exterior Wall Framing:	2x6

Foundation options:
Daylight basement (Plan H-946-1B).
Crawlspace (Plan H-946-1A).
Foundation & framing conversion
diagram available — see order form.)

Blueprint Price Code:	A

**UPPER FLOOR
PLANS H-946-1A & -1B**

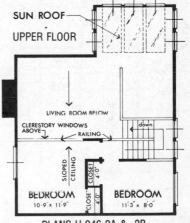

PLANS H-946-2A & -2B

Plans H-946-2A & -2B (Three Bedrooms)

Bedrooms: 3	Baths: 2

Space:	
Upper floor:	290 sq. ft.
Main floor:	814 sq. ft.

Total living area:	1,104 sq. ft.
Basement	approx. 814 sq. ft.
Garage:	315 sq. ft.

Exterior Wall Framing:	2x6

Foundation options:
Daylight basement (Plan H-946-2B).
Crawlspace (Plan H-946-2A).
Foundation & framing conversion
diagram available — see order form.)

Blueprint Price Code:	A

Narrow-Lot Solar Design

- This design offers your choice of foundation and number of bedrooms, plus it can be built on a narrow, sloping lot.
- The passive solar dining room has windows on three sides and a slate floor for heat storage. A French door leads to rear deck.
- The living room features a sloped ceiling, a wood stove in ceiling-high masonry, and sliding glass doors to the adjoining deck.
- The kitchen is open to the dining room but separated from the living room by a 7½-ft. high wall.
- The upper-level variations include a choice of one or two bedrooms. Clerestory windows above the balcony railing add drama to both versions.

MAIN FLOOR

Plans H-946-1A/1B & -2A/2B

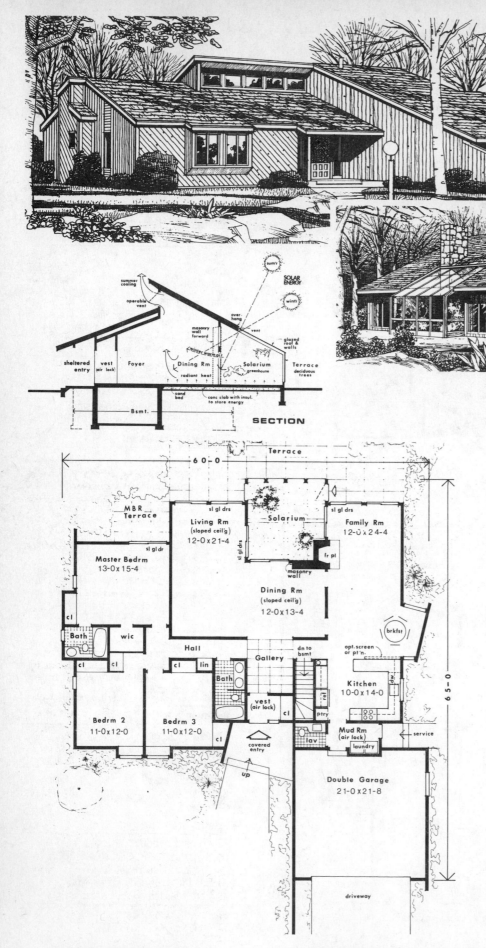

SECTION

summer cooling
operable vent
SOLAR ENERGY
sum'r
wint'r
overhang
masonry wall forward
vent
glazed roof & walls
sheltered entry
vest (air lock)
Foyer
winter warm air
Dining Rm
Solarium greenhouse
Terrace deciduous trees
radiant heat
sand bed
conc slab with insul. to store energy
Bsmt.

Terrace

60-0

M B R Terrace

Living Rm (sloped ceil'g) 12-0 x 21-4

sl gl drs

Solarium

sl gl drs

Family Rm 12-0 x 24-4

Master Bedrm 13-0 x 15-4

sl gl dr

sl gl drs

fr pl

masonry wall

Dining Rm (sloped ceil'g) 12-0 x 13-4

brkfst

cl

Bath

wic

Hall

cl

lin

Gallery

dn to bsmt

opt. screen or pt'n.

Kitchen 10-0 x 14-0

cl

Bath

vest (air lock)

cl

ptry

Bedrm 2 11-0 x 12-0

Bedrm 3 11-0 x 12-0

cl

covered entry

up

Mud Rm (air lock)

lav

laundry

service

65-0

Double Garage 21-0 x 21-8

driveway

Building into the Sunrise

This one-story passive solar energy home makes the most of the sun and provides great fuel savings. The key to this system is a south-facing solarium, glowing with natural light. All rooms except two bedrooms are oriented to maximize collection of the sun's energy by direct heat gain through large glazed openings. Thermal wall and insulated floor absorb and store heat energy for night time radiation.

In summer, eave overhang to the rear provides desirable shade, and high operable vents in the clerestory draw air out to produce natural ventilation. Many features are built into the design to aid in heat retention.

A central gallery efficiently channels traffic. To the right is the informal family room, with a rustic stone fireplace. A U-shaped kitchen and breakfast nook are situated off the dining and family rooms.

Isolated in one wing, away from family noise and traffic, are the sleeping quarters with two full baths. The master bedroom has a private terrace.

Total living area, excluding the solarium, is 1,816 sq. ft.; garage and mud room, 545 sq. ft.; optional basement, 1,043 sq. ft.

Basic House (excluding Solarium)	1,816 sq. ft.
Gar., Mud Rm., Etc.:	545 sq. ft.
Basement (optional):	1,043 sq. ft.

Blueprint Price Code B
Plan K-528-C

Passive Solar with Many Orientation Options

This angled passive solar design is planned to suit almost any plot and many orientation alternatives. Exterior siding of vertical natural wood and a high front chimney give the house an interesting appearance.

Inside, the central focus is the light-filled south-facing sun garden that greets occupants and visitors as they enter the reception hall. The large combination living room and dining room are highlighted by a dramatic sloped ceiling and a high-efficiency wood-burning fireplace. Glass around and above the fireplace contributes more light and provides a panoramic view of the rear landscaping. Sharing a second fireplace is the informal area that includes the family room and U-shaped kitchen.

Three bedrooms are located in the left wing of the house. The large master suite has a cheerful sitting area which borders on the sun garden. Living area, excluding the sun garden, is 1,574 sq. ft.; optional basement is 1,522 sq. ft.; garage is 400 sq. ft.

Total living area: 1,574 sq. ft.
(Not counting basement or garage)

Floor Plan labels

whirlpool tub · Terrace · 81-9 · Master Suite 13-0 × 22-0 · SITTING AREA · sl gl dr · Bath · w i c · cl · Bath · cl · Hall · Bedrm 2 13-4×11-0 · Bedrm 3 10-0×11-0 · cl · cl · lin · Vest (air lock) · Entry · shelf · Reception · sl gl dr · vent · Sun Garden · sl gl dr · Terrace · hi-efficiency fireplace · sl gl dr · window above · Living Rm · Dining Rm 17-0 × 23-0 (sloped ceil'g) · skylight · Family Rm 11-0 × 19-8 · Kitchen · ref · p'try · w d · eat'g bar · Mud Rm · d · hi-efficiency fireplace · Double Garage 20-0 × 20-0 · driveway · 46-11

FLOOR PLAN

Section labels

SOLAR ENERGY · sum'r · wint'r · summer vent · summer shade to reflect sun · deciduous trees for summer shade · winter warm air · Terrace · Sun Garden · Recep · Vest air lock · Sheltered Entry · thermal flr. with insul. to store energy · wd. const. · Bsmt. · wall insulation

SECTION
PASSIVE SOLAR AT WORK

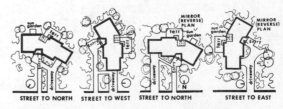

sun garden · terr · STREET TO NORTH · STREET TO WEST · MIRROR (REVERSE) PLAN · terr · sun garden · STREET TO NORTH · MIRROR (REVERSE) PLAN · sun garden · terr · STREET TO EAST

IMAGINE THE ORIENTATION POSSIBILITIES

Blueprint Price Code B

Plan K-526-C

TO ORDER THIS BLUEPRINT,
CALL TOLL-FREE 1-800-547-5570
(prices and details on pp. 12-15.)

Sun Room Adds Warmth to "Switched-Level" Contemporary

Solar warmth abounds in this dining area sun room, bolstered by a nearby free-standing wood fireplace and heat-storing masonry. An unusual feature of this design is that the active areas are on the second floor for a better view, and the sleeping rooms on the lower floor.

The spacious entry hall, with a door in from the double garage, has stairs with an open balcony railing leading up to the living-dining-kitchen floor, or down to the bedrooms, for complete traffic separation.

The open-plan upper floor, with vaulted ceiling, has an eight-foot wall screening the dining area from the stairway and the half-bath that is adjacent to the kitchen.

The glass roof and windows over and around the dining area are passive solar collectors and a brick or slate floor provides a storage mass.

A sliding glass door in the living room window wall opens onto the large wood deck, enhancing the view orientation of the house. Another small deck is reached by a French door next to the woodstove.

Downstairs, a hallway from the stairs leads to the master bedroom, with its own bath and large closets, and to the other two bedrooms, second bath and utility room.

The upper floor has 886 sq. ft., and there are 790 sq. ft. downstairs. Ceilings have R-30 insulation and the 2x6 stud walls hold R-19 batts.

Upper floor:	886 sq. ft.
Lower floor:	790 sq. ft.
Total living area:	1,676 sq. ft.
(Not counting garage)	

UPPER FLOOR
886 SQUARE FEET

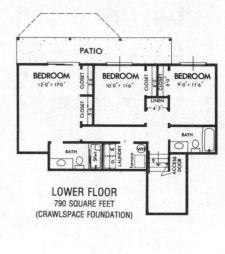

LOWER FLOOR
790 SQUARE FEET
(CRAWLSPACE FOUNDATION)

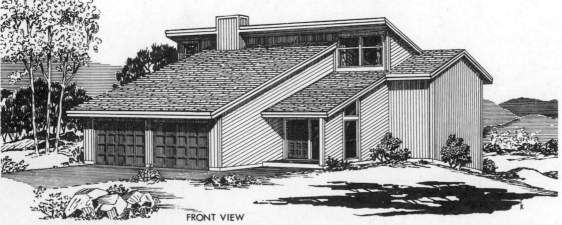

FRONT VIEW

TO ORDER THIS BLUEPRINT, CALL TOLL-FREE 1-800-547-5570 (prices and details on pp. 12-15.)

Blueprint Price Code B
Plan H-945-1A

Fresh Exterior Facade

- This two-story design with contemporary overhangs, exposed beams, gabled vertical windows, and multiple roof lines offers plenty of bright and spacious comfort.
- A sunlit vaulted entrance welcomes you inside, where cozy fireplaces in the living and activity rooms prove inviting.
- Highlights include a large sunken sun room with skylights and sloped ceilings plus a garden area off the family room, living room, and entry.
- A multi-level wood deck is accessible from the activity area, dining room, and sun room.
- Vaulted ceilings grace the dining room, living room, and entry, open stairs lead to the second floor.
- A large pantry and snack bar make food preparation more convenient.
- A rear master bedroom features adjacent spa and separate shower.

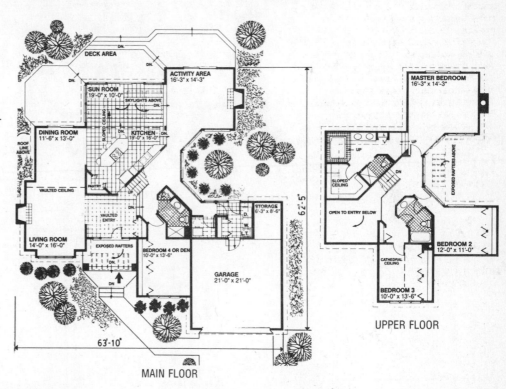

MAIN FLOOR

UPPER FLOOR

Plan N-1258

Bedrooms: 3	Baths: 3
Space:	
Upper floor:	1,127 sq. ft.
Main floor:	1,886 sq. ft.
Total living area:	3,013 sq. ft.
Garage:	441 sq. ft.
Storage area:	53 sq. ft.

Exterior Wall Framing: 2x4

Foundation options:
Standard basement.
Crawlspace with opt. slab.
(Foundation & framing conversion diagram available — see order form.)

Blueprint Price Code: E

Plan N-1258

Low-Cost Comfort

- Designed for the energy-conscious, this passive solar home provides year-round comfort at much lower fuel costs.
- The open, airy interior is a delight. In winter, sunshine penetrates deeply into the living spaces. In summer, wide overhangs shade the interior.
- The family room/breakfast/kitchen combination is roomy and bright for family activities.
- The living/dining areas flow together for more bright, open space.
- The master suite includes a private bath and walk-in closet. Two other bedrooms share another full bath.

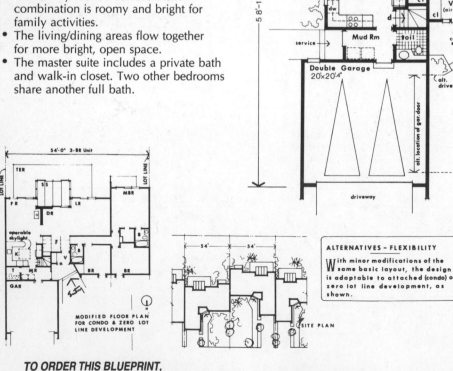

ALTERNATIVES - FLEXIBILITY

With minor modifications of the same basic layout, the design is adaptable to attached (condo) or zero lot line development, as shown.

Plan K-392-T

Bedrooms: 3	Baths: 2½
Space	
Main floor	1,592 sq. ft.
Total Living Area	**1,592 sq. ft.**
Basement	634 sq. ft.
Garage	407 sq. ft.
Exterior Wall Framing	2x4/2x6

Foundation options:
Partial Basement
Slab
(Foundation & framing conversion diagram available—see order form.)

Blueprint Price Code	B

TO ORDER THIS BLUEPRINT,
CALL TOLL-FREE 1-800-547-5570
(prices and details on pp. 12-15.)

Plan K-392-T

Solar Design Centers on Geometric Core

- This passive solar design, with a six-sided core, is angled to capture as much sunlight as possible.
- Finished in natural vertical cedar planks and stone veneer, this contemporary three-bedroom requires minimum maintenance.
- Double doors at the entry open into the spacious six-sided living-dining areas.
- The formal area, with its domed ceiling and free-standing fireplace, is enhanced by the two skylights overhead and the three sets of sliding glass doors, one of which leads to a glass-enclosed sunroom.
- The bright U-shaped kitchen is an extension of the den; sliding glass doors lead to one of the backyard terraces.
- The master bedoom, in a quiet sleeping wing, boasts ample closets, private terrace and a luxurious bath, complete with a whirlpool tub.

Plan K-534-L

Bedrooms: 3	Baths: 2

Space:	
Total living area:	1,495 sq. ft.
Basement:	1,505 sq. ft.
Garage:	400 sq. ft.
Mud room, etc.:	152 sq. ft.
Exterior Wall Framing:	2x4 or 2x6

Foundation options:
Standard basement.
Slab.
(Foundation & framing conversion diagram available — see order form)

Blueprint Price Code:	A

Plan K-534-L

Economical Design with Solar Option

Whether the solar room is built or not, this one-and-a-half story house is planned for energy savings and cost-effective construction. The focal theme is the combined family room and kitchen, facing the rear yard, which can accommodate a solar-room if opted. A fireplace, set within a glass wall, lends coziness and warmth. Sloped ceiling in the living room, with two operable skylights, rises over the second floor balcony.

Isolated on the upper level are three bedrooms. Master suite has a dressing room and a private bath, accented by a whirlpool tub. Operable skylights cool the house in the summer by convection. Total living area is 943 sq. ft. on the first floor and 690 on the second; optional basement is 943 sq. ft., and garage is 435 sq. ft.

Total living area: 1,633 sq. ft.
(Not counting basement or garage)

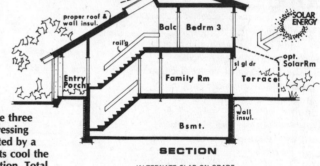

SECTION

(ALTERNATE SLAB-ON-GRADE
FOUNDATION PLAN INCLUDED)

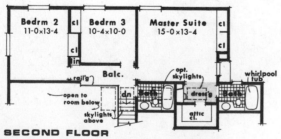

SECOND FLOOR

FIRST FLOOR

Blueprint Price Code B

Plan K-519-A

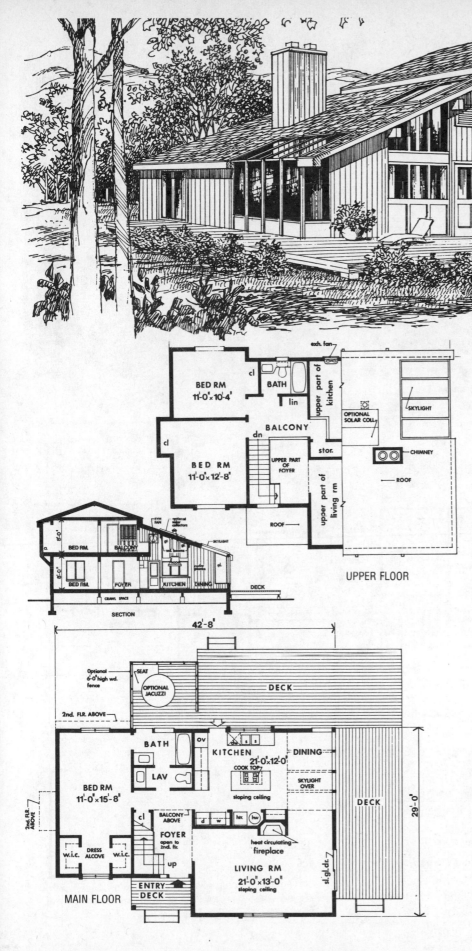

UPPER FLOOR

SECTION

42'-8"

29'-0"

MAIN FLOOR

Leisure Living at its Best

- This exciting contemporary is designed for leisure living, from the wraparound deck to the outdoor jacuzzi.
- The spacious combination kitchen and dining area has a glass wall and a vaulted, skylighted ceiling to create a greenhouse effect. Exposed wood beams and cedar board walls characterize the informal atmosphere.
- The large living room flows into the dining/kitchen area and also has a beamed ceiling. The living room features a heat-circulating fireplace and a slider that leads to the deck. The deck includes a sequestered area for a jacuzzi and extra seating space.
- The main-floor bedroom offers two walk-in closets, a dressing alcove and a private entrance to a full bath, which also can be reached from the jacuzzi area and the main hall.
- Two more bedrooms are upstairs and share another full bath. Note the balcony that overlooks the vaulted foyer and kitchen.

Plan HFL-1360-SN

Bedrooms: 3	Baths: 2
Space:	
Upper floor	426 sq. ft.
Main floor	1,106 sq. ft.
Total Living Area	**1,532 sq. ft.**
Exterior Wall Framing	2x6
Foundation options:	
Crawlspace	
(Foundation & framing conversion diagram available—see order form.)	
Blueprint Price Code	B

Plan HFL-1360-SN

Sunny Indoor or Outdoor Dining

- This cozy country-style home offers an inviting front porch and an interior just as welcoming.
- A spacious living room features a warming fireplace and windows that overlook the porch.
- The living room opens to the dining area, which leads to a rear porch and patio.
- The island kitchen has plenty of counter space, a sink view and an adjoining sun room that could be used as a sunny formal dining area.
- The private master suite is secluded to the rear. Dual walk-in closets, vanities and a large windowed tub are nice features in the master bath.

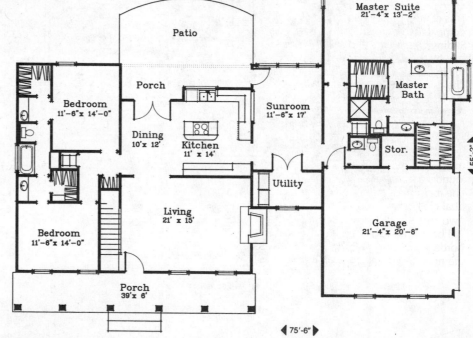

Plan J-90014

Bedrooms: 3	**Baths:** 2 ½

Space:

Main floor	2,190 sq. ft.
Total Living Area	**2,190 sq. ft.**
Basement	2,190 sq. ft.
Garage	465 sq. ft.
Storage	34 sq. ft.

Exterior Wall Framing	2x6

Foundation options:
Standard Basement
Crawlspace
Slab
(Foundation & framing conversion diagram available—see order form.)

Blueprint Price Code	C

Contemporary Saltbox

- This contemporary two-story saltbox is compactly designed.
- Sliding glass doors and a greenhouse bay off the dining area make the rear of the home almost all enclosed in glass.
- The huge living room at the center of the floor plan features a sloped ceiling, heat-circulating fireplace and a skylight in addition to the glass wall of the greenhouse.
- A sunny dinette and open, skylit kitchen merge together with a convenient laundry room and pantry nearby.
- The main-floor master bedroom has dual closets and an adjacent full bath.
- Two nice-sized bedrooms and a second full bath share the upper level; a railing borders the balcony that overlooks the main living areas below.

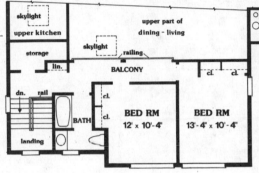

Plan HFL-1300-MS	
Bedrooms: 3	**Baths:** 2
Space:	
Upper floor	519 sq. ft.
Main floor	1,042 sq. ft.
Total Living Area	**1,561 sq. ft.**
Basement	1,000 sq. ft.
Garage	233 sq. ft.
Exterior Wall Framing	2x6
Foundation options:	
Standard Basement	
Slab	
(Foundation & framing conversion diagram available—see order form.)	
Blueprint Price Code	B

UPPER FLOOR

- skylight
- upper kitchen
- storage
- lin.
- dn. rail
- landing
- BATH
- cl.
- cl.
- upper part of dining - living
- skylight
- railing
- BALCONY
- cl. cl.
- BED RM 12' x 10'-4"
- BED RM 13'-4" x 10'-4"

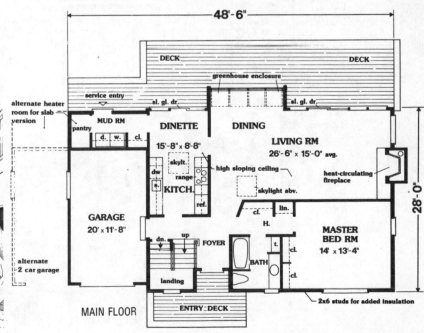

MAIN FLOOR

48'-6"

28'-0"

- DECK
- DECK
- greenhouse enclosure
- alternate heater room for slab version
- service entry
- sl. gl. dr.
- sl. gl. dr.
- pantry
- MUD RM
- d. w. cl.
- DINETTE 15'-8" x 8'-8"
- DINING
- LIVING RM 26'-6" x 15'-0" avg.
- skylt.
- range
- high sloping ceiling
- heat-circulating fireplace
- dw
- s.
- KITCH.
- ref.
- skylight abv.
- cl. lin.
- GARAGE 20' x 11'-8"
- dn. up
- FOYER
- H.
- MASTER BED RM 14' x 13'-4"
- landing
- BATH
- t.
- cl.
- cl.
- alternate 2 car garage
- ENTRY DECK
- 2x6 studs for added insulation

Plan HFL-1300-MS

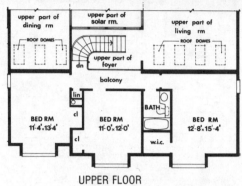

UPPER FLOOR

BED RM
11'-4"·13'-4"

BED RM
11'-0"·12'-0"

BED RM
12'-8"·15'-4"

upper part of dining rm
upper part of solar rm.
upper part of living rm
upper part of foyer
ROOF DOMES
ROOF DOMES
balcony
BATH
cl
lin
cl
w.i.c.
dn

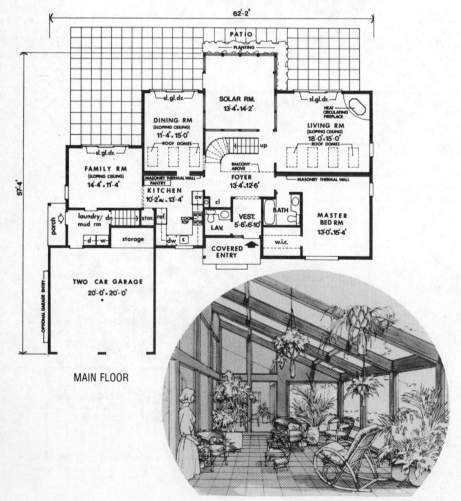

MAIN FLOOR

62'-2"
57'-4"

PATIO
PLANTING
SOLAR RM.
13'-4"·14'-2"
sl.gl.dr.
sl.gl.dr.
DINING RM
(SLOPING CEILING)
11'-4"·15'-0"
LIVING RM
(SLOPING CEILING)
18'-0"·15'-0"
HEAT CIRCULATING FIREPLACE
ROOF DOMES
ROOF DOMES
sl.gl.dr.
FAMILY RM
(SLOPING CEILING)
14'-4" x 11'-4"
MASONRY THERMAL WALL
PANTRY
FOYER
13'-4"·12'-6"
BALCONY ABOVE
up
MASONRY THERMAL WALL
KITCHEN
10'-2" x 13'-4"
ov
cl
laundry/ dn
mud rm
stor.
ref.
COOK TOP
LAV.
VEST.
5'-6"·6'-10"
BATH
MASTER BED RM
13'-0"·15'-4"
d w
storage
dw
s
COVERED ENTRY
w.i.c.
porch
TWO CAR GARAGE
20'-0"·20'-0"
OPTIONAL GARAGE ENTRY

A Stunning Solar Room

- The highlight in this exciting contemporary home is its central solar room. Bordering both the living and dining rooms, its ceiling and walls are glass with wood beam framing.
- Roof domes and sliders to a large rear patio are found in both the living room and the dining room, and a heat-circulating corner fireplace is an added touch in the living room.
- A covered entry leads to the dramatic central foyer that features a curved, open stair and a view of the solar room behind a 12-ft.-high glass wall.
- The main-floor master suite offers a huge walk-in closet and private bath.
- Three additional bedrooms and a second full bath occupy the upper level.

Plan HFL-1270-LN	
Bedrooms: 4	**Baths:** 2 ½
Space:	
Upper floor	752 sq. ft.
Main floor	1,490 sq. ft.
Total Living Area	**2,242 sq. ft.**
Partial Basement	281 sq. ft.
Garage	400 sq. ft.
Exterior Wall Framing	2x6
Foundation options:	
Partial Basement	
Slab	
(Foundation & framing conversion diagram available—see order form.)	
Blueprint Price Code	C

Plan HFL-1270-LN

FRONT VIEW

Sunny Family Living

- Pleasant-looking and unassuming from the front, this plan breaks into striking, sun-catching angles at the rear.
- The living room sun roof gathers passive solar heat, which is stored in the tile floor and the two-story high masonry backdrop to the wood stove.
- A 516-square-foot master suite with private bath and balcony makes up the second floor.
- The main floor offers two more bedrooms and a full bath.

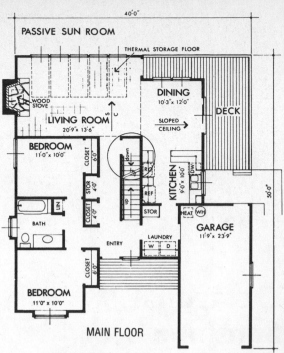

MAIN FLOOR

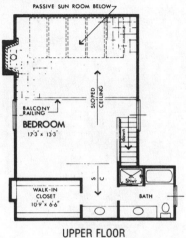

UPPER FLOOR

WITHOUT BASEMENT
(CRAWLSPACE FOUNDATION)

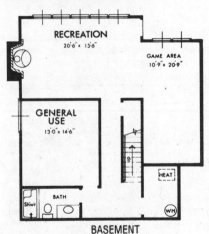

BASEMENT

Plans H-947-1A & -1B	
Bedrooms: 3	**Baths: 2-3**

Space:	
Upper floor:	516 sq. ft.
Main floor:	1,162 sq. ft.

Total without basement:	1,678 sq. ft.
Daylight basement:	966 sq. ft.

Total with basement:	2,644 sq. ft.
Garage:	279 sq. ft.

Exterior Wall Framing:	2x6

Foundation options:
Daylight basement (H-947-1B).
Crawlspace (H-947-1A).
(Foundation & framing conversion diagram available — see order form.)

Blueprint Price Code:	
Without basement:	B
With basement:	D

REAR VIEW

Plans H-947-1A & -1B

***TO ORDER THIS BLUEPRINT,
CALL TOLL-FREE 1-800-547-5570***
(prices and details on pp. 12-15.)

FRONT VIEW

Octagonal Sunshine Special

- Octagon homes offer the ultimate for taking advantage of a view, and are fascinating designs even for more ordinary settings.
- This plan offers a huge, house-spanning living/dining area with loads of glass and a masonry collector wall to store solar heat.
- The 700-square-foot upper level is devoted entirely to an enormous master suite, with a balcony overlooking the living room below, a roomy private bath and a large closet/dressing area.
- Scissor-trusses allow vaulted ceilings over the two-story-high living room and the master suite.
- A second roomy bedroom and full bath are offered downstairs, along with an efficient kitchen, a laundry area and inviting foyer.
- A daylight basement option offers the potential for more bedrooms, hobbies, work rooms or recreational space.

Plans H-948-1A & -1B

Bedrooms: 2-4	Baths: 2

Space:	
Upper floor:	700 sq. ft.
Main floor:	1,236 sq. ft.
Total without basement:	1,936 sq. ft.
Daylight basement:	1,236 sq. ft.
Total with basement:	3,172 sq. ft.
Garage:	550 sq. ft.
Exterior Wall Framing:	2x6

Foundation options:
Daylight basement (H-948-1B).
Crawlspace (H-948-1A).
(Foundation & framing conversion diagram available — see order form.)

Blueprint Price Code:

Without basement:	B
With basement:	E

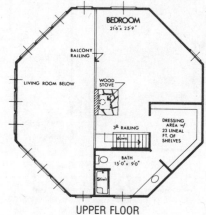

UPPER FLOOR

MAIN FLOOR

WITHOUT BASEMENT (CRAWLSPACE FOUNDATION)

SCALE
0 1 2 3 4 5 6 7 8 9 10

BASEMENT

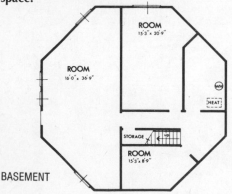

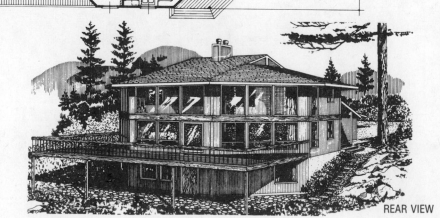

REAR VIEW

Plans H-948-1A & -1B

Simple and Economical Chalet

- This home away from home is relatively simple to construct; it is also an enjoyable reason to spend your weekends in the mountains or at the beach.
- The main level is largely devoted to open living space, other than the kitchen and master bedroom, which could also be used as a study or hobby room.
- Second-floor bedrooms are larger and share a full bath and large storage areas.

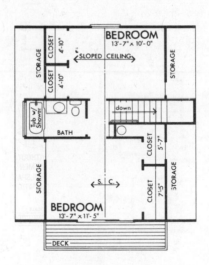

UPPER FLOOR

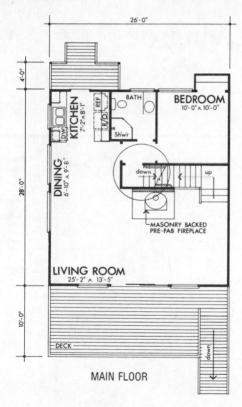

MAIN FLOOR

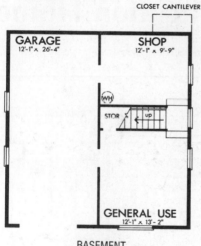

BASEMENT
PLAN H-26-1
DAYLIGHT BASEMENT

PLAN H-26-1A
WITHOUT BASEMENT

Plans H-26-1 & -1A

Bedrooms: 3	Baths: 2

Space:

Upper floor:	476 sq. ft.
Main floor:	728 sq. ft.
Total living area:	**1,204 sq. ft.**
Basement:	approx. 728 sq. ft.
Garage: (included in basement)	318 sq. ft.

Exterior Wall Framing:	2x4

Foundation options:
Daylight basement (Plan H-26-1).
Crawlspace (Plan H-26-1A).
(Foundation & framing conversion diagram available — see order form.)

Blueprint Price Code:	A

Plans H-26-1 & -1A

For Year-Round Living or Vacation Home

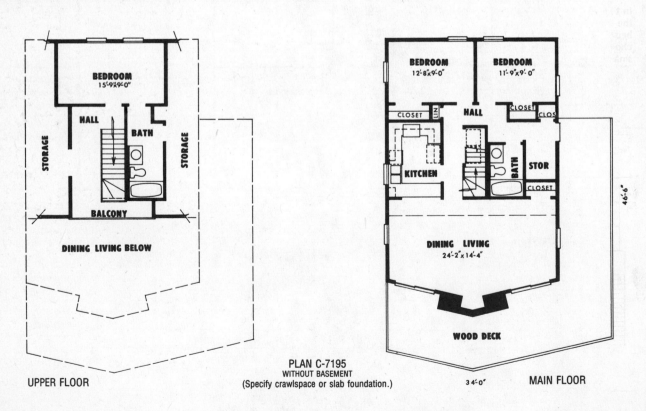

STORAGE

BEDROOM
15'-9"x9'-0"

HALL

BATH

STORAGE

BALCONY

DINING LIVING BELOW

UPPER FLOOR

PLAN C-7195
WITHOUT BASEMENT
(Specify crawlspace or slab foundation.)

BEDROOM
12'-8"x9'-0"

BEDROOM
11'-9"x9'-0"

CLOSET

HALL

CLOSET   **CLOS**

KITCHEN

BATH

STOR

CLOSET

DINING LIVING
24'-2"x14'-4"

46'-6"

WOOD DECK

3'-0"   **MAIN FLOOR**

Total living area: 1,260 sq. ft.

Blueprint Price Code A
Plan C-7195

A-Frame Offers Options

In this versatile A-frame, the main floor is the same in all versions, and includes one bedroom. The upper floor gives you a choice of one large bedroom or two smaller ones.

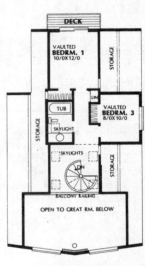

UPPER FLOOR
PLAN P-530-5A
WITH CRAWLSPACE

PLAN P-530-5D
WITH BASEMENT

UPPER FLOOR
PLAN P-530-2A
WITH CRAWLSPACE

PLAN P-530-2D
WITH BASEMENT

Upper floor:	400 sq. ft.
Main floor:	761 sq. ft.
Total living area: (Not counting basement or garage)	1,161 sq. ft.
Basement:	938 sq. ft.
Total living area with daylight basement:	2,099 sq. ft.

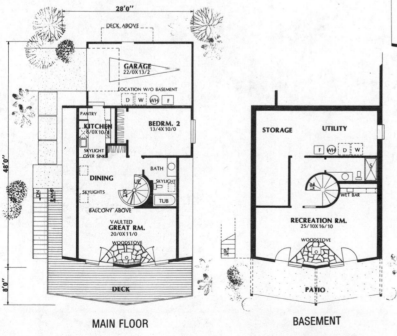

MAIN FLOOR

BASEMENT

Blueprint Price Code C With Basement
Blueprint Price Code A Without Basement

Plans P-530-2A/2D & -5A/5D

TO ORDER THIS BLUEPRINT,
CALL TOLL-FREE 1-800-547-5570
(prices and details on pp. 12-15.)

Indoor-Outdoor Living

- Attention-getting pentagonal-shaped home is ideal for full-time or vacation living.
- Huge, two-story high living/dining area takes up half of the main floor, ideal for family gatherings.
- Compact, but functional kitchen features breakfast bar and adjacent laundry room that can also serve as a pantry and/or mudroom.
- Open stairway leads to second-floor balcony hallway overlooking the main level living area.
- Upper level has room for two additional bedrooms and a second bath.

Plans H-855-2 & -2A

Bedrooms: 3	Baths: 2
Space:	
Upper floor:	660 sq. ft.
Main floor:	1,174 sq. ft.
Total living area:	1,834 sq. ft.
Basement:	approx. 1,174 sq. ft.
Garage:	277 sq. ft.
Exterior Wall Framing:	2x4

Foundation options:
Daylight basement (Plan H-855-2).
Crawlspace (Plan H-855-2A).
(Foundation & framing conversion diagram available — see order form.)

Blueprint Price Code:

Without basement	B
With basement	E

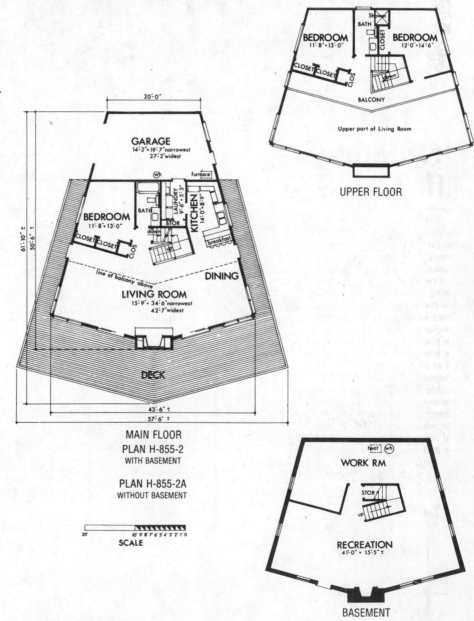

UPPER FLOOR

MAIN FLOOR
PLAN H-855-2
WITH BASEMENT

PLAN H-855-2A
WITHOUT BASEMENT

SCALE

BASEMENT

Plans H-855-2 & -2A

Dramatic and Affordable Chalet

This year-round vacation home is an "upside-down" house, with the main living areas on the upper floor and the sleeping quarters at the ground level. The main entrance on the side of the house opens into a two-story foyer, conveying the feel of being part of the main level, which is just a few steps up.

Once in the living room, one immediately experiences the drama of the open planning and the views beyond. The large front deck has a stairway that can be used as a secondary entrance way. The U-shaped kitchen is illuminated by an operable skylight. A railing in the living room overlooks the foyer below.

Lower level includes two bedrooms and a den which can become a third bedroom. Total living area is 488 sq. ft. on the first floor and 492 sq. ft. on the second.

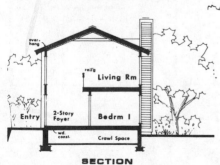

SECTION

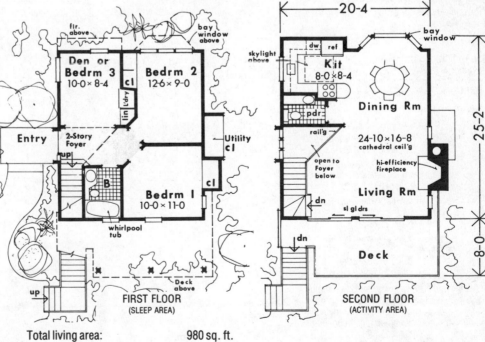

Total living area: 980 sq. ft.

Blueprint Price Code A

Plan K-532-L

TO ORDER THIS BLUEPRINT, CALL TOLL-FREE 1-800-547-5570
(prices and details on pp. 12-15.)

45

FRONT VIEW

Versatile, Open Plan

One enters this home from a side entry approached by the elevated deck and gains access to a spacious entry that controls traffic to all portions of the home. The entrance immediately reveals the open character of the home where you can see the spacious living room with central fireplace located at one end of the building.

Besides an expansive view through clerestory windows, one will notice the sliding glass doors that flank each side of the log-sized fireplace.

Connected to the living room by a 10' wide opening, a dining area is located in such manner as to provide an expandable dining table arrangement. Combination living-dining area opens all living space for entertaining.

First floor: 1,056 sq. ft.
Second floor: 336 sq. ft.

Total living area: 1,392 sq. ft.
(Not counting basement or garage)

FOR PLAN WITH NO BASEMENT
AND BEDROOM/BATH ON SECOND FLOOR, ORDER
PLAN H-893-1A

FOR PLAN WITH NO BASEMENT
AND DORMITORY ON SECOND FLOOR, ORDER
PLAN H-893-2A

FOR PLAN WITH STANDARD BASEMENT
AND BEDROOM/BATH ON SECOND FLOOR, ORDER
PLAN H-893-1B

FOR PLAN WITH STANDARD BASEMENT
AND DORMITORY ON SECOND FLOOR, ORDER
PLAN H-893-2B

FOR PLAN WITH DAYLIGHT BASEMENT
AND BEDROOM/BATH ON SECOND FLOOR, ORDER
PLAN H-893-1C

FOR PLAN WITH DAYLIGHT BASEMENT
AND DORMITORY ON SECOND FLOOR, ORDER
PLAN H-893-2C

TO ORDER THIS BLUEPRINT,
CALL TOLL-FREE 1-800-547-5570
46 (prices and details on pp. 12-15.)

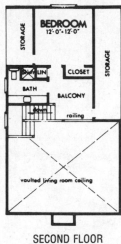

SECOND FLOOR
WITH BATHROOM
336 SQUARE FEET

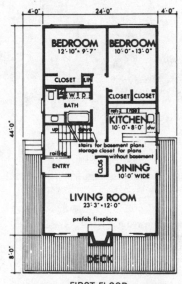

FIRST FLOOR
1056 SQUARE FEET

(NON-BASEMENT VERSIONS
HAVE CRAWLSPACE
FOUNDATIONS)

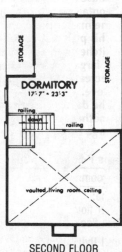

SECOND FLOOR
WITHOUT BATHROOM
336 SQUARE FEET

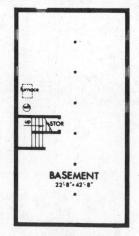

STANDARD BASEMENT

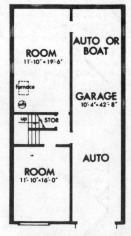

DAYLIGHT BASEMENT

Blueprint Price Code A

Plans H-893-1A, -2A, -1B, -2B, -1C & -2C

An Octagonal Home with a Lofty View

- There's no better way to avoid the ordinary than by building an octagonal home and escaping from square corners and rigid rooms.
- The roomy main floor offers plenty of space for full-time family living or for a comfortable second home retreat.
- The vaulted entry hall leads to the bedrooms on the right or down the hall to the Great Room.
- Warmed by a wood stove, the Great Room offers a panoramic view of the surrounding scenery.
- The center core of the main floor houses two baths, one of which contains a spa tub and is private to the master bedroom.
- This plan also includes a roomy kitchen and handy utility area.
- A large loft is planned as a recreation room, also with a wood stove.
- The daylight basement version adds another bedroom, bath, garage and large storage area.

Plans P-532-3A & -3D

Bedrooms: 3-4	Baths: 2-3

Space:

Upper floor:	355 sq. ft.
Main floor:	1,567 sq. ft.

Total living area:	**1,922 sq. ft.**
Basement living area:	430 sq. ft.
Garage (included in basement):	
	approx. 735 sq. ft.
Storage:	approx. 482 sq. ft.

FRONT VIEW

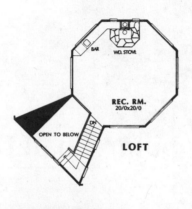

LOFT

BAR — WD. STOVE — REC. RM. 20/0x20/0 — OPEN TO BELOW — DN

Exterior Wall Framing:	2x6

Foundation options:
Daylight basement (Plan P-532-3D).
Crawlspace (Plan P-532-3A).
(Foundation & framing conversion diagram available — see order form.)

Blueprint Price Code:

Without basement:	B
With basement:	C

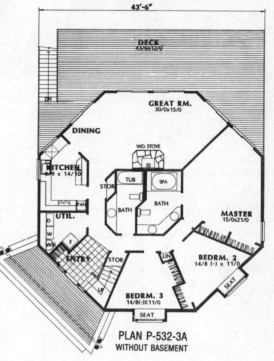

PLAN P-532-3A
WITHOUT BASEMENT

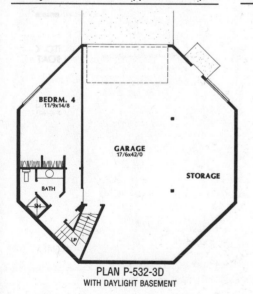

PLAN P-532-3D
WITH DAYLIGHT BASEMENT

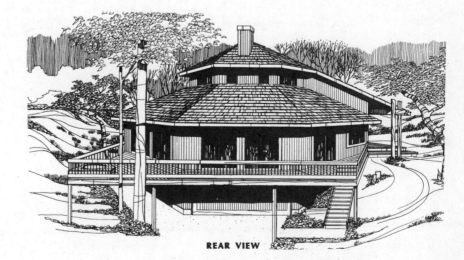

REAR VIEW

Plans P-532-3A & -3D

Ever-Popular Chalet Style

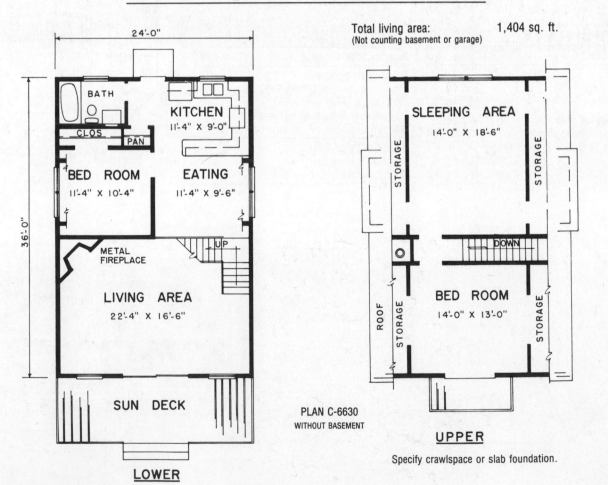

Total living area: 1,404 sq. ft.
(Not counting basement or garage)

24'-0"

BATH

KITCHEN
11'-4" X 9'-0"

CLOS
PAN

BED ROOM
11'-4" X 10'-4"

EATING
11'-4" X 9'-6"

36'-0"

METAL
FIREPLACE

UP

LIVING AREA
22'-4" X 16'-6"

SUN DECK

LOWER

SLEEPING AREA
14'-0" X 18'-6"

STORAGE

STORAGE

DOWN

ROOF

STORAGE

STORAGE

BED ROOM
14'-0" X 13'-0"

PLAN C-6630
WITHOUT BASEMENT

UPPER

Specify crawlspace or slab foundation.

Blueprint Price Code A
Plan C-6630

Panoramic View Embraces Outdoors

- This geometric design takes full advantage of scenic sites.
- Living area faces a glass-filled wall and wrap-around deck.
- Open dining/living room arrangement is complemented by vaulted ceilings, an overhead balcony, and a 5-ft-wide fireplace.
- 12' deep main deck offers generous space for outdoor dining and entertaining.

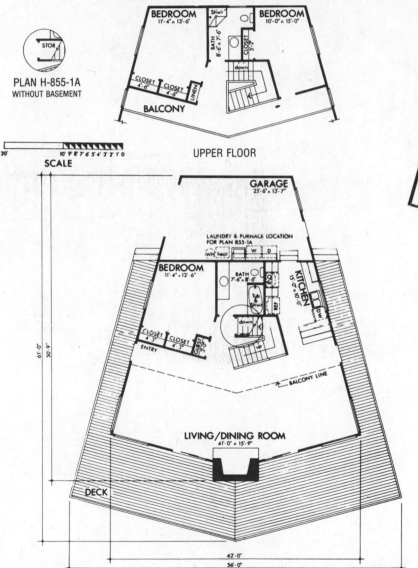

STOR

PLAN H-855-1A
WITHOUT BASEMENT

SCALE

BEDROOM 11'-4" x 13'-6"
BEDROOM 10'-0" x 15'-0"
Sh'w'r
BATH 8'-6" x 7'-6"
CLOSET 5'-2"
down
CLOSET 4'-6"
CLOSET 4'-6"
LINEN
BALCONY

UPPER FLOOR

GARAGE 25'-6" x 13'-7"

LAUNDRY & FURNACE LOCATION FOR PLAN 855-1A
WH heat W D

BEDROOM 11'-4" x 13'-6"
BATH 7'-6" x 8'-6"
Tub
KITCHEN 15'-0" x 10'-0"
REF
DW
CLOSET 4'-3"
CLOSET 4'-3"
GUEST 3'-0"
ENTRY
down
up
BALCONY LINE

LIVING/DINING ROOM 41'-0" x 15'-9"

DECK

42'-0"
56'-0"

61'-0"
50'-9"

MAIN FLOOR

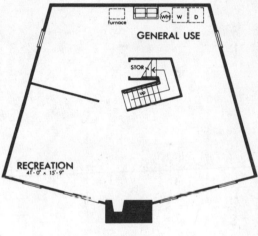

furnace
WH W D
GENERAL USE
STOR
down up

RECREATION
41'-0" x 15'-9"

BASEMENT

Plans H-855-1 & -1A

Bedrooms: 3		**Baths:** 2

Space:

Upper floor:	625 sq. ft.
Main floor:	1,108 sq. ft.

Total living area:	1,733 sq. ft.
Basement:	approx. 1,108 sq. ft.
Garage:	346 sq. ft.

Exterior Wall Framing:	2x6

Foundation options:
Daylight basement (Plan H-855-1).
Crawlspace (Plan H-855-1A).
(Foundation & framing conversion diagram available — see order form.)

Blueprint Price Code:

Without basement	B
With basement	D

Plans H-855-1 & -1A

Spacious Octagon

- Highly functional main floor plan makes traffic easy and minimizes wasted hall space.
- Double-sized entry opens to spacious octagonal living room with central fireplace and access to all rooms.
- U-shaped kitchen and attached dining area allow for both informal and formal occasions.
- Contiguous bedrooms each have independent deck entrances.
- Exciting deck borders entire home.

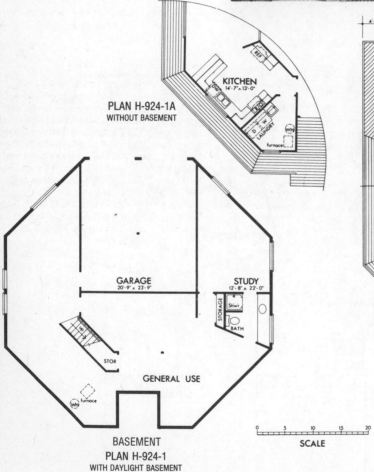

PLAN H-924-1A
WITHOUT BASEMENT

KITCHEN
14'-7" x 13'-0"

GARAGE
20'-9" x 23'-9"

STUDY
12'-8" x 22'-0"

STORAGE

BATH

STOR

GENERAL USE

furnace

BASEMENT
PLAN H-924-1
WITH DAYLIGHT BASEMENT

SCALE
0 5 10 15 20

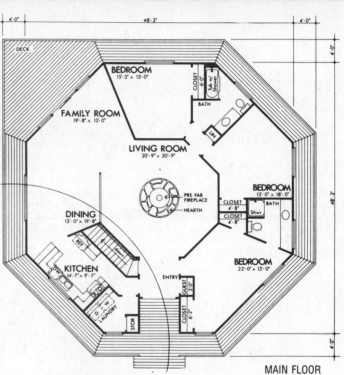

DECK

BEDROOM
15'-3" x 13'-0"

CLOSET

BATH

FAMILY ROOM
19'-8" x 13'-0"

LIVING ROOM
20'-9" x 20'-9"

PRE-FAB FIREPLACE
HEARTH

BEDROOM
13'-0" x 18'-0"

CLOSET
4'-8"

CLOSET
4'-8"

BATH

DINING
13'-0" x 19'-8"

KITCHEN
14'-7" x 9'-7"

LAUNDRY

STOR

ENTRY

CLOSET
6'-2"

GUEST
3'-0"

BEDROOM
22'-0" x 13'-0"

MAIN FLOOR

48'-3"

4'-0"

4'-0"

4'-0"

48'-3"

4'-0"

Plans H-924-1 & -1A

Bedrooms: 3-4	Baths: 2-3
Space:	
Main floor:	1,888 sq. ft.
Total without basement:	1,888 sq. ft.
Basement:	1,395 sq. ft.
Total with basement:	3,283 sq. ft.
Garage:	493 sq. ft.
Exterior Wall Framing:	2x4

Foundation options:
Daylight basement (Plan H-924-1).
Crawlspace (Plan H-924-1A).
(Foundation & framing conversion diagram available — see order form.)

Blueprint Price Code:

Without basement:	B
With basement:	E

Plans H-924-1 & -1A

FRONT VIEW

Compact, Economical A-Frame

A huge living room with cathedral-like vaulted ceilings charmingly interrupted midway by an overhanging balcony provides a breath-taking introduction to this home — after you finish marvelling over the expansive entry deck. Furniture arranges itself naturally around the cozy warmth of the free-standing prefabricated fireplace or wood stove. A functional U-shaped kitchen area occupies one open corner of this great room.

This A-Frame boasts a laundry space, complete with washer and dryer. The practical-minded will surely note the central location of the water heater within fuel-saving inches of every hot water tap. A small but functional bathroom is also located in this area. Placement near the rear door allows easy daytime use by children without forcing them to track through the rest of the house with muddy feet.

Two large sleeping areas are located upstairs. One is a balcony room, which might also serve as a charming studio for indoor projects. It should be noted that in none of the rooms except the balcony do the slanting exterior walls intersect directly with the floor to create areas that are useless because of restricted head room. All rooms have a five foot high "knee-wall" located a few feet inboard to assure head space.

If you prefer a home with a basement, Plan H-6B is shown as an alternate, offering garage and recreation space as well as additional plumbing facilities.

BASEMENT
676 SQUARE FEET

PLAN H-6B
WITH BASEMENT
(LAUNDRY IN BASEMENT)

MAIN FLOOR
760 SQUARE FEET

PLAN H-6LA
WITHOUT BASEMENT

SECOND FLOOR PLAN
303 SQUARE FEET

Main floor:	760 sq. ft.
Second floor:	303 sq. ft.
Total living area:	1,063 sq. ft.
(Not counting basement or garage)	

Blueprint Price Code A

Plans H-6LA & H-6B

TO ORDER THIS BLUEPRINT, CALL TOLL-FREE 1-800-547-5570
(prices and details on pp. 12-15.)

Photo by: Karl Bischoff

NOTE:
The above photographed home may have been modified by the homeowner. Please refer to floor plan and/or drawn elevation shown for actual blueprint details.

Unique Octagon Design

- **Irregularly shaped rooms are oriented around an entrance hall paralleling the octagonal exterior.**
- **Short directional hallways eliminate cross-room traffic and provide independent room access to the front door.**
- **Spacious living and dining rooms form a continuous area more than 38' wide.**
- **Oversized bathroom serves a large master suite which features a deck view and dual closets.**
- **This plan is also available with a stucco exterior (Plans H-942-2, with daylight basement, and H-942-2A, without basement).**

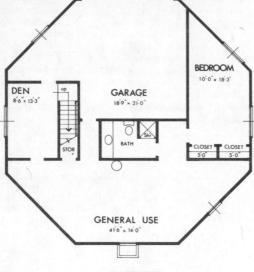

DEN
8'-6" x 13'-3"

up

GARAGE
18'-9" x 21'-0"

BEDROOM
10'-0" x 18'-3"

STOR

BATH

Shr.

CLOSET 5'-0"

CLOSET 5'-0"

GENERAL USE
41'-6" x 14'-0"

BASEMENT

1/16" = 1'

0 1 2 3 4 5 6 7 8 9 10

Plans H-942-1 & -1A (Wood)
Plans H-942-2 & -2A (Stucco)

Bedrooms: 3-4	Baths: 2-3
Space:	
Main floor:	1,564 sq. ft.
Basement:	approx. 1,170 sq. ft.
Total with basement:	**2,734 sq. ft.**
Garage:	394 sq. ft.
Exterior Wall Framing	**2x6**

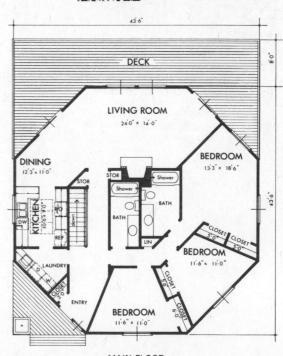

43'-6"

8'-0"

DECK

LIVING ROOM
24'-0" x 14'-0"

DINING
12'-3" x 11'-0"

STOR

Shower

Shower

BEDROOM
13'-3" x 18'-6"

43'-6"

KITCHEN
10'-6" x 9'-0"

DW

REF

down

BATH

BATH

LIN

CLOSET 5'-0"

CLOSET 5'-0"

BEDROOM
11'-6" x 11'-0"

LAUNDRY

W

CLOSET 3'-0"

ENTRY

CLOSET 5'-0"

CLOSET 6'-0"

BEDROOM
11'-6" x 11'-0"

MAIN FLOOR

Foundation options:
Daylight basement (Plans H-942-1 & -2).
Crawlspace (Plans H-942-1A & -2A).
(Foundation & framing conversion diagram available — see order form.)

Blueprint Price Code:
Without basement: B
With basement: D

Weekend Retreat

For those whose goal is a small, affordable retreat at the shore or in the mountains, this plan may be the answer. Although it measures less tha 400 sq. ft. of living space on the main floor, it lacks nothing in comfort and convenience. A sizeable living room boasts a masonry hearth on which to mount your choice of a wood stove or a pre-fab fireplace. There is plenty of room for furniture, including a dining table.

The galley-type kitchen is a small marvel of compact convenience and utility, even boasting a dishwasher and space for a stackable washer and dryer. The wide open nature of the first floor guarantees that even the person working in the kitchen area will still be included in the party. On the floor plan, a dashed line across the living room indicates the limits of the balcony bedroom above. In front of this line, the A-frame shape of the living room soars from the floor boards to the ridge beam high above. Clerestory windows lend a further note of spaciousness and unity with nature's outdoors. A huge planked deck adds to the indoor-outdoor relationship.

A modest-sized bedroom on the second floor is approached by a standard stairway, not an awkward ladder or heavy pull-down stairway as is often the case in small A-frames. The view over the balcony rail to the living room below adds a note of distinction. The unique framing pattern allows a window at either end of the bedroom, improving both outlook and ventilation.

A compact bathroom serves both levels and enjoys natural daylight through a skylight window.

First floor:	391 sq. ft.
Upper level:	144 sq. ft.
Total living area:	535 sq. ft.

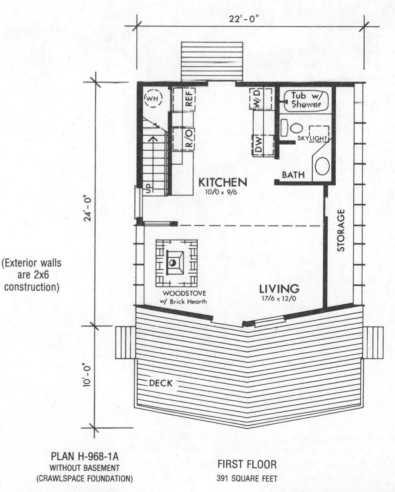

(Exterior walls are 2x6 construction)

UPPER LEVEL
144 SQUARE FEET

PLAN H-968-1A
WITHOUT BASEMENT
(CRAWLSPACE FOUNDATION)

FIRST FLOOR
391 SQUARE FEET

Blueprint Price Code A
Plan H-968-1A

TO ORDER THIS BLUEPRINT,
CALL TOLL-FREE 1-800-547-5570
(prices and details on pp. 12-15.)

Handsome Chalet Design Features View

- Roomy floor plan will make this chalet something you'll yearn for all year long.
- Massive fireplace in living room is a pleasant welcome after a day in the cold outdoors.
- Open kitchen has two entrances for smoother traffic.
- Generous laundry facilities and large bath are unexpected frills you'll appreciate.
- Upper floor bedrooms feature sloped ceilings and plenty of storage space.
- Optional basement plan affords more storage and general use space.

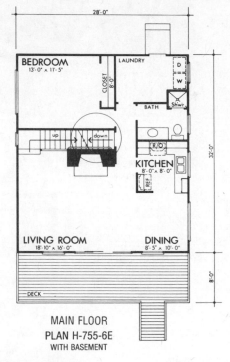

MAIN FLOOR
PLAN H-755-6E
WITH BASEMENT

UPPER FLOOR

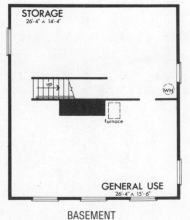

BASEMENT

PLAN H-755-5E
WITHOUT BASEMENT

WATER HEATER & FURNACE
LOCATED IN LAUNDRY RM.

Plans H-755-5E & -6E

Bedrooms: 3	Baths: 2

Space:

Upper floor:	454 sq. ft.
Main floor:	896 sq. ft.
Total without basement:	1,350 sq. ft.
Basement:	896 sq. ft.
Total with basement:	2,246 sq. ft.
Exterior Wall Framing:	2x4

Foundation options:
Daylight basement (Plan H-755-6E).
Crawlspace (Plan H-755-5E).
(Foundation & framing conversion diagram available — see order form.)

Blueprint Price Code:

Without basement:	A
With basement:	C

Plans H-755-5E & -6E

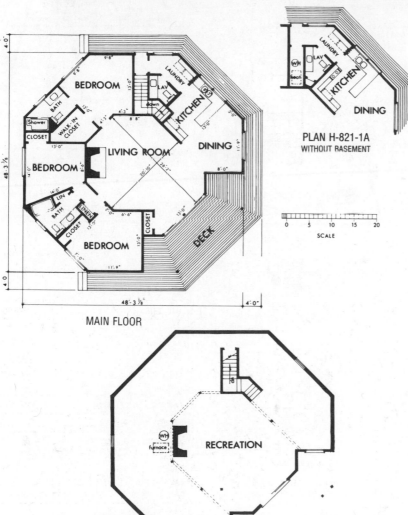

MAIN FLOOR

PLAN H-821-1A
WITHOUT BASEMENT

SCALE
0   5   10   15   20

BASEMENT

Versatile Octagon

- Popular octagonal design features a secondary raised roof to allow light into the 500 sq. ft. living room.
- Unique framing design allows you to divide the living space any way you choose: left open, with 3 or more bedrooms, a den, library or other options.
- Large, winding deck can accommodate outdoor parties and guests.
- Optional basement expands recreational opportunities.

Plans H-821-1 & -1A

Bedrooms: 3	Baths: 2½

Space:	
Main floor:	1,699 sq. ft.

Total living area:	1,699 sq. ft.
Basement:	approx. 1,699 sq. ft.

Exterior Wall Framing:	2x4

Foundation options:
Daylight basement (Plan H-821-1).
Crawlspace (Plan H-821-1A).
(Foundation & framing conversion diagram available — see order form.)

Blueprint Price Code:	
Without basement	B
With basement	E

Plans H-821-1 & -1A

Photo by Carren Strock

Proven Plan Features Passive Sun Room

- A passive sun room, energy-efficient wood stove, and a panorama of windows make this design highly economical.
- Open living/dining room features attractive balcony railing, stone hearth, and adjoining sun room with durable stone floor.
- Well-equipped kitchen is separated from dining area by a convenient breakfast bar.
- Second level sleeping areas border a hallway and balcony.
- Optional basement plan provides extra space for entertaining or work.

Plans H-855-3A & -3B

Bedrooms: 3	Baths: 2-3

Space:	
Upper floor:	586 sq. ft.
Main floor:	1,192 sq. ft.
Sun room:	132 sq. ft.

Total living area:	1,910 sq. ft.
Basement:	approx. 1,192 sq. ft.
Garage:	520 sq. ft.

Exterior Wall Framing:	2x6

Foundation options:
Daylight basement (Plan H-855-3B).
Crawlspace (Plan H-855-3A).
(Foundation & framing conversion diagram available — see order form.)

Blueprint Price Code:

Without basement	B
With basement	E

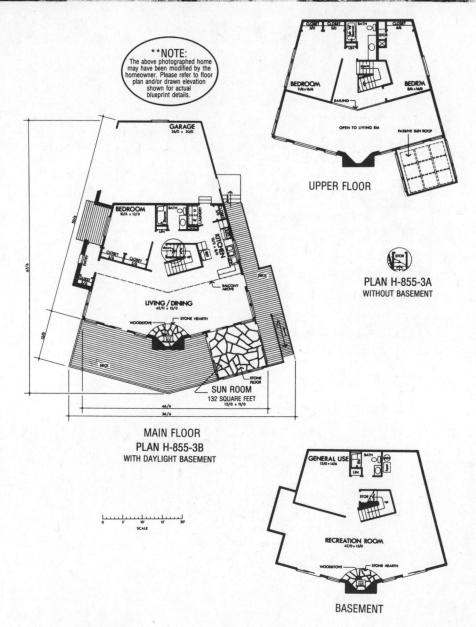

NOTE:
The above photographed home may have been modified by the homeowner. Please refer to floor plan and/or drawn elevation shown for actual blueprint details.

UPPER FLOOR

PLAN H-855-3A
WITHOUT BASEMENT

MAIN FLOOR
PLAN H-855-3B
WITH DAYLIGHT BASEMENT

SUN ROOM
132 SQUARE FEET
12/0 x 11/0

BASEMENT

RECREATION ROOM
42/0 x 13/0

GENERAL USE
12/0 x 14/6

TO ORDER THIS BLUEPRINT, CALL TOLL-FREE 1-800-547-5570 (prices and details on pp. 12-15.)

Plans H-855-3A & -3B

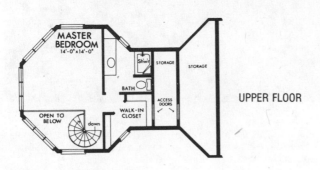

MASTER BEDROOM
14'-0" x 14'-0"

Shwr

STORAGE

STORAGE

BATH

OPEN TO BELOW

down

WALK-IN CLOSET

ACCESS DOORS

UPPER FLOOR

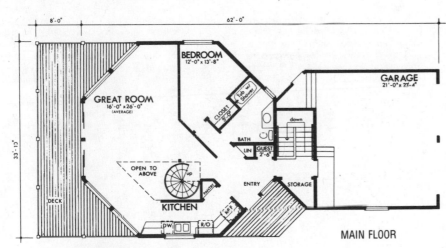

8'-0"

62'-0"

33'-13"

BEDROOM
12'-0" x 13'-8"

GARAGE
21'-0" x 27'-4"

GREAT ROOM
16'-0" x 26'-0"
(AVERAGE)

CLOSET
5'-0"

Tub w/ Shower

down

BATH

LIN

GUEST
2'-6"

OPEN TO ABOVE

up

ENTRY

STORAGE

DECK

KITCHEN

PANTRY

REF.

DW

R/O

MAIN FLOOR

BEDROOM
22/0 x 10/0

CLOSET

CLOSET

Shwr

RECREATION
16/0 x 21/6

BATH

up

W   D
LAUNDRY

LIN

CLOSET
7/6

STORAGE

STOR
3/6

WH

furnace

BASEMENT

0 1 2 3 4 5 6 7 8 9 10   15   20
SCALE

Octagonal Vacation Retreat

- Octagonal shape offers a view on all sides.
- Living, dining, and meal preparation are combined in a single Great Room, interrupted only by a provocative spiral staircase.
- Winding staircase allows continuous observance of activities below.
- Extraordinary master suite is bordered by glass, a private bath, and dressing room.
- Attached garage has room for boat, camper, or extra automobile.

Plans H-964-1A & -1B

Bedrooms: 2-3	Baths: 2-3
Space:	
Upper floor:	346 sq. ft.
Main floor:	1,067 sq. ft.
Total living area:	**1,413 sq. ft.**
Basement:	approx. 1,045 sq. ft.
Garage:	512 sq. ft.
Storage (2nd floor)	134 sq. ft.
Exterior Wall Framing:	**2x6**

Foundation options:
Daylight basement (Plan H-964-1B).
Crawlspace (Plan H-964-1A).
Foundation & framing conversion
diagram available — see order form.)

Blueprint Price Code:
Without basement:	A
With basement:	C

Plans H-964-1A & -1B

All-Season Chalet

A guided tour from the front entry of this home takes you into the central hallway that serves as the hub of traffic to the main floor level. From here, convenience extends in every direction and each room is connected

in a step-saving manner. Besides the master bedroom with twin closets, a full bathroom with stall shower is placed adjacent to a common wall that also serves the laundry equipment.

The living room and dining area are connected to allow for the expandable use of the dining table should the need arise for additional seating. The kitchen is open ended onto the dining area and has all the modern conveniences and built-in details.

A raised deck flanks the gable end of the living zone and extends outward for a distance of 8'.

A full basement is reached via a stairway connecting with the central hallway. The basement provides ample storage plus room for the central heating system. Another interesting feature is the garage placed under the home where the owner may not only store his automobile but such things as a boat and trailer and other sporting equipment.

First floor: 1,008 sq. ft.
Second floor: 462 sq. ft.

Total living area: 1,470 sq. ft.
(Not counting basement or garage)

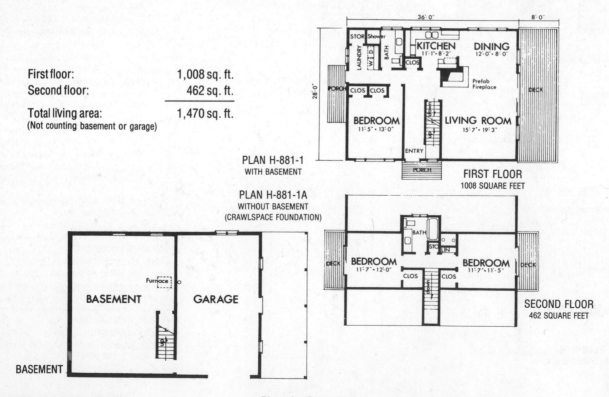

PLAN H-881-1
WITH BASEMENT

PLAN H-881-1A
WITHOUT BASEMENT
(CRAWLSPACE FOUNDATION)

FIRST FLOOR
1008 SQUARE FEET

SECOND FLOOR
462 SQUARE FEET

BASEMENT

Blueprint Price Code A

Plans H-881-1 & H-881-1A

Carefree Vacation Home

Scoffers and non-believers had a field day when the A-Frame first began to appear. Impractical, some said; uncomfortable, declared others; too expensive, ugly and more. And yet people built them and enjoyed them — and like the Volkswagen Bug, found them to be economical and practical, and yes, even beautiful to many beholders. Through the years, there has been a steady demand for these ubiquitous structures, and Plan H-15-1 is one of our more popular models. With this design, you will not be experimenting or pioneering because it has been built sucessfully many times.

Though it covers only 654 sq. ft. of main floor living space, it boasts an oversized living/dining room, a U-shaped kitchen, large bedroom and closet spaces, fully equipped bath plus a standard stairway (not a ladder) to the large second floor balcony dormitory. An old fashioned wood stove or a modern pre-fabricated fireplace adds warmth and cheer to the main living room.

The huge glass wall that dominates the front facade enhances the romantic atmosphere of the vaulted interior. And in ideal locations, where this wall can face south, a surprising amount of solar energy can help minimize heating costs.

One particular advantage of the A-Frame as a part-time or holiday home is easy maintenance. Use of penetrating stains that resist flaking and powdering on the small areas of siding and trim at the front and rear of the building is all that is required. The rest is roofing which resists weather without painting or other treatment.

MAIN FLOOR

26'-0"

DECK

BATH

STORAGE

BEDROOM
11'-8" x 10'-0"

4'-0"

Shwr

KITCHEN
9'-2" x 8'-8"

RFF

LIN

CLOSET
5'-0"

DW

STOR

up

STORAGE

28'-0"

R/O

WOODSTOVE

LIVING ROOM
23'-8" x 11'-6"

DECK

10'-0"

MAIN FLOOR

PLAN H-15-1
CRAWLSPACE FOUNDATION

UPPER LEVEL

DECK

S. C.

BALCONY ROOM
15'-6" x 12'-4"

RAILINGS

down

OPEN TO
LIVING RM.

SLOPED CEILING

UPPER LEVEL

Main floor:	654 sq. ft.
Upper floor:	254 sq. ft.
Total living area:	908 sq. ft.

(Not counting basement or garage)

Blueprint Price Code A

Plan H-15-1

TO ORDER THIS BLUEPRINT,
CALL TOLL-FREE 1-800-547-5570
(prices and details on pp. 12-15.) **59**

Five-Bedroom Chalet

Realizing that there are situations that require the maximum number of bedrooms, we have created this modest-sized home containing five bedrooms. One of these, especially the one over the garage, would serve very well as a private den, card room or library. The plan is available with or without basement.

This is an excellent example of the classic chalet. Close study will reveal how hall space has been kept at an absolute minimum. As a result, a modest first floor area of 952 sq. ft. and a compact second floor plan of 767 sq. ft. make the five bedrooms possible.

Also notice the abundance of storage space and built-ins with many other conveniences. Plumbing is provided in two complete bathrooms, and a washer and dryer has been tucked into one corner of the central hall on the main floor.

A clever technique has been used in the design of the staircase as it progresses halfway up to a landing midway between the two floors. From here it branches in two directions to a bedroom over the garage and to a hallway common to other rooms.

First floor:	952 sq. ft.
Second floor:	767 sq. ft.
Total living area: (Not counting basement or garage)	1,719 sq. ft.

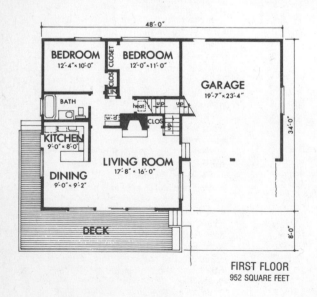

FIRST FLOOR
952 SQUARE FEET

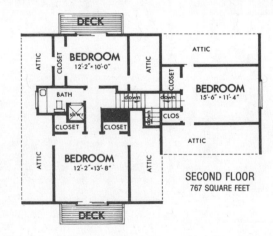

SECOND FLOOR
767 SQUARE FEET

PLAN H-804-2
WITH BASEMENT
PLAN H-804-2A
WITHOUT BASEMENT
(CRAWLSPACE FOUNDATION)

Blueprint Price Code B
Plans H-804-2 & -2A

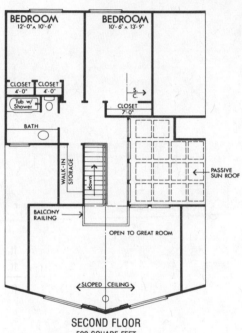

SECOND FLOOR
590 SQUARE FEET

First floor:	1,074 sq. ft.
Passive sun room:	136 sq. ft.
Second floor:	590 sq. ft.
Total living area:	**1,800 sq. ft.**

(Not counting basement or garage)

A Truly Livable Retreat

For a number of years the A-Frame idea has enjoyed great acceptance and popularity, especially in recreational areas. Too often, however, hopeful expectations have led to disappointment because

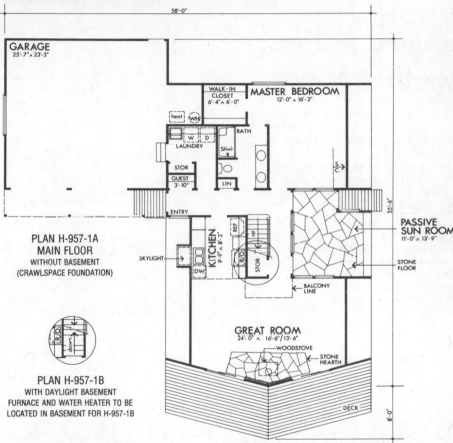

PLAN H-957-1A
MAIN FLOOR
WITHOUT BASEMENT
(CRAWLSPACE FOUNDATION)

PLAN H-957-1B
WITH DAYLIGHT BASEMENT
FURNACE AND WATER HEATER TO BE
LOCATED IN BASEMENT FOR H-957-1B

economic necessity resulted in small and restricted buildings. Not so with this plan. Without ignoring the need for economy, the designers allowed themselves enough freedom to create a truly livable and practical home with a main floor of 1,210 sq. ft., exclusive of the garage area. The second floor has 590 sq. ft., and includes two bedrooms, a bath and ample storage space.

Take special note of the multi-use passive sun room. Its primary purpose is to collect, store and redistribute the sun's heat, not only saving a considerable

amount of money but contributing an important function of keeping out dampness and cold when the owners are elsewhere. Otherwise the room might serve as a delightful breakfast room, a lovely arboretum, an indoor exercise room or any of many other functions limited only by the occupants' ingenuity.

A truly livable retreat, whether for weekend relaxation or on a daily basis as a primary residence, this passive solar A-Frame is completely equipped for the requirements of today's active living. Exterior walls are framed with 2x6 studs.

Blueprint Price Code B

Plans H-957-1A & -1B

TO ORDER THIS BLUEPRINT,
CALL TOLL-FREE 1-800-547-5570
(prices and details on pp. 12-15.)

Every Room with a View

- Unique, octagonal design allows an outdoor view from each room.
- Three bordering decks extend first-level living areas.
- Generous living room features dramatic stone fireplace and central skylight open to second floor.
- Second level features circular balcony connecting all bedrooms.
- Alternate second-floor plan replaces one bedroom with a viewing deck.

Plan H-27: 4-Bedroom Version

Bedrooms: 4	Baths: 2½
Space:	
Upper floor:	1,167 sq. ft.
Main floor:	697 sq. ft.
Total living area:	1,864 sq. ft.
Exterior Wall Framing:	2x4

Foundation options:
Crawlspace only.
(Foundation & framing conversion diagram available — see order form.)

Blueprint Price Code:	B

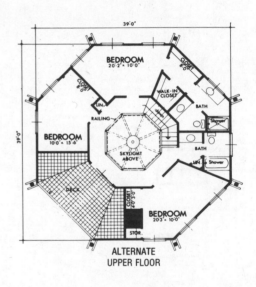

ALTERNATE
UPPER FLOOR

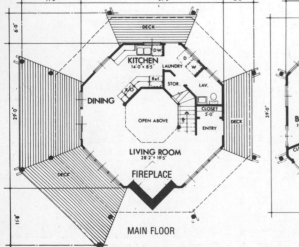

MAIN FLOOR

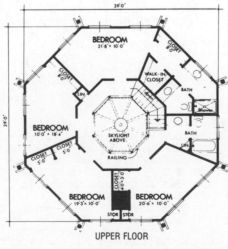

UPPER FLOOR

Plan H-27: 3-Bedroom Version

Bedrooms: 3	Baths: 2½
Space:	
Upper floor:	960 sq. ft.
Main floor:	697 sq. ft.
Total living area:	1,657 sq. ft.
Exterior Wall Framing:	2x4

Foundation options:
Crawlspace only.
(Foundation & framing conversion diagram available — see order form.)

Blueprint Price Code:	B

Plan H-27

UPPER FLOOR

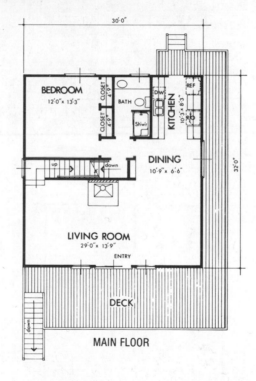

MAIN FLOOR

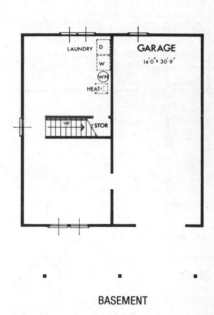

BASEMENT

Chalet for All Seasons

- Rustic exterior makes this design suitable for a lakefront, beach, or wooded setting.
- Patterned railing and wood deck edge the front and side main level, while a smaller deck assumes a balcony role.
- Designed for relaxed, leisure living, the main level features a large L-shaped Great Room warmed by a central free-standing fireplace.
- Upper level offers a second bath and added sleeping accommodations.

Plan H-858-2

Bedrooms: 3	Baths: 2
Space:	
Upper floor:	576 sq. ft.
Main floor:	960 sq. ft.
Total living area:	**1,536 sq. ft.**
Basement:	530 sq. ft.
Garage:	430 sq. ft.

Exterior Wall Framing: 2x6

Foundation options:
Daylight basement.
(Foundation & framing conversion diagram available — see order form.)

Blueprint Price Code: B

Plan H-858-2

TO ORDER THIS BLUEPRINT,
CALL TOLL-FREE 1-800-547-5570
(prices and details on pp. 12-15.)

Soaring Design
Lifts the Human Spirit

Photo by Bob Hallinen

- Suitable for level or sloping lots, this versatile design can be expanded or finished as time and budget allow.
- Surrounding deck accessible from all main living areas.
- Great living room enhanced by vaulted ceilings, second-floor balcony, skylights and dramatic window wall.
- Rear entrance has convenient access to full bath and laundry room.
- Two additional bedrooms on upper level share second bath and balcony room.

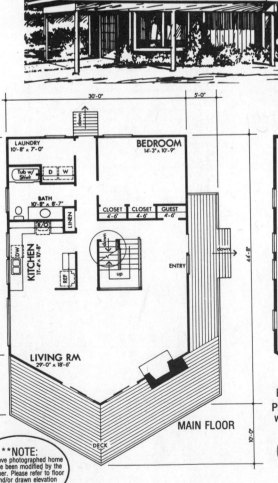

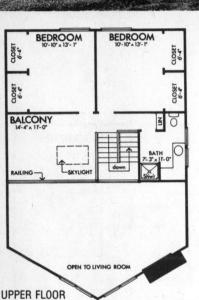

UPPER FLOOR

Plans H-930-1 & -1A

Bedrooms: 3	Baths: 2

Space:

Upper floor:	710 sq. ft.
Main floor:	1,210 sq. ft.

Total living area:	1,920 sq. ft.
Basement:	1,210 sq. ft.
Garage:	(Included in basement).

Exterior Wall Framing:	2x6

Foundation options:
Daylight basement (Plan H-930-1).
Crawlspace (Plan H-930-1A).
(Foundation & framing conversion diagram available — see order form.)

Blueprint Price Code:

Without basement:	B
With basement:	D

TO ORDER THIS BLUEPRINT, CALL TOLL-FREE 1-800-547-5570

64 (prices and details on pp. 12-15.)

**NOTE:
The above photographed home may have been modified by the homeowner. Please refer to floor plan and/or drawn elevation shown for actual blueprint details.

MAIN FLOOR

BASEMENT
PLAN H-930-1
WITH BASEMENT

PLAN H-930-1A
WITHOUT BASEMENT
(CRAWLSPACE FOUNDATION)

Plans H-930-1 & -1A

Eye-Catching Prow-Shaped Chalet

- Steep pitched roof lines and wide cornices give this chalet a distinct alpine appearance.
- Prowed shape, large windows, and 10' deck provide view and enhancement of indoor/outdoor living.
- Functional division of living and sleeping areas by hallway and first floor full bath.
- Laundry facilities conveniently located near bedroom wing.
- U-shaped kitchen and spacious dining/living areas make the main floor perfect for entertaining.

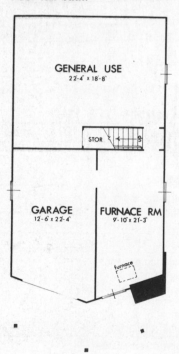

BASEMENT

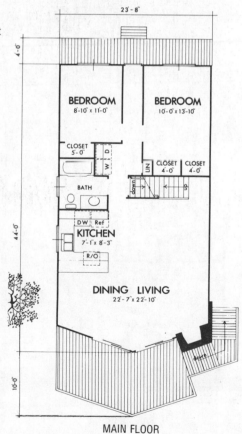

MAIN FLOOR

UPPER FLOOR

Plans H-886-3 & -3A

Bedrooms: 3	Baths: 2

Space:	
Upper floor:	486 sq. ft.
Main floor:	994 sq. ft.

Total without basement:	1,480 sq. ft.
Basement:	approx. 715 sq. ft.
Garage:	279 sq. ft.

Exterior Wall Framing:	2x6

Foundation options:
Daylight basement (Plan H-886-3).
Crawlspace (Plan H-886-3A).
(Foundation & framing conversion diagram available — see order form.)

Blueprint Price Code:	A

Plans H-886-3 & -3A

TO ORDER THIS BLUEPRINT, CALL TOLL-FREE 1-800-547-5570
(prices and details on pp. 12-15.)

UPPER FLOOR

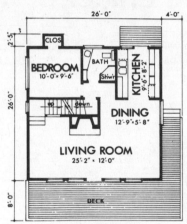

**MAIN FLOOR
PLAN H-720-11**

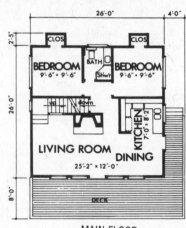

**MAIN FLOOR
PLAN H-720-10**

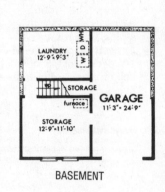

BASEMENT

Chalet with Variations

- Attractive chalet offers several main level variations, with second floor and basement layouts identical.
- All versions feature well-arranged kitchen, attached dining area, and large living room.
- Second-floor amenities include private decks off each bedroom and storage space in every corner!

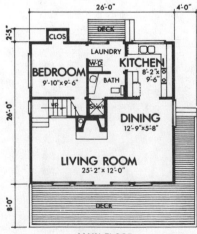

**MAIN FLOOR
PLAN H-720-12A
WITHOUT BASEMENT**

Plans H-720-10, -11 & -12A

Bedrooms: 3-4	Baths: 2

Space:

Upper floor:	328 sq. ft.
Main floor:	686 sq. ft.

Total living area:	**1,014 sq. ft.**
Basement:	approx. 686 sq. ft.
Garage: (incl. in basement)	278 sq. ft.

Exterior Wall Framing:	2x4

Foundation options:
Daylight basement
 (Plans H-720-10 or -11).
Crawlspace (Plan H-720-12A)
(Foundation & framing conversion
diagram available — see order form.)

Blueprint Price Code:

Without basement:	A
With basement:	B

**TO ORDER THIS BLUEPRINT,
CALL TOLL-FREE 1-800-547-5570**
(prices and details on pp. 12-15.)

66

Plans H-720-10, -11 & -12A

A-Frame Chalet with Popular Features

Ski chalets bring to mind Alpine comforts and evenings by the hearth. Schussing down nearby slopes is much more enjoyable when you don't have to worry about long drives home. Also, being on hand means you won't miss the fresh snowfall. In addition, summer time finds the mountain setting ideal for refreshing weekends away from the crowds and heat.

This class A-Frame is designed for optimum comfort and minimum cost, yet allows for variety and individual taste in setting and decor. Your home away from home can vary from plush to rustic, depending on personal preferences.

A special feature of this plan is the natural stone fireplace located where it can be enjoyed from indoors and outdoors. It serves the dual function of being a standard fireplace indoors and a handy barbecue outdoors. Two sleeping rooms on the main floor are a further advantage. Upstairs, there is a third bedroom plus a half bath. A balcony room provides space for overflow guests or a playroom for the kids. All the rooms in the house have "knee walls" so the space is usable right to the wall. These walls provide handy storage places as well as space for insulation.

First floor:	845 sq. ft.
Second floor:	375 sq. ft.
Total living area:	1,220 sq. ft.

PLAN H-6
WITHOUT BASEMENT
(CRAWLSPACE FOUNDATION)

SECOND FLOOR
375 SQUARE FEET

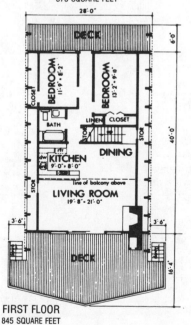

FIRST FLOOR
845 SQUARE FEET

Blueprint Price Code A

Plan H-6

A-Frame Offered in Three Versions

Why is the A-frame so popular? One reason may be that the spirit of the A-frame is a complete opposite of most of our full time box houses, and its soaring, free, unfettered lines carry with it an unusual appeal.

Its simplicity is another reason for its popularity.

To make this home all the more desirable, we have designed three ways for you to build it. A plan with a standard basement and no garage is Plan H-726-3. A plan without any basement whatsoever is Plan H-726-3A. If you would like a daylight basement and a garage you should then order Plan H-726-3B.

First floor: 720 sq. ft.
Second floor: 250 sq. ft.

Total living area: 970 sq. ft.
(Not counting basement or garage)

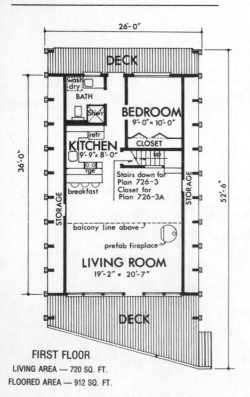

FIRST FLOOR
LIVING AREA — 720 SQ. FT.
FLOORED AREA — 912 SQ. FT.

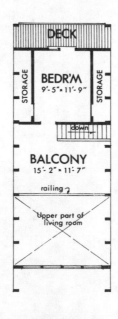

SECOND FLOOR
LIVING AREA — 250 SQ. FT.
FLOORED AREA — 370 SQ. FT.

PLAN H-726-3
WITH STANDARD BASEMENT
(NO GARAGE)

PLAN H-726-3A
WITHOUT BASEMENT
(CRAWLSPACE FOUNDATION)

PLAN H-726-3B
WITH DAYLIGHT BASEMENT & GARAGE

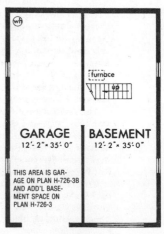

THIS AREA IS GARAGE ON PLAN H-726-3B AND ADD'L BASEMENT SPACE ON PLAN H-726-3

PLAN H-726-3B
BASEMENT

TO ORDER THIS BLUEPRINT, CALL TOLL-FREE 1-800-547-5570 (prices and details on pp. 12-15.)

Blueprint Price Code A
Plans H-726-3, -3A & -3B

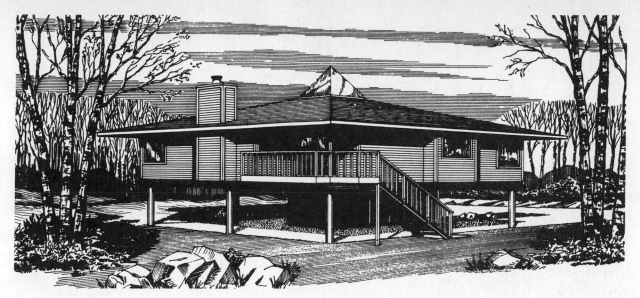

Skylighted Timber-Topper for Four-Way Views

This up, up and away design for open country or sweeping views has some of the sophisticated elegance of a townhouse. It's built atop an entry and service core that gives you two ways to get to the main living area.

One is a dramatic spiral staircase. But there's also provision for a dumbwaiter opening into the upstairs hallway. Getting this design off the ground gives you all kinds of sheltered space for boats, cars and equipment needing some protection from the full force of the weather. It also adds vast spaces to the available views.

The skylight over the stairwell will flood one end of the living room and kitchen-dining space with light. Even though there are three generous-sized bedrooms, there's still space for a 23' x 14' living room.

Brightly painted plywood accent panels and textured plywood siding are tastefully employed to create a dramatically handsome exterior.

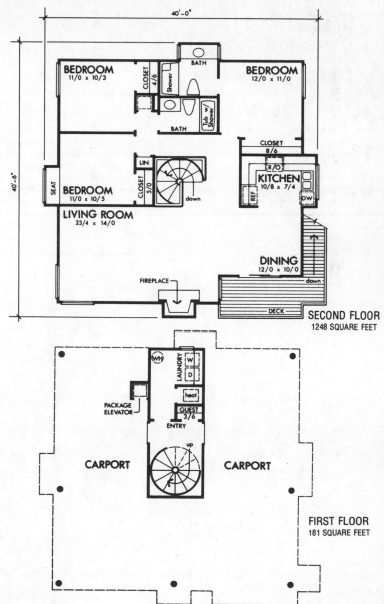

SECOND FLOOR
1248 SQUARE FEET

FIRST FLOOR
181 SQUARE FEET

Blueprint Price Code A

Plan H-111-1

TO ORDER THIS BLUEPRINT,
CALL TOLL-FREE 1-800-547-5570
(prices and details on pp. 12-15.)

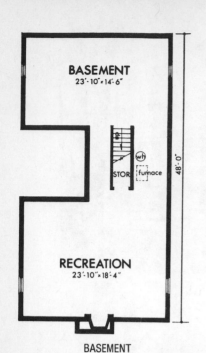

BASEMENT
23'-10" × 14'-6"

STOR

wh

furnace

RECREATION
23'-10" × 18'-4"

48'-0"

BASEMENT

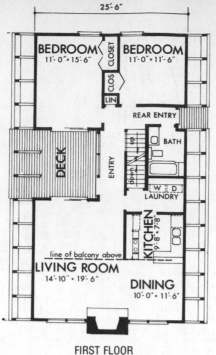

25'-6"

BEDROOM
11'-0" × 15'-6"

BEDROOM
11'-0" × 11'-6"

CLOSET

CLOS

LIN

REAR ENTRY

DECK

ENTRY

up

down

BATH

W D
LAUNDRY

line of balcony above

LIVING ROOM
14'-10" × 19'-6"

KITCHEN
9'-8" × 7'-8"

DINING
10'-0" × 11'-6"

FIRST FLOOR
1089 SQUARE FEET

BATH

W D

wh

LAUNDRY

furnace

KITCHEN
9'-8" × 7'-8"

FIRST FLOOR
WITHOUT BASEMENT

PLAN H-770-2
WITH BASEMENT

PLAN H-770-2A
WITHOUT BASEMENT
(CRAWLSPACE FOUNDATION)

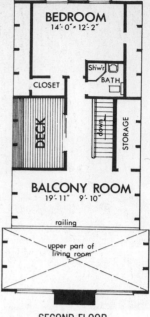

BEDROOM
14'-0" × 12'-2"

Sh'wr

BATH

CLOSET

DECK

down

STORAGE

BALCONY ROOM
19'-11" × 9'-10"

railing

upper part of
living room

SECOND FLOOR
546 SQUARE FEET

A-Frame with Side Entry

Quite unusual for an A-frame home, the functional entry serves as the hub of traffic flow to all of the lower floor areas. At one end is the living room and dining space connected in semi-L-shaped fashion and centered around a generous-sized fireplace. A well equipped kitchen with auxiliary counter space is located between the expandable dining area and a custom styled laundry room.

A 546 sq. ft. second floor is reached via the open staircase that starts from the central entry hall. A spacious master bedroom with private bath is located at one gable end of the structure. A central hall connects with the balcony room that overlooks the living room below, and sliding glass doors open to a second story deck.

First floor: 1,089 sq. ft.
Second floor: 546 sq. ft.

Total living area: 1,635 sq. ft.
(Not counting basement)

FRONT VIEW

Blueprint Price Code B

Plans H-770-2 & -2A

Loaded With Options

- This rustic A-frame offers an optional solar heating system and attached screened porch; other exciting features include a large rear deck, an attached outdoor shower, and a second floor balcony off the upper level bedrooms.
- The dramatic living/dining area below boasts a heat-circulating fireplace with opposite-facing barbecue, sliding glass doors on four sides and a snack bar off the kitchen; it is open to the second floor balcony.
- A whirlpool tub is located in the main floor bath, shared by both the master and secondary bedrooms.
- Two additional bedrooms and a second bath are found on the upper level.

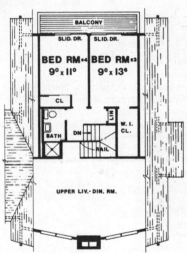

UPPER FLOOR

Plan AX-97729

Bedrooms: 4	Baths: 2
Space:	
Upper floor:	450 sq. ft.
Main floor:	988 sq. ft.
Total living area:	1,438 sq. ft.
Basement:	905 sq. ft.
Garage:	264 sq. ft.
Exterior Wall Framing:	2x4

Foundation options:
Standard basement.
Slab.
(Foundation & framing conversion diagram available — see order form.)

Blueprint Price Code:	B

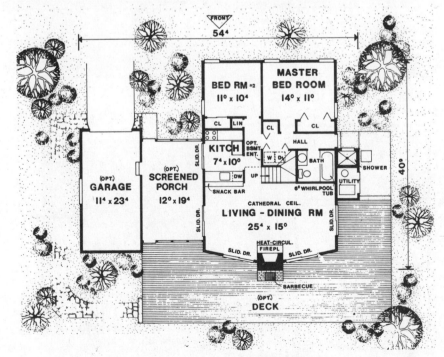

MAIN FLOOR

Plan AX-97729

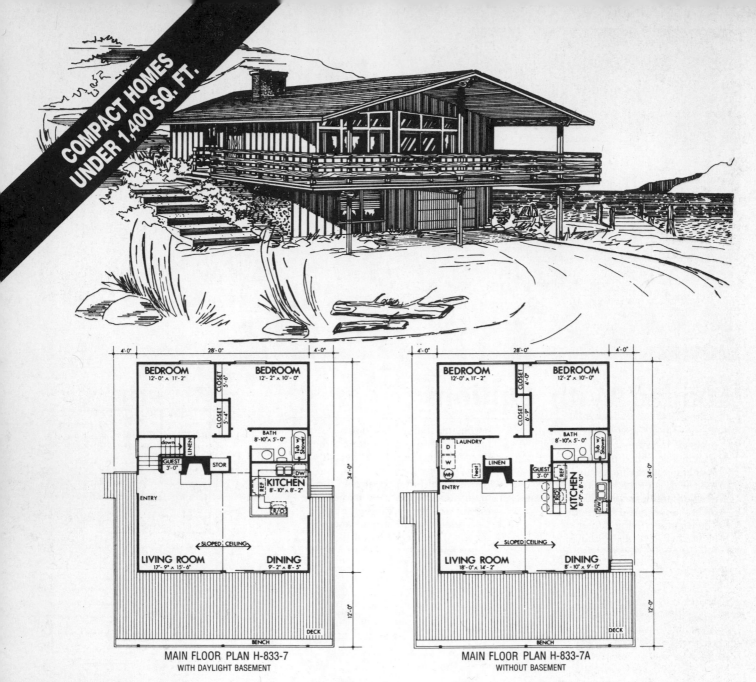

MAIN FLOOR PLAN H-833-7
WITH DAYLIGHT BASEMENT

MAIN FLOOR PLAN H-833-7A
WITHOUT BASEMENT

An Owner-Builder Special

- Everything you need for a leisure or retirement retreat is neatly packaged in just 952 square feet.
- The basic rectangular design features a unique wraparound deck, which is entirely covered by the projecting roof-line.
- Vaulted ceilings and a central fireplace visually enhance the cozy living/dining room.
- The daylight-basement option is suitable for building on a sloping lot.

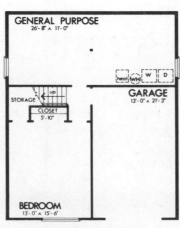

DAYLIGHT BASEMENT

Plans H-833-7 & -7A	
Bedrooms: 2-3	**Baths:** 1
Living Area:	
Main floor	952 sq. ft.
Optional daylight basement	676 sq. ft.
Total Living Area:	**952/1,628 sq. ft.**
Garage	276 sq. ft.
Exterior Wall Framing:	2x6
Foundation Options:	**Plan #**
Daylight basement	H-833-7
Crawlspace	H-833-7A
(Typical foundation & framing conversion diagram available—see order form.)	
BLUEPRINT PRICE CODE:	A/B

 (prices and details on pp. 12-15.)

TO ORDER THIS BLUEPRINT,
CALL TOLL-FREE 1-800-547-5570

Plan H-833-7 & -7A

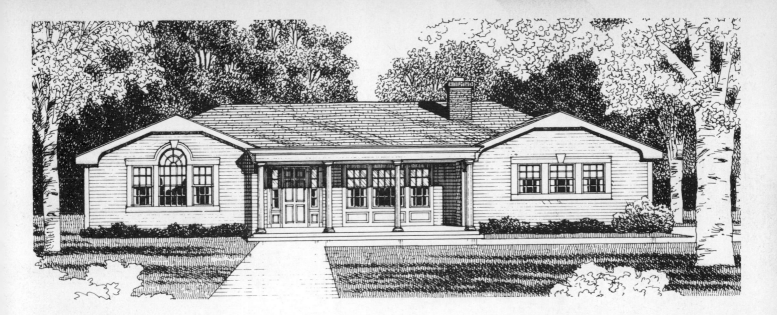

Design Harmony

- This house combines several different architectural styles to achieve a design harmony all its own.
- The columns of the front porch are reminiscent of ancient Greece, while the Palladian window in the master bedroom originates from the Renaissance period. The sleek rectangular shape of the home is in keeping with more contemporary times.
- The columns are repeated inside, where they are used to visually divide the foyer from the living room and to dramatize the cathedral ceiling. Columns also frame the heat-circulating fireplace.
- Note the twin closets in the foyer. Straight ahead is the combination dining room and kitchen, which basks in an abundance of natural light from two skylights, a large bow window, plus a sliding glass door that opens to the terrace.
- Another back entrance separates the kitchen from the large mud room. The mud room has loads of closet space, with two closets and cabinets above the washer and dryer.
- The sleeping wing has three large bedrooms and two full baths. Here, as elsewhere, closet space is well accounted for.

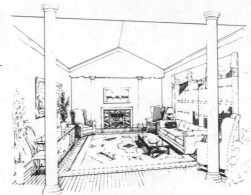

View into living room from entry foyer.

Plan HFL-1200-FH	
Bedrooms: 3	**Baths:** 2
Space:	
Main floor	1,397 sq. ft.
Total Living Area	**1,397 sq. ft.**
Basement	1,434 sq. ft.
Garage and Storage	463 sq. ft.
Exterior Wall Framing	2x6
Foundation options:	
Standard Basement	
Slab	
(Foundation & framing conversion diagram available—see order form.)	
Blueprint Price Code	**A**

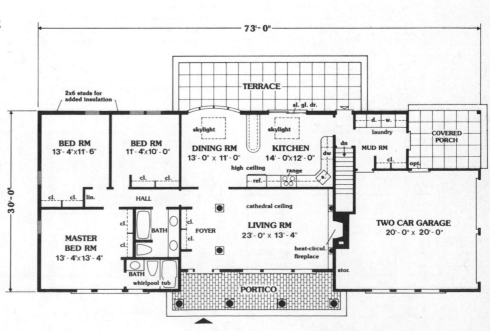

Plan HFL-1200-FH

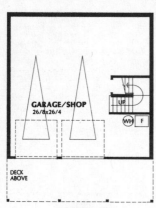

GARAGE/SHOP
26/8x26/4

UP

WH F

DECK ABOVE

BASEMENT
PLAN P-520-D
WITH DAYLIGHT BASEMENT

Neatly Packaged Leisure Home

This pitched-roof two-story contemporary leisure home is accented with solid wood siding, placed vertically and diagonally, and it neatly packages three bedrooms and a generous amount of living space into a 1,271 sq. ft. plan that covers a minimum of ground space.

Half the main floor is devoted to the vaulted Great Room, which is warmed by a woodstove and opens out through sliding glass doors to a wide deck. The U-shaped kitchen adjacent to the Great Room has a

window looking onto the deck and a circular window in the front wall. The master bedroom, a full bath and the utility room complete the 823 sq. ft. first floor.

Stairs next to the entry door lead down to the daylight basement, double garage and workroom, or up to the second floor. An open railing overlooking the Great Room and clerestory windows add natural light and enhance the open feeling of the home. The two bedrooms share another full bathroom.

Main floor:	823 sq. ft.
Upper floor:	448 sq. ft.
Total living area:	1,271 sq. ft.
(Not counting basement or garage)	

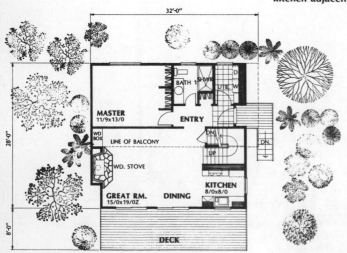

32'-0"

28'-0"

8'-0"

BATH 1 SHWR D
UTIL W

MASTER
11/9x13/0

ENTRY

WD BOX
LINE OF BALCONY

WD. STOVE

DN

UP

DN

GREAT RM.
15/0x19/0Z

DINING

KITCHEN
8/0x8/0

DECK

MAIN FLOOR

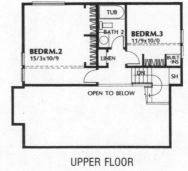

TUB

BATH 2

BEDRM.3
11/9x10/0

BEDRM.2
15/3x10/9

LINEN

BUILT-INS

OPEN TO BELOW

DN

SH

UPPER FLOOR

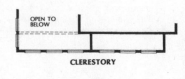

OPEN TO BELOW

CLERESTORY

Blueprint Price Code A
Plan P-520-D

Open Floor Plan, Large Deck

Total living area: 1,358 sq. ft.

STAIRS DOWN
RAIL
BEDROOM
14'-6" x 9'-6"
LIVING BELOW
BALCONY
CLOS
CLOS
BATH
BEDROOM
14'-6" x 11'-4"

UPPER FLOOR

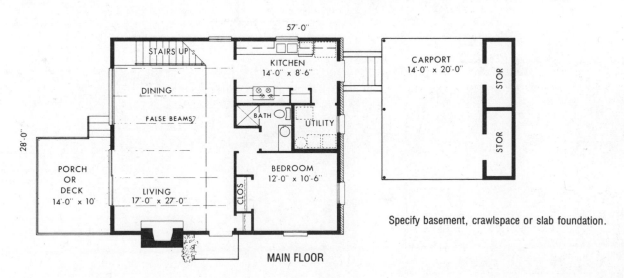

57'-0"
STAIRS UP
KITCHEN
14'-0" x 8'-6"
CARPORT
14'-0" x 20'-0"
STOR
DINING
FALSE BEAMS
BATH
UTILITY
STOR
28'-0"
PORCH
OR
DECK
14'-0" x 10'
LIVING
17'-0" x 27'-0"
CLOS
BEDROOM
12'-0" x 10'-6"

MAIN FLOOR

Specify basement, crawlspace or slab foundation.

Blueprint Price Code A

Plan C-7070

Designed for Easy Living

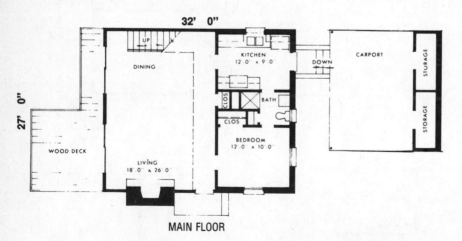

MAIN FLOOR

32' 0"

27' 0"

WOOD DECK

DINING

UP

KITCHEN
12'-0" x 9'-0"

CLOS
BATH
CLOS

LIVING
18'-0" x 26'-0"

BEDROOM
12'-0" x 10'-0"

DOWN

CARPORT

STORAGE

STORAGE

UPPER FLOOR

DOWN

BEDROOM
12'-0" x 10'-0"

BALCONY

CLOS
CLOS
BATH

OPEN BELOW

BEDROOM
12'-0" x 10'-0"

PLAN C-7020
WITHOUT BASEMENT
(Specify crawlspace or slab foundation.)

Total living area: 1,224 sq. ft.

Blueprint Price Code A
Plan C-7020

FRONT VIEW

Compact Plan Fits Narrow Building Site

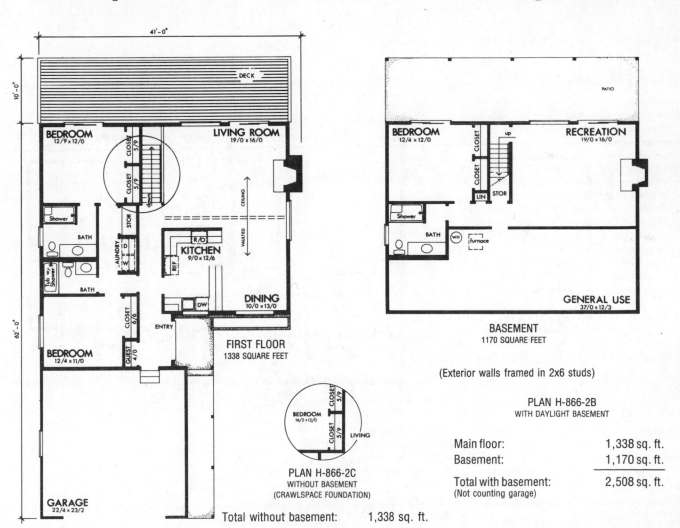

41'-0"

10'-0"

DECK

BEDROOM
12/9 x 12/0

CLOSET 5/9

CLOSET 5/9

LIVING ROOM
19/0 x 16/0

STOR

CEILING

VAULTED

Shower

BATH

AUNDRY

R/O

KITCHEN
9/0 x 12/6

REF

W

D

Tub w/ Shower

BATH

DW

DINING
10/0 x 13/0

CLOSET 6/6

GUEST 4/0

ENTRY

62'-0"

BEDROOM
12/4 x 11/0

GARAGE
22/4 x 23/2

FIRST FLOOR
1338 SQUARE FEET

CLOSET 5/9

CLOSET 5/9

BEDROOM
16/2 x 12/0

LIVING

PLAN H-866-2C
WITHOUT BASEMENT
(CRAWLSPACE FOUNDATION)

Total without basement: 1,338 sq. ft.

PATIO

BEDROOM
12/4 x 12/0

CLOSET

CLOSET

up

RECREATION
19/0 x 16/0

LIN

STOR

Shower

BATH

WH

furnace

GENERAL USE
37/0 x 12/3

BASEMENT
1170 SQUARE FEET

(Exterior walls framed in 2x6 studs)

PLAN H-866-2B
WITH DAYLIGHT BASEMENT

Main floor:	1,338 sq. ft.
Basement:	1,170 sq. ft.
Total with basement: (Not counting garage)	2,508 sq. ft.

Blueprint Price Code D With Basement
Blueprint Price Code A Without Basement

Plans H-866-2B & H-866-2C

TO ORDER THIS BLUEPRINT, CALL TOLL-FREE 1-800-547-5570
(prices and details on pp. 12-15.)

Build It On Weekends

- The basic design and use of truss roof framing promote easy and speedy erection.
- See-through kitchen allows a look into the living or dining rooms.
- Living room reveals the outdoors and surrounding deck through sliding glass doors.
- Separate bedroom/bathroom area eliminates cross-room traffic and wasted hall space.
- Plan H-921-2A utilizes the sealed crawlspace as an air distribution chamber for a Plen-Wood heating system.
- Plan H-921-1A has a standard crawlspace foundation and optional solar heating system.

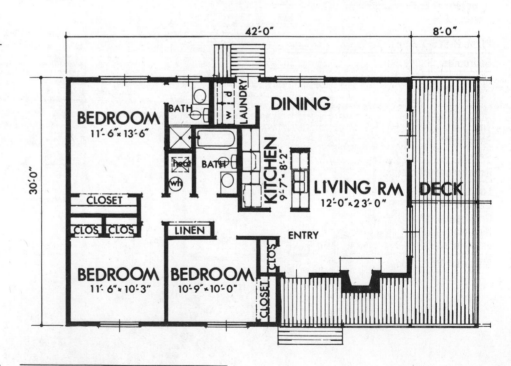

Plans H-921-1A & -2A

Bedrooms: 3	Baths: 2

Space:

Main floor:	1,164 sq. ft.
Total living area:	1,164 sq. ft.

Exterior Wall Framing:	2x6

Foundation options:
Plen-Wood crawlspace system (Plan H-921-2A).
Standard crawlspace (Plan H-921-1A).
(Foundation & framing conversion diagram available — see order form.)

Blueprint Price Code: A

Plans H-921-1A & -2A

Easy Living

- Large, beautiful living area with sloped ceiling and fireplace lies five steps below entry and sleeping areas.
- Attached dining room and kitchen separated by eating bar.
- Convenient main floor laundry near kitchen and side entrance.
- Secluded master suite includes personal bath and private access to sun deck.

Plans H-925-1 & -1A

Bedrooms: 3	Baths: 2

Space:

Upper floor:	288 sq. ft.
Main floor:	951 sq. ft.
Total living area:	**1,239 sq. ft.**
Basement:	approx. 951 sq. ft.
Garage:	266 sq. ft.

Exterior Wall Framing:	2x4

Foundation options:
Daylight basement (Plan H-925-1)
Crawlspace (Plan H-925-1A).
(Foundation & framing conversion diagram available — see order form.)

Blueprint Price Code:	A

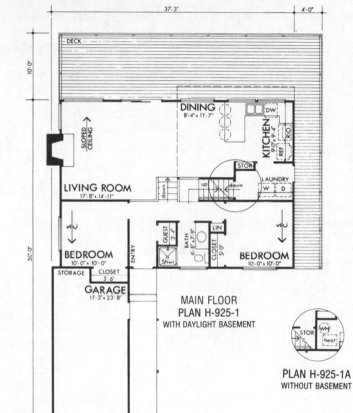

DECK

DINING
8'-4" x 11'-7"

KITCHEN
9'-0" x 9'-4"

SLOPED CEILING

LIVING ROOM
17'-8" x 14'-11"

LAUNDRY
W D

STOR

GUEST

BATH
6'-6" x 7'-6"

LIN

CLOSET
5'-0"

BEDROOM
10'-0" x 10'-0"

ENTRY

BEDROOM
10'-0" x 10'-0"

STORAGE

CLOSET
5'-6"

GARAGE
11'-3" x 23'-8"

37'-3"

4'-0"

10'-0"

50'-0"

MAIN FLOOR
PLAN H-925-1
WITH DAYLIGHT BASEMENT

STOR

WH heat

PLAN H-925-1A
WITHOUT BASEMENT

DECK

WALK-IN CLOSET
7'-4" x 5'-0"

Tub w/ Shwr

BEDROOM
12'-0" x 13'-6"

BATH
9'-2" x 5'-0"

down

S. SLOPED C. CEILING

UPPER FLOOR

Plans H-925-1 & -1A

MAIN FLOOR

UPPER FLOOR

Multi-Level Design

- This open and attractive design features multi-level construction and efficient use of living space.
- Elevated den and high ceilings with exposed rafters enhance the spacious feeling of the living room.
- Washer/dryer and kitchen are separated from the dining area by an eating counter.
- Third level comprises the master bedroom and bath.
- Garage and storage space are combined in the basement level.

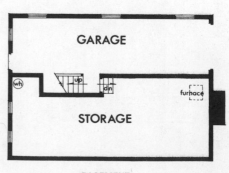

BASEMENT

Plan H-863-2

Bedrooms: 2-3		**Baths:** 2	

Space:
Upper floor: 252 sq. ft.
Main floor: 936 sq. ft.

Total living area: 1,188 sq. ft.
Basement: approx. 936 sq. ft.
(includes garage)

Exterior Wall Framing: 2x4

Foundation options:
Daylight basement only.
(Foundation & framing conversion diagram available — see order form.)

Blueprint Price Code: A

Plan H-863-2

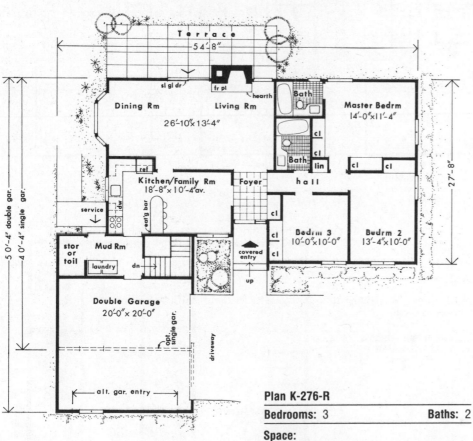

Compact, Economical to Build

- This economically-structured L-shaped ranch puts a great many desirable features into a mere 1,193 sq. ft. of living space. A wood-burning fireplace highlights the living area. Sliding glass doors open to the backyard terrace.
- The kitchen/family room features an eating bar.
- Covered entry welcomes you to the central foyer for easy channeling to any part of the house.
- Located in a wing of their own are three bedrooms and two baths.
- For a narrow lot, the garage door could face the front.

Plan K-276-R

Bedrooms: 3	Baths: 2

Space:

Total living area:	1,193 sq. ft.
Basement:	1,193 sq. ft.
Garage, mud room, etc.:	551 sq. ft.

Exterior Wall Framing:	2x4 or 2x6

Foundation options:
Standard basement.
Crawlspace.
Slab.
(Foundation & framing conversion diagram available — see order form)

Blueprint Price Code:	A

TO ORDER THIS BLUEPRINT,
CALL TOLL-FREE 1-800-547-5570
(prices and details on pp. 12-15.)

Plan K-276-R

FRONT VIEW

Wide Open Spaces

This home is applicable to just about any lot and housing need. For year-round residence, the possibilities include a finished basement and an upstairs master bedroom suite. For a second home, the upstairs dormitory can be used as a game room and the basement for storage.

Sliding glass doors and clerestory windows in the living room take advantage of the deck and the view beyond. The stairway to the second floor is flooded with light from another clerestory window.

Like plan H-893, the open kitchen, dining and living rooms are at the heart of the design. What sets this plan apart are the distinctive twin roof peaks over the side entrance.

SECOND FLOOR
WITH BATHROOM
336 SQUARE FEET

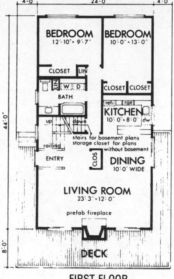

FIRST FLOOR
1056 SQUARE FEET

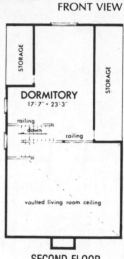

SECOND FLOOR
WITHOUT BATHROOM
336 SQUARE FEET

FOR PLAN WITH NO BASEMENT
AND BEDROOM/BATH ON SECOND FLOOR, ORDER
PLAN H-894-1A

FOR PLAN WITH NO BASEMENT
AND DORMITORY ON SECOND FLOOR, ORDER
PLAN H-894-2A

FOR PLAN WITH STANDARD BASEMENT
AND BEDROOM/BATH ON SECOND FLOOR, ORDER
PLAN H-894-1B

FOR PLAN WITH STANDARD BASEMENT
AND DORMITORY ON SECOND FLOOR, ORDER
PLAN H-894-2B

FOR PLAN WITH DAYLIGHT BASEMENT
AND BEDROOM/BATH ON SECOND FLOOR, ORDER
PLAN H-894-1C

FOR PLAN WITH DAYLIGHT BASEMENT
AND DORMITORY ON SECOND FLOOR, ORDER
PLAN H-894-2C

All Versions:
First floor: 1,056 sq. ft.
Second floor: 336 sq. ft.
_____
Total living area: 1,392 sq. ft.
(Not counting basement)

(NON-BASEMENT VERSIONS
HAVE CRAWLSPACE
FOUNDATIONS)

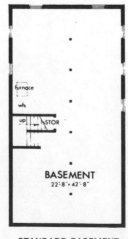

STANDARD BASEMENT

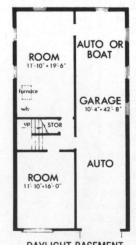

DAYLIGHT BASEMENT

Blueprint Price Code A

Plans H-894-1A, -2A, -1B, -2B, -1C & -2C

TO ORDER THIS BLUEPRINT, CALL TOLL-FREE 1-800-547-5570
(prices and details on pp. 12-15.)

REAR

FRONT

Small Home Generous with Living Comforts

- Open, space-saving Great Room with vaulted ceilings and stone fireplace; expansive front adjoining deck.
- Open staircase and balcony overlook living area below.
- U-shaped kitchen with pantry and snack bar.
- All three bedrooms feature private access to rear decks.

Plan H-5

Bedrooms: 3	Baths: 1

Space:	
Upper floor:	660 sq. ft.
Main floor:	332 sq. ft.
Total living area:	**992 sq. ft.**
Exterior Wall Framing:	2x4

Foundation options:
Crawlspace only.
(Foundation & framing conversion diagram available — see order form.)

Blueprint Price Code: A

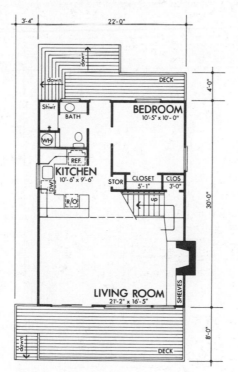

MAIN FLOOR

UPPER FLOOR

Plan H-5

Compact, Easy to Build

This compact vacation or retirement home is economical and easy to construct. Only 24' x 46' for the daylight basement version, it nonetheless contains all the necessities and some of the luxuries one desires in a three-bedroom home. The non-basement version measures 24' x 44'.

Overall width for both versions including deck and carport is 50'.

One luxury is the separate, private bath adjoining the master bedroom; another is the double "His & Hers" wardrobe closets for the same room. The other two bedrooms are equipped with good-sized closets and share a second bathroom. Even if you choose the basement version, the convenience of first floor laundry facilities is yours.

The open stairway to the basement adds 3' to the visual size of the living room. A

pre-fab fireplace is located to allow enjoyment of a cozy hearth and a beautiful view from the same chair.

The plans are so completely detailed that a handyman amateur might frame this building (with the help of a few friends). Why not try it? (Be sure to order a materials list, too!).

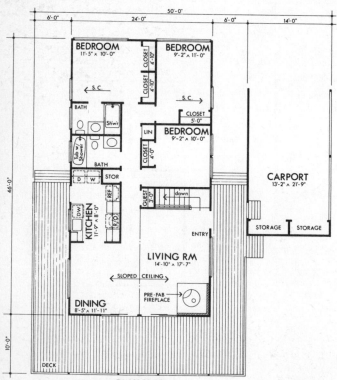

PLAN H-18
WITH DAYLIGHT BASEMENT
1104 SQUARE FEET

PLAN H-18-A
WITH CRAWLSPACE
1056 SQUARE FEET

Total living area: 1,104 sq. ft.
(Not counting basement or carport)

Blueprint Price Code A

Plans H-18 & H-18-A

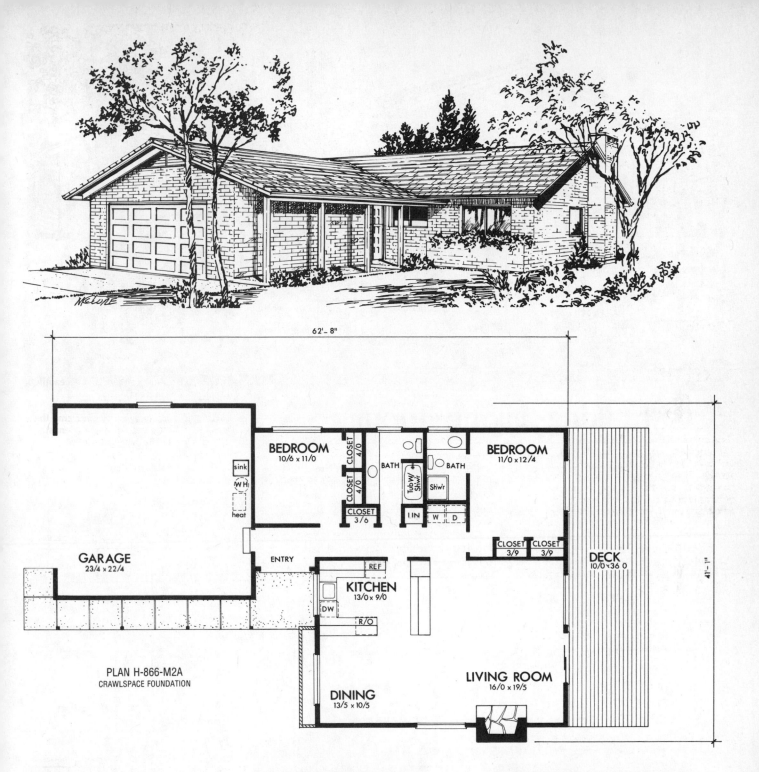

62'- 8"

BEDROOM
10/6 x 11/0

CLOSET 4/0

CLOSET 4/0

BATH

BEDROOM
11/0 x 12/4

BATH

sink

W H

heat

Tub W Shwr

Sh'wr

W D

CLOSET 3/6

LIN

GARAGE
23/4 x 22/4

ENTRY

CLOSET 3/9

CLOSET 3/9

DECK
10/0 x 36 0

41'-1"

REF

DW

R/O

KITCHEN
13/0 x 9/0

PLAN H-866-M2A
CRAWLSPACE FOUNDATION

DINING
13/5 x 10/5

LIVING ROOM
16/0 x 19/5

Designed for a Small Lot

Desiring to create a two-bedroom home with less than 1,200 sq. ft., it was essential for the designers to devise a scheme that avoided the usual series of small, cramped spaces labelled living room, dining and

kitchen. The solution was to remove interior walls, vault the ceilings and combine all three rooms into one huge 600 sq. ft. space visually changing the plan from a very ordinary two-bedroom home to a remarkably spacious and liveable arrangement.

A very large U-shaped kitchen with one 9' long wall devoid of equipment and devoted solely to cabinets, cupboards and a convenient pantry closet will prove to be a homemaker's delight. An oversize masonry

fireplace is another feature of this huge, open living space. A standard-sized bedroom located near the entry would be an ideal home office when needed. The master bedroom boasts separate "his and hers" closets as well as a private bathroom.

Concrete brick veneer units laid in a running bond pattern provide an attractive and durable exterior, which is matched by a roof covered with flat, shake-style concrete tiles.

Total living area: 1,199 sq. ft.
(Not counting garage)

Blueprint Price Code A

Plan H-866-M2A

TO ORDER THIS BLUEPRINT, CALL TOLL-FREE 1-800-547-5570
(prices and details on pp. 12-15.)

85

Karl Swanson

Breathtaking Living Room

- Stone veneer, log cabin siding, and a large covered porch are some of this rustic cabin's exterior attractions.
- Dramatic, contemporary and informal living is encompassed in the breathtaking living room with a massive stone fireplace flanked by sliding glass doors and a soaring cathedral ceiling that sweeps up to the second floor.
- A breakfast counter separates the living room from the adjoining kitchen; a bath and utility room are convenient to both the kitchen and the master bedroom.
- Two additional bedrooms are located on the upper level, reached by an eye-catching circular stairway.

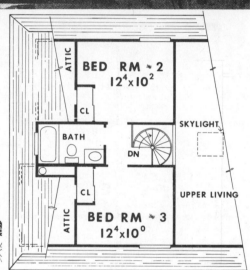

UPPER FLOOR

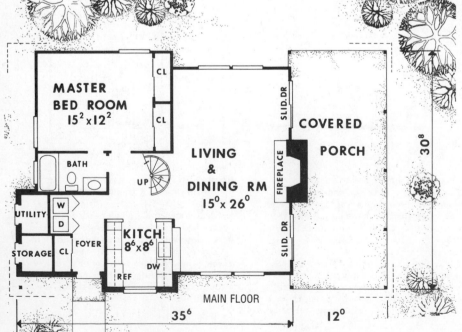

MAIN FLOOR

Plan AX-7836-A

Bedrooms: 3	Baths: 2

Space:	
Upper floor:	375 sq. ft.
Main floor:	970 sq. ft.

Total living area:	1,345 sq. ft.
Basement:	970 sq. ft.

Exterior Wall Framing:	2x4

Foundation options:
Standard basement.
Slab.
(Foundation & framing conversion diagram available — see order form.)

Blueprint Price Code:	A

Affordable Alternative

- A rustic contemporary exterior surrounds an efficient plan to create an affordable rec home.
- The design would be well-suited to a ski or water location for winter or summer enjoyment.
- The heart of the plan is the dramatic vaulted fireside living room with fireplace and an optional built-in sofa.
- The informal galley ktichen serves the dining room while enjoying plenty of views on three sides.
- The sleeping quarters upstairs can accommodate up to two bedrooms with a second full bath in-between.

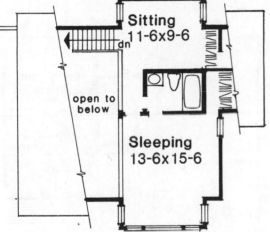

Sitting 11-6x9-6

dn

open to below

Sleeping 13-6x15-6

UPPER FLOOR

Plan B-7635

Bedrooms: 1-2	Baths: 2
Space:	
Upper floor:	452 sq. ft.
Main floor:	700 sq. ft.
Total living area:	1,152 sq. ft.
Exterior Wall Framing:	2x4

Foundation options:
Crawlspace.
(Foundation & framing conversion diagram available — see order form.)

Blueprint Price Code:	A

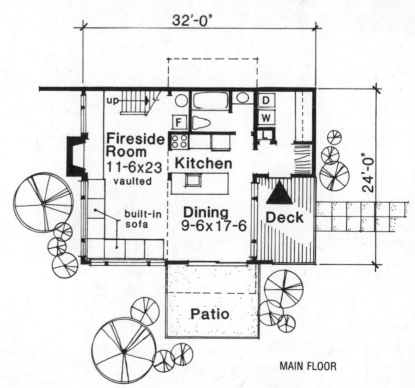

32'-0"

24'-0"

up

Fireside Room 11-6x23 vaulted

Kitchen

F

D
W

built-in sofa

Dining 9-6x17-6

Deck

Patio

MAIN FLOOR

Plan B-7635

Compact Cabin

- An open stairway in the entryway of this compact two-story cabin leads to an open loft hall above.
- The Great Room to the left offers a cathedral ceiling and an inviting fireplace that welcomes guests.
- A screened porch to the rear of the adjoining dining room is close to the kitchen for convenient outdoor dining; a private sun deck off the master bedroom is located above.
- The kitchen features a counter bar and nearby toilet and laundry facilities.

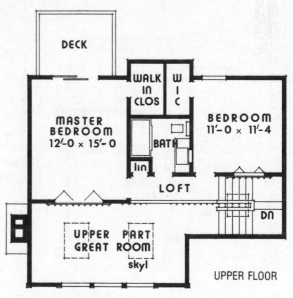

DECK

WALK IN CLOS

WIC

MASTER BEDROOM 12'-0 × 15'-0

BATH

lin

BEDROOM 11'-0 × 11'-4

LOFT

DN

UPPER PART GREAT ROOM
skyl

UPPER FLOOR

Plan CPS-1077-SE

Bedrooms: 2	Baths: 1½
Space:	
Upper floor:	528 sq. ft.
Main floor:	760 sq. ft.
Total living area:	1,288 sq. ft.
Basement:	760 sq. ft.
Exterior Wall Framing:	2x6

Foundation options:
Standard basement.
(Foundation & framing conversion diagram available — see order form.)

Blueprint Price Code: A

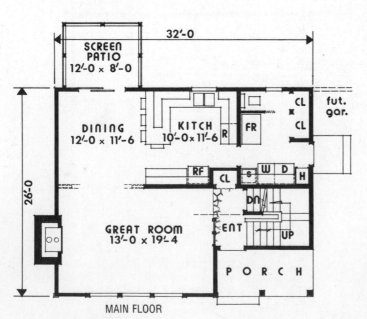

32'-0

SCREEN PATIO
12'-0 × 8'-0

CL

CL

fut. gar.

DINING
12'-0 × 11'-6

KITCH
10'-0 × 11'-6

R

FR

26'-0

RF

CL

S

W

D

H

DN

GREAT ROOM
13'-0 × 19'-4

ENT

UP

PORCH

MAIN FLOOR

Plan CPS-1077-SE

Multi-Level Contemporary

- Multiple levels in this exciting contemporary home allow it to step down the side of a mountain or sloping lakeside site.
- A wooden deck skirts three sides of the home to maximize views outside while an abundance of windows and glass doors allow enjoyment of the views while inside.
- The entry opens to a view of the sunken living room with a dramatic 21-foot ceiling.
- The U-shaped kitchen flows into the spacious dining area with sliders to the deck.
- A main-level bedroom has handy access to a bath with a large shower.
- The upper level includes two more bedrooms, a bath with a tub, and a balcony overlooking the living room below.

MAIN FLOOR

UPPER FLOOR

Plan CAR-78019

Bedrooms: 3	Baths: 2

Space:

Upper floor:	572 sq. ft.
Main floor:	769 sq. ft.
Total living area:	**1,341 sq. ft.**
Basement:	540 sq. ft.

Exterior Wall Framing:	2x6

Foundation options:
Standard basement.
Slab.
(Foundation & framing conversion diagram available — see order form.)

Blueprint Price Code:	A

Plan CAR-78019

Open Living for Weekend or Forever

- This cozy, 1 1/2 story home is perfect for a weekend retreat, summer home, or casual permanent residence.
- A large, open living area on the first level combines the kitchen, dining area and living room for a spacious setting; sliding doors to the front offer an outdoor relaxing or dining alternative.
- Two bedrooms and a full bath are located at the rear, both with closet space.
- The upper loft would be ideal for a private master bedroom or quiet study area.

Plan CPS-1095

Bedrooms: 2-3	Baths: 1
Space:	
Upper floor	320 sq. ft.
Main floor	784 sq. ft.
Total Living Area	**1,104 sq. ft.**
Basement	784 sq. ft.
Exterior Wall Framing	2x6

Foundation options:

Standard Basement

(Foundation & framing conversion diagram available—see order form.)

Blueprint Price Code	**A**

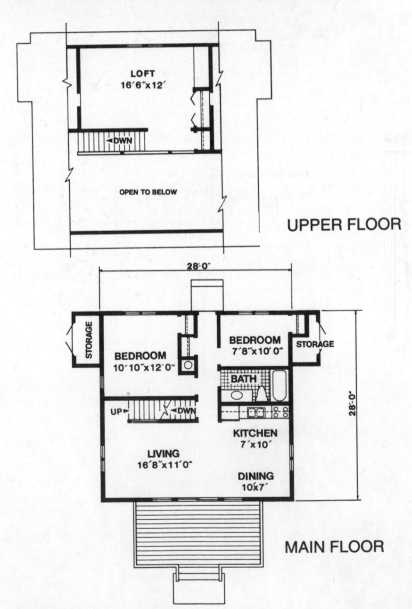

UPPER FLOOR

MAIN FLOOR

Plan CPS-1095

Living With Sunpower

Angled wood siding accentuates the architectural geometry of this flexible leisure home. The house is designed to exploit sun power and conserve energy. Focal point of the plan is an outsized living lounge that has pitched ceiling and overall dimensions of 18'-8" by 26'-0". Note the glass wall that leads to the spacious sun deck. A roomy kitchen is accessible from another sun deck and serves two eating bars as well as the dining room. The three bedrooms are well isolated from noise and traffic. Adjacent to the kitchen is the utility-storage room that can accommodate laundry facilities.

As an option, two solar collectors can be installed on the roof, either over the living lounge, or on the opposite roof, depending on the southern exposure. Solar equipment may be installed now or in the future.

Total living area: 1,077 sq. ft.
(Not counting garage)

FLOOR PLAN
Plan includes crawlspace foundation.

42-0 · 6-4 · 30-0 · 26-0 · 18-8

Sun Deck

up

laundry or toilet
utility & stor.
eat'g bar
solar stor. tank
Kitchen 8-0 x 12-0
dw
opt hi window
htr.
Bath
Bedrm 1 11-0 x 13-2

dining

eat'g bar
clerestory above
cl
opt. ldry space
hall
cl cl cl

Living Lounge (sloped ceil'g)
fireplace
lin
Bedrm 3 9-0 x 10-0
cl
Bedrm 2 10-0 x 12-4

Sun Deck

sl'g dr

cl

entry

up

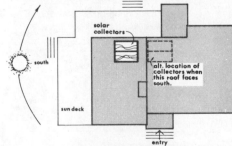

ORIENTATION FEASIBILITY
mirror plan also possible
home may be built without solar system

solar collectors
alt. location of collectors when this roof faces south.
south
sun deck
entry

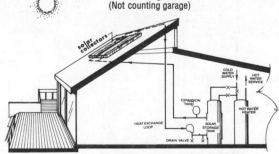

CONCEPT OF SOLAR SYSTEM FOR DOMESTIC HOT WATER

solar collectors
COLD WATER SUPPLY
HOT WATER SERVICE
EXPANSION TANK
HOT WATER HEATER
HEAT EXCHANGE LOOP
SOLAR STORAGE TANK
DRAIN VALVE

Blueprint Price Code A

Plan K-166-T

**TO ORDER THIS BLUEPRINT,
CALL TOLL-FREE 1-800-547-5570**
(prices and details on pp. 12-15.)

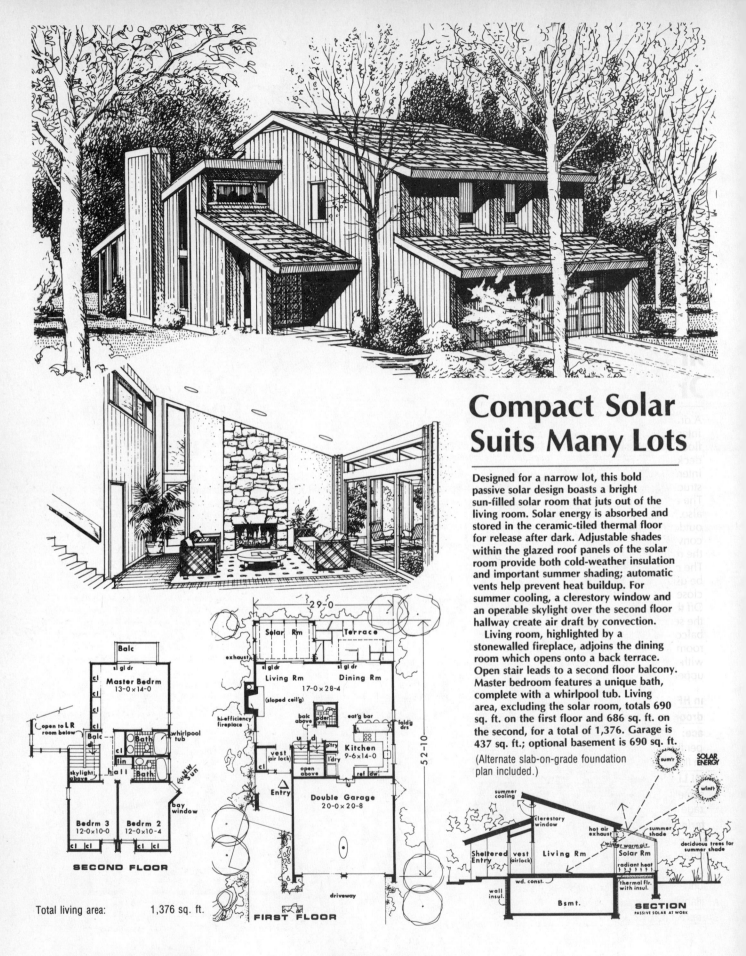

Compact Solar Suits Many Lots

Designed for a narrow lot, this bold passive solar design boasts a bright sun-filled solar room that juts out of the living room. Solar energy is absorbed and stored in the ceramic-tiled thermal floor for release after dark. Adjustable shades within the glazed roof panels of the solar room provide both cold-weather insulation and important summer shading; automatic vents help prevent heat buildup. For summer cooling, a clerestory window and an operable skylight over the second floor hallway create air draft by convection.

Living room, highlighted by a stonewalled fireplace, adjoins the dining room which opens onto a back terrace. Open stair leads to a second floor balcony. Master bedroom features a unique bath, complete with a whirlpool tub. Living area, excluding the solar room, totals 690 sq. ft. on the first floor and 686 sq. ft. on the second, for a total of 1,376. Garage is 437 sq. ft.; optional basement is 690 sq. ft.

(Alternate slab-on-grade foundation plan included.)

Master Bedrm 13-0×14-0

Bedrm 3 12-0×10-0

Bedrm 2 12-0×10-4

SECOND FLOOR

Solar Rm   **Terrace**

Living Rm   **Dining Rm**
17-0×28-4

Kitchen 9-6×14-0

Double Garage 20-0×20-8

FIRST FLOOR

Total living area: 1,376 sq. ft.

SECTION PASSIVE SOLAR AT WORK

Blueprint Price Code A
Plan K-521-C

Simple, but Dramatic

- A dramatic sloped roof exterior and interior living room with sloped ceiling, floor-to-ceiling windows, an adjoining deck and wood stove give this home an interesting, but easy and affordable structure under 1,500 square feet.
- The attached kitchen and dining area also has access to the deck, for an outdoor dining alternative; a pantry and convenient laundry room is secluded to the rear.
- The main-level bedroom could ideally be used as the master; it offers dual closets and nearby bath.
- Off the two-story foyer is the stairway to the second level which ends in a balcony area that overlooks the living room. Two good-sized bedrooms, one with unique dressing vanity, share the upper level with a second bath.

Plan HFL-1382

Bedrooms: 3	Baths: 2
Space:	
Upper floor	465 sq. ft.
Main floor (Without mudroom)	917 sq. ft.
Total Living Area	**1,382 sq. ft.**
Basement	811 sq. ft.
Garage	220 sq. ft.
Exterior Wall Framing	**2x6**

Foundation options:
Standard Basement
Slab
(Foundation & framing conversion diagram available—see order form.)

Blueprint Price Code	**A**

TO ORDER THIS BLUEPRINT,
CALL TOLL-FREE 1-800-547-5570
(prices and details on pp. 12-15.)

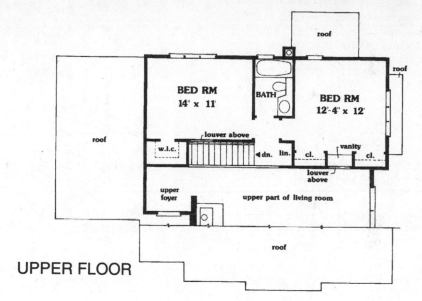

UPPER FLOOR

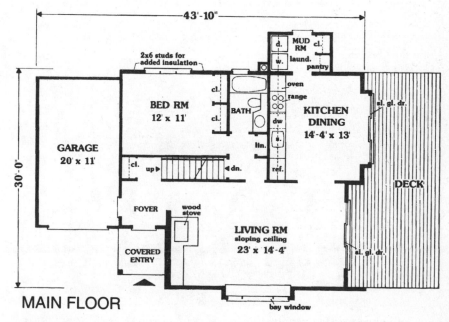

MAIN FLOOR

Plan HFL-1382

More for Less

- Big in function but small in footage, this two-story passive solar plan puts every inch of space to efficient use, and is designed in such a way that it can be built as a free-standing unit or as part of a multiple unit complex.
- The plan flows visually from its entry, through its high-ceilinged Great Room, to a brilliant south-facing sun room.
- The master bedroom includes a deluxe private bath and two roomy closets.
- Upstairs, two more bedrooms share a second bath, and one bedroom offers a private balcony.

K-507-S

Bedrooms: 3	Baths: 2½
Space:	
Upper floor	397 sq. ft.
Main floor	942 sq. ft.
Total Living Area	**1,339 sq. ft.**
Basement	915 sq. ft.
Garage	400 sq. ft.
Exterior Wall Framing	**2x4/2x6**

Foundation options:

Standard Basement

Slab

(Foundation & framing conversion diagram available—see order form.)

Blueprint Price Code	**A**

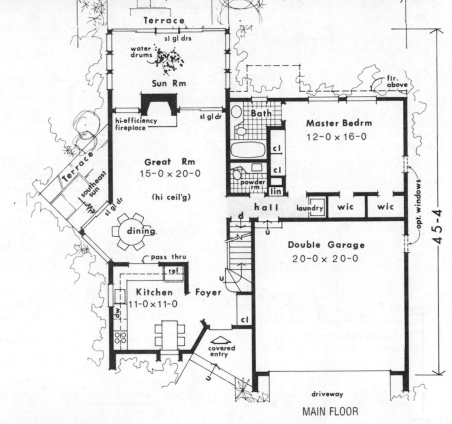

MAIN FLOOR

UPPER FLOOR

TO ORDER THIS BLUEPRINT, CALL TOLL-FREE 1-800-547-5570

(prices and details on pp. 12-15.)

Plan K-507-S

The Simple & Economical Housing Solution

- This compact plan could serve as a second home or a primary residence for a small family.
- Spacious Great Room features woodstove and a large adjoining deck.
- Efficent kitchen is close to storage and laundry area.
- Large, overlooking loft offers infinite possibilities, such as extra sleeping quarters, a home office, art studio, or recreation room.
- Clerestory window arrangement and sloped-ceilings top the loft for added light.

Plan H-963-2A	
Bedrooms: 1	**Baths:** 1
Space:	
Loft:	432 sq. ft.
Main floor:	728 sq. ft.
Total living area:	1,160 sq. ft.
Lower level/garage:	728 sq. ft.
Exterior Wall Framing:	2x4
Foundation options: Slab. (Foundation & framing conversion diagram available — see order form.)	
Blueprint Price Code:	A

LOFT
25'-3" x 16'-2"

SLOPED CEILING

down → RAILING S. C.

CLERESTORY LINE S. C.

OPEN TO GREAT ROOM

SKYLIGHTS

LOFT

CLERESTORY WINDOWS OVER LOFT AND STAIRS

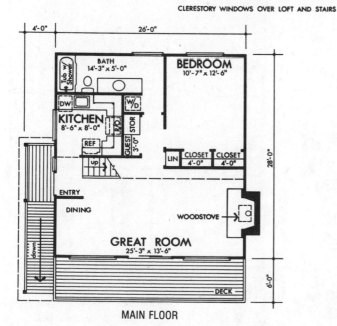

MAIN FLOOR

4'-0" 26'-0"

BATH 14'-3" x 5'-0"

BEDROOM 10'-7" x 12'-6"

DW

KITCHEN 8'-6" x 8'-0"

W/D

GUEST STOR 3'-0"

REF

LIN CLOSET 4'-0" CLOSET 4'-0"

up

28'-0"

ENTRY

DINING

WOODSTOVE →

GREAT ROOM 25'-3" x 13'-6"

down

DECK

6'-0"

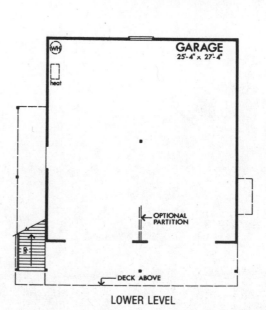

LOWER LEVEL

WH

heat

GARAGE 25'-4" x 27'-4"

OPTIONAL PARTITION

DECK ABOVE

Plan H-963-2A

An Exciting Entertainment Center

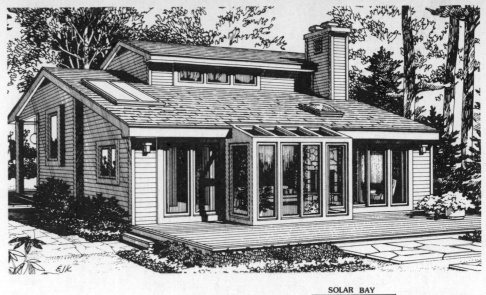

- This leisure home is designed to provide optimum media entertainment into your living room.
- The kitchen, dining area and living room flow together into one large space with a huge corner fireplace, server bar and sloped ceiling open to the upper level. A bubble skylight and a solar bay flood the rooms with daylight. Both the living and the dining areas offer access to the large, rear deck.
- The main level also includes a large master bedroom with dual closets and a nearby bath.
- Two additional bedrooms and a second full bath share the upper level.

Plan HFL-1340-PW

Bedrooms: 3	Baths: 2
Space:	
Upper floor	389 sq. ft.
Main floor	967 sq. ft.
Total Living Area	**1,356 sq. ft.**
Basement	885 sq. ft.
Exterior Wall Framing	**2x6**

Foundation options:

Standard Basement

Slab

(Foundation & framing conversion diagram available—see order form.)

Blueprint Price Code	**A**

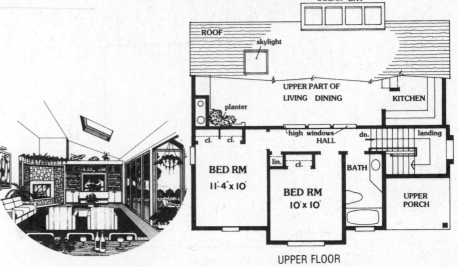

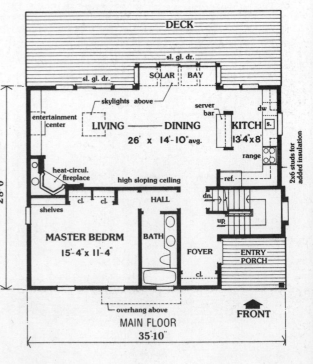

UPPER FLOOR

MAIN FLOOR

TO ORDER THIS BLUEPRINT, CALL TOLL-FREE 1-800-547-5570 (prices and details on pp. 12-15.)

Plan HFL-1340-PW

Cozy Vacation Retreat

- This cozy cabin is at home in the mountains or on a lake, river or coastline.
- Large enough to provide comfortable living quarters and small enough to fit a modest budget, this is an ideal vacation retreat.
- The openness and minimum number of walls give it a spacious feel. Expanses of glass and a two-story-high ceiling give volume to the living and dining space.
- The kitchen offers a window view and a pass-through to the dining area.
- One bedroom is located on the main level and an optional second bedroom can occupy the loft area above.

Plan I-880-A

Bedrooms: 1-2	Baths: 1
Space:	
Upper floor	308 sq. ft.
Main floor	572 sq. ft.
Total Living Area	**880 sq. ft.**
Exterior Wall Framing	2x6

Foundation options:

Crawlspace
(Foundation & framing conversion diagram available—see order form.)

Blueprint Price Code	**A**

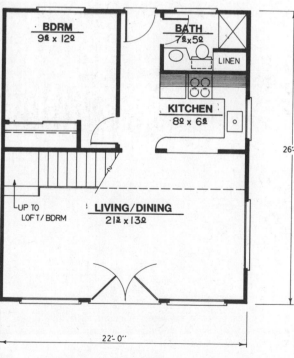

LOFT/BDRM.
308 SQ. FT.

← DOWN

UPPER FLOOR

BDRM
9² x 12²

BATH
7² x 5²

LINEN

KITCHEN
8² x 6²

UP TO
LOFT/BDRM

LIVING/DINING
21² x 13²

26'-0''

22'- 0''

MAIN FLOOR

Plan I-880-A

Compact, Easy to Build

This compact vacation or retirement home is economical and easy to construct. Only 24' x 46' for the daylight basement version, it nonetheless contains all the necessities and some of the luxuries one desires in a three-bedroom home. The non-basement version measures 24' x 44'.

Overall width for both versions including deck and carport is 50'.

One luxury is the separate, private bath adjoining the master bedroom; another is the double "His & Hers" wardrobe closets for the same room. The other two bedrooms are equipped with good-sized closets and share a second bathroom. Even if you choose the basement version, the convenience of first floor laundry facilities is yours.

The open stairway to the basement adds 3' to the visual size of the living room. A

pre-fab fireplace is located to allow enjoyment of a cozy hearth and a beautiful view from the same chair.

The plans are so completely detailed that a handyman amateur might frame this building (with the help of a few friends). Why not try it? (Be sure to order a materials list, too!).

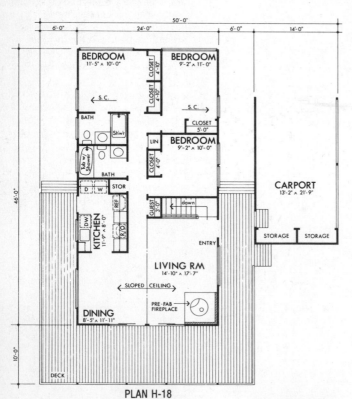

PLAN H-18
WITH DAYLIGHT BASEMENT
1104 SQUARE FEET

PLAN H-18-A
WITH CRAWLSPACE
1056 SQUARE FEET

Total living area: 1,104 sq. ft.
(Not counting basement or carport)

Blueprint Price Code A

Plans H-18 & H-18-A

TO ORDER THIS BLUEPRINT, CALL TOLL-FREE 1-800-547-5570
(prices and details on pp. 12-15.)

Sunny, Cost-Efficient Spaces

- This home keeps costs down without sacrificing aethestics.
- The entry is brightened by clerestory windows, while the vaulted living room features floor-to-ceiling windows.
- The dining room has sliding glass doors opening to the rear deck. The U-shaped kitchen includes a space-saving laundry closet.
- The vaulted master bedroom has a wonderful view of the backyard. The private master bath is adjacent to the main bath for more cost-effective plumbing runs.
- Two more bedrooms round out the main floor.
- The full basement can be finished to provide more living space.

Plan B-90066

Bedrooms: 3	Baths: 2
Living Area:	
Main floor	1,135 sq. ft.
Total Living Area:	**1,135 sq. ft.**
Standard basement	1,135 sq. ft.
Garage	288 sq. ft.
Exterior Wall Framing:	2x4

Foundation Options:

Standard basement
(Typical foundation & framing conversion diagram available—see order form.)

BLUEPRINT PRICE CODE: **A**

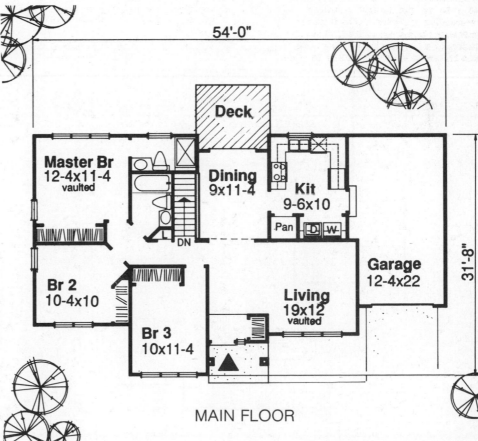

MAIN FLOOR

Plan B-90066

Small Pleasures

- A raised living area over a tuck-under garage gives improved views with multiple decks and windows aplenty.
- Vaulted ceilings in the living area and over the entry give a feeling of spaciousness.
- The living and dining rooms share a fireplace and a front-facing deck.
- The bright kitchen overlooks the dining room and the deck beyond.
- The master bedroom offers private access to the bathroom and has its own deck with French doors.
- A second bedroom rounds out the living floor.
- A two-car garage and a sunny, future living area at the rear make up the lower floor (not shown).

Plan I-1144-A

Bedrooms: 2	Baths: 1

Living Area:	
Main floor	1,144 sq. ft.

Total Living Area:	**1,144 sq. ft.**
Daylight basement	275 sq. ft.
Garage	857 sq. ft.

Exterior Wall Framing:	2x6

Foundation Options:

Daylight basement
(Typical foundation & framing conversion diagram available—see order form.)

BLUEPRINT PRICE CODE: A

Floor plan labels:

34'-6"

42'-6"

MASTER BD. RM.
17⁴ x 11³

DECK
5⁶ x 11⁰

B-1

KITCHEN
9⁸ x 9⁸

BED-2
10⁸ x 10⁰

LIN.

DINING
12⁰ x 10⁰

LIVING RM.
17⁴ x 15⁶

DN   UP

DECK
10⁶ x 8⁶

Plan I-1144-A

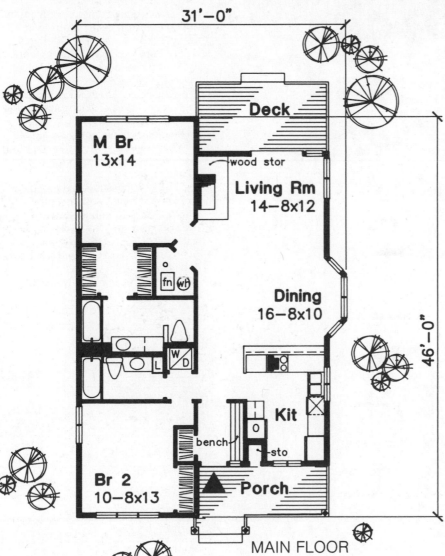

31'-0"

Deck

M Br
13x14

wood stor

Living Rm
14—8x12

fn wh

Dining
16—8x10

L
W D

Kit

bench

sto

Br 2
10—8x13

Porch

46'-0"

MAIN FLOOR

B-91007

Creative Cottage Design

- This creative cottage design features an efficient, open floor plan along with a unique exterior look. At 31 feet wide, it will fit on almost any lot.
- The covered front porch provides a charming welcome. The entry offers a built-in bench and an immediate view of the living room straight ahead.
- The living room flows into the dining room and kitchen to allow for flexible living space. The living area is made even more spacious by adding vaulted ceilings, lots of glass and access to a large deck.
- The kitchen shares a snack bar with the bay-windowed dining area. The living room is highlighted by a fireplace with built-in storage space for wood.
- The plan provides for other amenities as well, including a luxurious master bedroom suite. Another full bath is adjacent to the second bedroom.

Plan B-91007

Bedrooms: 2	Baths: 2
Space:	
Main floor	1,199 sq. ft.
Total Living Area	**1,199 sq. ft.**
Exterior Wall Framing	2x6
Foundation options:	
Slab	
(Foundation & framing conversion diagram available—see order form.)	
Blueprint Price Code	**A**

Mediterranean Delight

- Perfect for sunny climes, this delightful stucco home offers luxurious living spaces within a narrow-lot design.
- A clerestory window above the front door spotlights the plant shelves that frame the Great Room.
- The spectacular Great Room features a vaulted ceiling, a fireplace and access to a secluded patio.
- An efficient kitchen and a sunny breakfast room are easy to reach from the Great Room and from the two-car garage.
- The master suite is isolated at the rear of the home. It offers vaulted ceilings and a luxurious bath with garden tub.
- The bedroom adjacent to the master suite makes a great den.
- The main bath is centrally located to provide easy access from the living areas as well as from the two smaller bedrooms.

Plan B-90502	
Bedrooms: 2-3	**Baths:** 2
Space:	
Main floor	1,200 sq. ft.
Total Living Area	**1,200 sq. ft.**
Garage	387 sq. ft.
Exterior Wall Framing	2x4
Foundation options:	
Slab	
(Foundation & framing conversion diagram available—see order form.)	
Blueprint Price Code	**A**

MAIN FLOOR

Plan B-90502

Unexpected Amenities

- This good-looking design has a casual exterior but an interior filled with amenities you'd expect to find in a much larger and more elegant home.
- Open living areas are created with the use of vaulted ceilings and a minimum number of walls.
- The living room, dining room and kitchen merge in a comfortable setting that overlooks a fireplace and a huge side patio through a pair of sliding glass doors.
- One bedroom and bath, plus an oversized utility room with washer and dryer, extra freezer and storage space for recreational equipment complete the main level.
- Located on the upper level, a spacious master suite with a walk-in closet, private bath and a loft area that overlooks the living room.

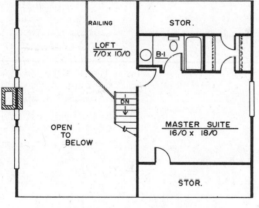

UPPER FLOOR

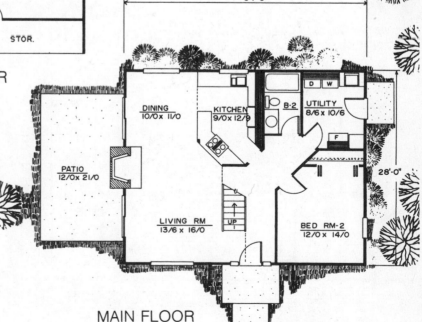

MAIN FLOOR

Plan I-1249-A

Bedrooms: 2	Baths: 2
Space:	
Upper floor	297 sq. ft.
Main floor	952 sq. ft.
Total Living Area	**1,249 sq. ft.**
Exterior Wall Framing	2x6
Foundation options:	

Crawlspace

(Foundation & framing conversion diagram available—see order form.)

Blueprint Price Code	A

Plan I-1249-A

Plan AX-7622-A

Bedrooms: 3	**Baths:** 2

Living Area:

Upper floor	343 sq. ft.
Main floor:	924 sq. ft.
Total Living Area:	**1,267 sq. ft.**
Standard basement	924 sq. ft.

Exterior Wall Framing: 2x4

Foundation Options:
Standard basement
Slab
(Typical foundation & framing conversion diagram available—see order form.)

BLUEPRINT PRICE CODE: A

True A-Frame

- This stylish A-frame has perfect outdoor complements including two side porches, one of which is screened, a second floor deck off the attic bedroom and an optional front deck.
- Interior highlights include a 24' living room with a corner stone fireplace, cathedral ceiling and two sets of sliding glass doors. An attractive circular stairway leads to the second level balcony which overlooks this high-activity area.
- The kitchen offers direct access to the attached porch with built-in stone barbecue for outdoor dining.

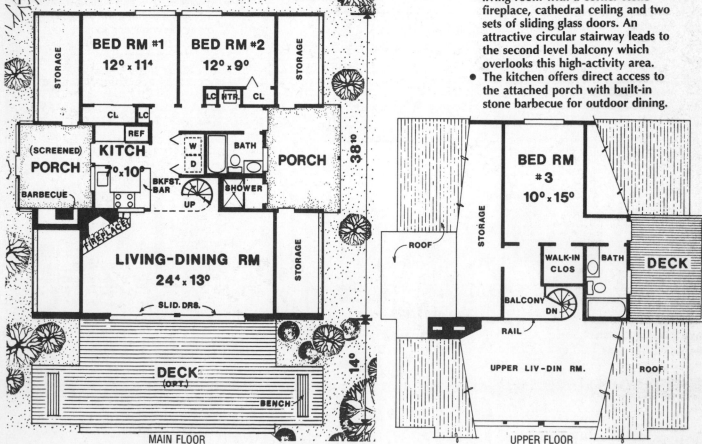

MAIN FLOOR

UPPER FLOOR

TO ORDER THIS BLUEPRINT,
CALL TOLL-FREE 1-800-547-5570

Plan AX-7622-A

DESIGN A - 3 BEDROOMS

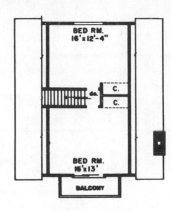

26'-0"

DINE

BATH

BED RM.
10'x13'-4"

KIT.
8'-10"x12'-4"

30'-0"

C.

LIVING RM.
25'-2"x13'

DECK

MAIN FLOOR

BED RM.
16'x12'-4"

da.

C.

C.

BED RM.
16'x13'

BALCONY

UPPER FLOOR

DESIGN B - 4 BEDROOMS

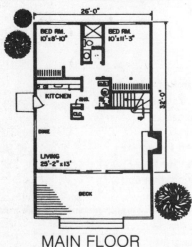

26'-0"

BED RM.
10'x8'-10"

BED RM.
10'x11'-3"

KITCHEN

32'-0"

DINE

LIVING
25'-2"x13'

DECK

MAIN FLOOR

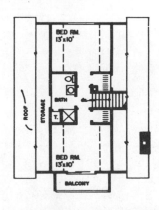

ROOF

STORAGE

BED RM.
13'x10'

BATH

T.

BED RM.
13'x10'

BALCONY

UPPER FLOOR

Design Your Vacation Home

- When it's time to build your dream vacation chalet, consider this versatile three- or four-bedroom design.
- The main level in either floor plan offers a large living area with fireplace and deck access, a compact kitchen, a dining area, a full bath and one or two bedrooms.
- The upper level in both plans features two bedrooms. The bedrooms in the four-bedroom design are smaller in size to accommodate a second bath.
- One upstairs bedroom features sliding glass doors accessing a dramatic outdoor balcony.
- Please specify Design A or Design B when ordering.

Plan N-Brentwood

Bedrooms: 3-4		Baths: 1-2
Living Area:	**Design A**	**Design B**
Upper floor	500 sq. ft.	448 sq. ft.
Main floor	780 sq. ft.	832 sq. ft.
Total Living Area:		**1,280 sq. ft.**
Exterior Wall Framing:		2x4

Foundation Options:
Crawlspace
Slab
(Typical foundation & framing conversion diagram available—see order form.)

BLUEPRINT PRICE CODE:	**A**

Plan N-Brentwood

Leisurely Appeal

- Although ideally designed as a leisure home, this affordable ranch could serve as a permanent residence in the city as well as near a mountain or lake.
- The spectacular living room features a cathedral ceiling with exposed beams, a decorative stone wall that frames a massive heat-circulating fireplace and three sets of sliding glass doors that beckon you to the exciting adjoining deck.
- A casual dining area separates the living room from the centrally located kitchen. The laundry room to the rear is also easily reached from the kitchen.
- The sleeping wing houses three bedrooms and two baths.

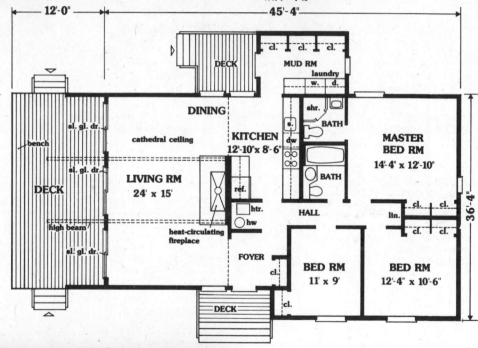

VIEW OF LIVING ROOM AND DECK.

Plan HFL-1140-BY

Bedrooms: 3	Baths: 2

Space:	
Main floor	1,299 sq. ft.
Total Living Area	**1,299 sq. ft.**
Exterior Wall Framing	**2x4**

Foundation options:
Crawlspace
(Foundation & framing conversion diagram available—see order form.)

Blueprint Price Code	**A**

**TO ORDER THIS BLUEPRINT,
CALL TOLL-FREE 1-800-547-5570**

Plan HFL-1140-BY

Contemporary Vacation Home

- If you're ready for summertime living or need a place near your favorite lake, you'll applaud this contemporary vacation home.
- A huge living area with a sloped ceiling, a fireplace, easy deck access and a balcony above reaches from one side of the home to the other.
- Behind the living area is a dining room with window seat and an open kitchen.
- A full bath separates the kitchen from the main-floor bedroom.
- The upper level provides two bedrooms of equal size. Both have closet space and share a second full bath. One also features a raised private deck.

Plan N-Kingsport

Bedrooms: 3	Baths: 2
Living Area:	
Upper floor	488 sq. ft.
Main floor	811 sq. ft.
Total Living Area:	**1,299 sq. ft.**
Exterior Wall Framing:	2x4

Foundation Options:

Pier

(Typical foundation & framing conversion diagram available—see order form.)

BLUEPRINT PRICE CODE: **A**

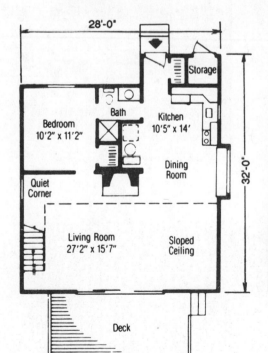

MAIN FLOOR

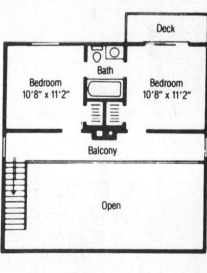

UPPER FLOOR

Plan N-Kingsport

TO ORDER THIS BLUEPRINT, CALL TOLL-FREE 1-800-547-5570

(prices and details on pp. 12-15.)

A Chalet for Today

- This new, up-to-date chalet design is ideal for recreational living, whether year-round or part-time. The home's rustic appeal and soaring windows are ideally suited to scenic sites.
- The living and dining rooms are combined to take advantage of the dramatic cathedral ceiling, the view through the spectacular windows and the rugged stone fireplace.
- A quaint balcony adds to the warm country feeling of the living area, which is further expanded by a wrap-around deck. The open, peninsula kitchen includes a breakfast bar that connects it to the living area.
- The first-floor study or den is an added feature rarely found in a home of this size and style.
- A convenient main-floor laundry is adjacent to two bedrooms and a full bath.
- The master bedroom retreat takes up the entire second floor. Cathedral ceilings, sweeping views from the balcony and a private bath with spa tub are highlights here.
- The optional basement plan calls for a tuck-under garage, a large family room, plus utility and storage space.

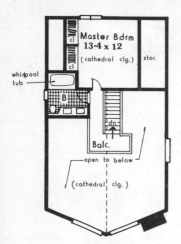

UPPER FLOOR

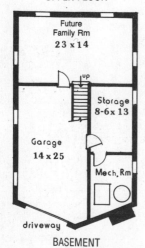

BASEMENT

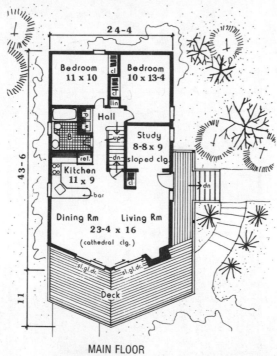

MAIN FLOOR

Plan AHP-9340

Bedrooms: 3-4	Baths: 2
Living Area:	
Upper floor	332 sq. ft.
Main floor	974 sq. ft.
Total Living Area:	**1,306 sq. ft.**
Basement	624 sq. ft.
Garage	350 sq. ft.
Exterior Wall Framing:	2x4 or 2x6

Foundation Options:
Daylight basement
Standard basement
Crawlspace
Slab
(Typical foundation & framing conversion diagram available—see order form.)

BLUEPRINT PRICE CODE: A

Plan AHP-9340

FRONT VIEW

Sunshine Floods Rustic Design

- The main floor is virtually one huge room divided into areas for lounging, eating and cooking.
- A spacious deck, spanning the entire rear of the home, provides for outdoor living and entertaining.
- Upstairs, one large bedroom serves as a master suite, while the balcony room can be used for a variety of purposes, if not needed as a second bedroom.
- Five huge skylight windows across the rear slope of the roof flood the entire home with sunlight and solar heat, achieving a dramatic effect throughout the home.

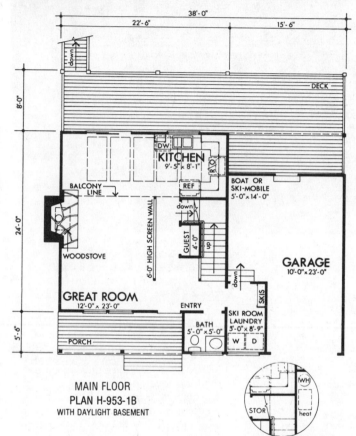

MAIN FLOOR
PLAN H-953-1B
WITH DAYLIGHT BASEMENT

PLAN H-953-1A
WITHOUT BASEMENT

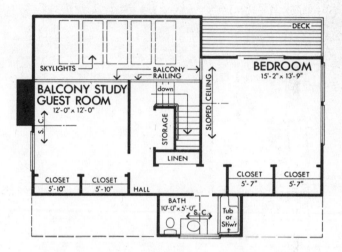

UPPER FLOOR

Plans H-953-1A & -1B	
Bedrooms: 2	**Baths:** 1½
Space:	
Upper floor	689 sq. ft.
Main floor	623 sq. ft.
Total Living Area	**1,312 sq. ft.**
Basement	540 sq. ft.
Garage	319 sq. ft.
Storage	70 sq. ft.
Exterior Wall Framing	2x6
Foundation options:	**Plan #**
Daylight Basement	H-953-1B
Crawlspace	H-953-1A
(Foundation & framing conversion diagram available—see order form.)	
Blueprint Price Code	A

REAR VIEW

Plans H-953-1A & -1B

TO ORDER THIS BLUEPRINT,
CALL TOLL-FREE 1-800-547-5570
(prices and details on pp. 12-15.) **109**

Casual Living with Luxury Features

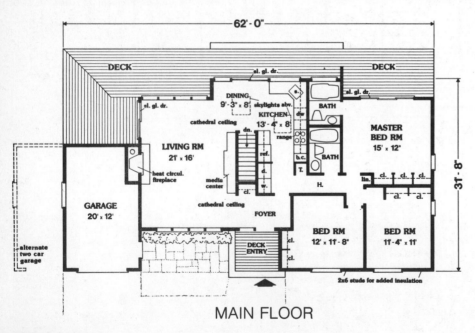

DECK

DECK

62' - 0"

sl. gl. dr.

DINING
9'-3" x 8'

skylights abv.

BATH

sl. gl. dr.

KITCHEN
13'-4" x 8'

sl. gl. dr.

cathedral ceiling

dw

MASTER
BED RM
15' x 12'

LIVING RM
21' x 16'

dn.

range

ref.

heat circul.
fireplace

media
center

b.c.

BATH

cl.

d.

w.

T.

lin.

cl. cl. cl.

cathedral ceiling

FOYER

H.

d.

d.

GARAGE
20' x 12'

DECK
ENTRY

BED RM
12' x 11'-8"

BED RM
11'-4" x 11'

cl.

cl.

31' - 8"

alternate
two car
garage

2x6 studs for added insulation

MAIN FLOOR

* This exciting home has the features of a luxury home and the extras the casual outdoors lover will enjoy.
* The gigantic living room, the kitchen and dining area, and the master bedroom all look out over the expansive rear deck through walls of windows and sliding glass doors.
* A cathedral ceiling and a fireplace add more volume to the living room. A built-in media center along one wall saves space and promotes order.
* The open kitchen and dining area features skylights and a nearby washer and dryer.
* Three bedrooms and two baths are included in the sleeping wing.

Plan HFL-1470-TE

Bedrooms: 3	Baths: 2
Space:	
Main floor	1,324 sq. ft.
Total Living Area	**1,324 sq. ft.**
Basement	1,298 sq. ft.
Garage	266 sq. ft.

Exterior Wall Framing 2x6

Foundation options:
Standard Basement
(Foundation & framing conversion diagram available—see order form.)

Blueprint Price Code A

VIEW OF LIVING ROOM AND DECK.

TO ORDER THIS BLUEPRINT,
CALL TOLL-FREE 1-800-547-5570

Plan HFL-1470-TE

Avant-Garde A-Frame

- This new A-frame design packs three bedrooms plus a loft into less than 1,400 sq. ft. of space, with room left over for storage areas in what is usually wasted kneewall space.
- Geared for sites with a great view, the open floor plan features a combination living/dining room with a corner fireplace, vaulted ceiling and lots of glass. Two sets of sliding doors lead to the large deck.
- The compact kitchen has a snack bar and an adjoining screened-in porch. A laundry closet is close to the kitchen and to the full bath and two bedrooms on the first floor.
- The bathroom and a separate shower room are accessible from another side porch, allowing easy cleanup after a day of swimming or skiing.
- A spiral staircase winds its way to the second floor. Here, a balcony/loft offers a striking view of the living room below and the outdoors beyond. The loft could also be used as an impressive guest room or study.
- The secluded second-floor bedroom has a walk-in closet, its own bath and a private deck.

Plan AX-98274

Bedrooms: 3-4	Baths: 2
Space:	
Upper floor	432 sq. ft.
Main floor	964 sq. ft.
Total Living Area	**1,396 sq. ft.**
Basement	964 sq. ft.
Exterior Wall Framing	2x4

Foundation options:
Standard Basement
Slab
(Foundation & framing conversion diagram available—see order form.)

Blueprint Price Code	**A**

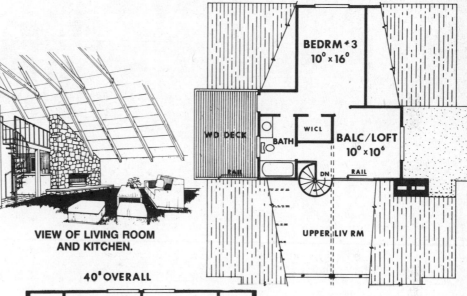

VIEW OF LIVING ROOM AND KITCHEN.

UPPER FLOOR

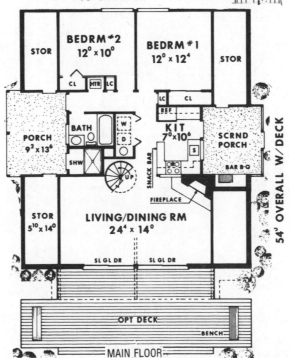

Plan AX-98274

Dramatic Skewed Prow

- This cleverly modified A-frame combines a dramatic exterior with an exciting interior that offers commanding views through its many windows.
- The central foyer opens to a spacious living room and dining room combination with a soaring cathedral ceiling and a massive stone fireplace.
- Directly ahead is the kitchen with sliding glass doors that open to the wraparound deck.
- Two bedrooms are located at the rear near the full bath and the laundry room.
- A third bedroom and a loft area that could sleep overnight guests are found on the upper level.

Plan HFL-1160-CW

Bedrooms: 3	Baths: 2
Space:	
Upper floor	400 sq. ft.
Main floor	1,016 sq. ft.
Total Living Area	**1,416 sq. ft.**
Exterior Wall Framing	**2x4**

Foundation options:
Crawlspace
(Foundation & framing conversion diagram available—see order form.)

Blueprint Price Code	**A**

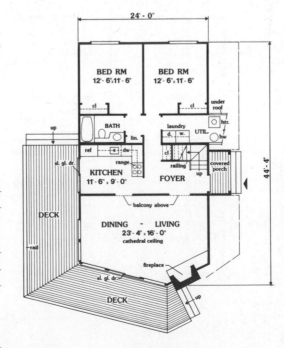

MAIN FLOOR

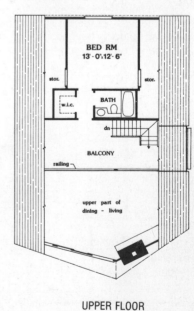

UPPER FLOOR

Plan HFL-1160-CW

At One with the Sun

- This two-bedroom ranch home combines an open floor plan with large expanses of glass to get the most out of the sun.
- The vaulted kitchen faces a cheerful sun porch on one side and opens to the dining and living rooms on the other.
- The dining and living rooms are combined to create one huge area, which is enhanced by vaulted ceilings and views of the large rear deck. A corner fireplace radiates warmth to the entire living area.
- The master bedroom has twin walk-in closets and a private bath. Another full bath, a laundry closet and a den or second bedroom complete the efficient plan.
- The full basement offers more potential living space.

Plan B-91012

Bedrooms: 2	**Baths: 2**

Space:

Main floor	1,421 sq. ft.
Total Living Area	**1,421 sq. ft.**
Basement	1,421 sq. ft.
Garage	440 sq. ft.
Exterior Wall Framing	**2x4**

Foundation options:

Standard Basement

(Foundation & framing conversion diagram available—see order form.)

Blueprint Price Code	**A**

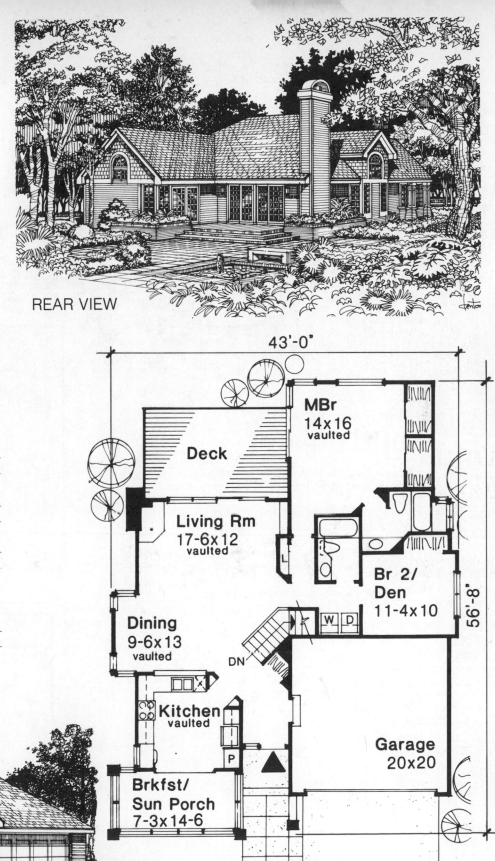

REAR VIEW

MAIN FLOOR

FRONT VIEW

Plan B-91012

Loft Lookout

- Unique lakeside living is possible with this getaway home that can be built on posts.
- Inside, a large living and dining space with a dramatic cathedral ceiling is surrounded by an expansive deck.
- A nice-sized kitchen, two baths and three bedrooms complete the main floor.
- The versatile loft could be used as a rec room, a lookout station or extra sleeping space.

Plan PH-1440

Bedrooms: 3	Baths: 2
Space:	
Upper floor	144 sq. ft.
Main floor	1,296 sq. ft.
Total Living Area	**1,440 sq. ft.**
Exterior Wall Framing	2x6

Foundation options:
Crawlspace
Pole
Slab
(Foundation & framing conversion diagram available—see order form.)

Blueprint Price Code	**A**

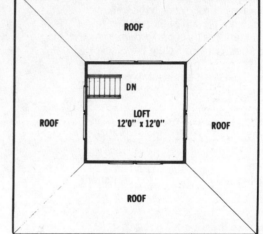

UPPER FLOOR

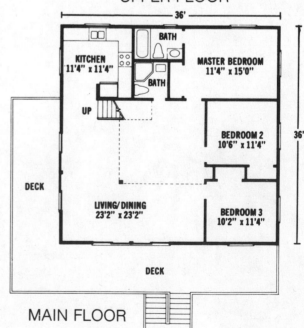

MAIN FLOOR

Plan PH-1440

Fantastic Patio Home

- This design gives you a choice of three different exterior treatments, allowing you to create a home that blends with its surroundings. The blueprints include details for finishing the exterior with stucco (shown), brick or wood siding.
- The interior is geared for indoor/outdoor living, with all of the main rooms featuring lots of glass and views to the secluded patio.
- Tall windows flank the fireplace in the living room, and a French door opens to the large patio. The dining room has a large picture window viewing out to the patio and backyard. Vaulted ceilings further enhance the bright, airy look of the open living and dining rooms.
- The bayed breakfast room is a natural extension of the kitchen and has a French door to the patio. Note the handy laundry closet in the kitchen and the easy access to the garage.
- The master bedroom suite enjoys a quiet corner of the house, with private access to the patio. The fantastic master bath, entered through double doors, includes a vaulted ceiling, a garden tub and a separate shower.

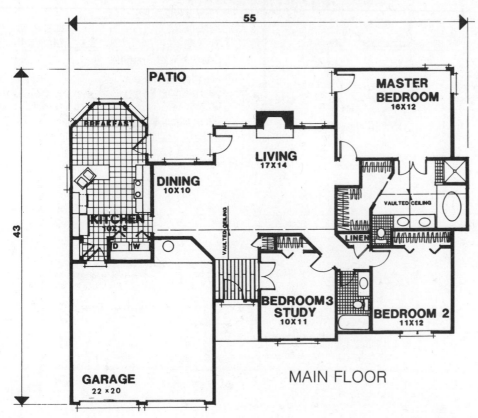

MAIN FLOOR

Plan APS-1404

Plan APS-1404	
Bedrooms: 2-3	**Baths:** 2
Space:	
Main floor	1,477 sq. ft.
Total Living Area	**1,477 sq. ft.**
Garage	440 sq. ft.
Exterior Wall Framing	2x4
Foundation options:	
Slab	
(Foundation & framing conversion diagram available—see order form.)	
Blueprint Price Code	**A**

Unique, Dramatic Floor Plan

- An expansive and impressive Great Room, warmed by a wood stove, features an island kitchen that's completely open in design.
- A passive solar sun room is designed to collect and store heat from the sun, while also providing a good view of the surroundings.
- Upstairs, you'll see a glamorous master suite with a private bath and a huge walk-in closet.
- The daylight basement adds a sunny sitting room, a third bedroom and a large recreation room.

UPPER FLOOR

Plans P-536-2A & -2D	
Bedrooms: 2-3	**Baths: 2-3**
Space:	
Upper floor:	642 sq. ft.
Main floor:	863 sq. ft.
Total living area:	1,505 sq. ft.
Basement:	863 sq. ft.
Garage:	445 sq. ft.
Exterior Wall Framing:	2x4
Foundation options:	Plan #
Daylight basement	P-536-2D
Crawlspace	P-536-2A
(Foundation & framing conversion diagram available — see order form.)	
Blueprint Price Code:	
Plan P-536-2A	B
Plan P-536-2D	C

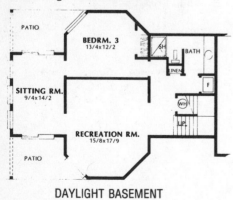

DAYLIGHT BASEMENT

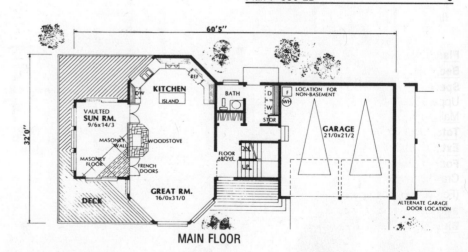

MAIN FLOOR

Plans P-536-2A & -2D

Compact Chalet

- This compact and efficient leisure home is ideal for weekends or getaways.
- The main living area consists of a large living room and dining room arrangement that overlooks the sun deck and the outdoors.
- Room for four comfortably-sized bedrooms makes the home accommodating for several weekend guests. The large master bedroom on the upper level has a private deck and a balcony that overlooks the living room, fireplace and deck below.
- A second bath and a laundry closet are located near the kitchen on the main floor.

Plan CPS-970-L

Bedrooms: 4	Baths: 1-2

Space:

Upper floor	688 sq. ft.
Main floor	832 sq. ft.
Total Living Area	**1,520 sq. ft.**
Exterior Wall Framing	**2x6**

Foundation options:

Crawlspace

(Foundation & framing conversion diagram available—see order form.)

Blueprint Price Code	**B**

MAIN FLOOR

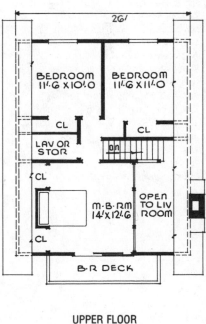

UPPER FLOOR

Plan CPS-970-L

Energy-Saving Sun Room

- This unique angled design offers spectacular rear views.
- From the high-ceilinged reception area is a view of the large inviting atmosphere created by the living room and the dining room. More high ceilings, a stone fireplace and a rear wall of glass that overlooks the terrace are attractions in this huge setting.
- The adjoining family room features an entertainment wall and a pair of sliders that access the attached energy-saving sun room.
- The comfortable kitchen has a handy snack counter and a sunny dinette.
- The bedroom wing offers three bedrooms, including the master suite, which has a sloped ceiling, a large walk-in closet, a personal bath with whirlpool tub and a private terrace.

Plan AHP-9330

Bedrooms: 3	Baths: 2
Space:	
Main floor	1,528 sq. ft.
Total Living Area	**1,528 sq. ft.**
Basement	1,542 sq. ft.
Garage	400 sq. ft.
Exterior Wall Framing	2x4 or 2x6

Foundation options:
Standard Basement
Crawlspace
Slab
(Foundation & framing conversion diagram available—see order form.)
Blueprint Price Code   **B**

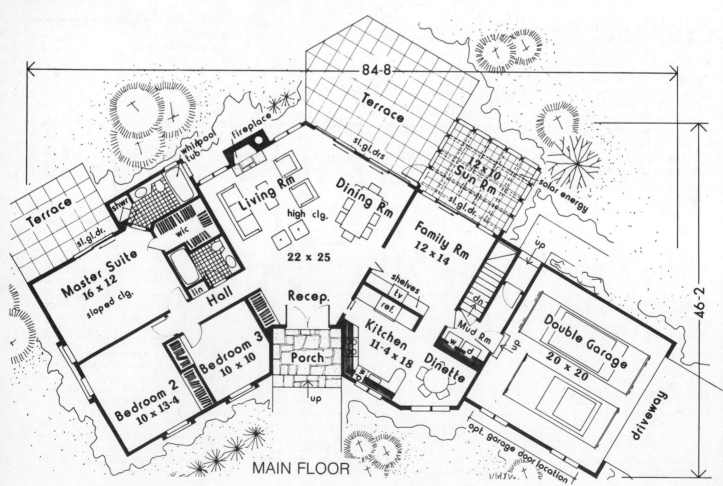

MAIN FLOOR

Plan AHP-9330

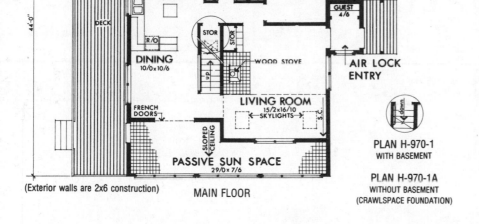

(Exterior walls are 2x6 construction)

MAIN FLOOR

PLAN H-970-1
WITH BASEMENT

PLAN H-970-1A
WITHOUT BASEMENT
(CRAWLSPACE FOUNDATION)

SECOND FLOOR

First floor:	817 sq. ft.
Sunspace:	192 sq. ft.
Second floor:	563 sq. ft.
Total living area:	1,572 sq. ft.
(Not counting basement or garage)	
Airlock entry:	40 sq. ft.
Garage:	288 sq. ft.

The Simple Life at Its Best in a Passive Solar Design

This home's rustic exterior is suggestive of Carpenter Gothic Style homes or early barn designs. The wood shake roof and "board-and-batten" style siding help to carry out this theme. An air-lock entry provides a protected place to remove outer garments as well as serving as an energy-conserving heat loss barrier. As you pass from the entry into the cozy living room, there is an immediate perception of warmth and light. This room features a centrally located woodstove and two skylights.

Between the living room and the sun space are two double-hung windows to provide heat circulation as well as admit natural light. Further inspection of the ground floor reveals a delightful flow of space. From the dining room it is possible to view the kitchen, the wider portion of the sun space and part of the living room. An open staircase connects this room with the second floor.

The kitchen boasts modern appliances, large pantry and storage closets and a convenient peninsula open to the dining room. The remainder of the first floor includes a handy laundry room, an easily accessible half-bath and a bonus room with an unlimited number of possibilities. One such use may be as a home computer/study area. Upstairs, two bedrooms with an abundance of closet space share the fully appointed, skylighted bathroom.

A word about the passive sun room: It seems that solar design has come full circle, returning us to the concept that less is more. This sun room uses masonry floor pavers as heat storage and natural convection as the primary means of heat circulation. This serves to reduce both the potential for system failures and the heavy operating workload often found in more elaborate solar designs, not to mention the high cost of such systems.

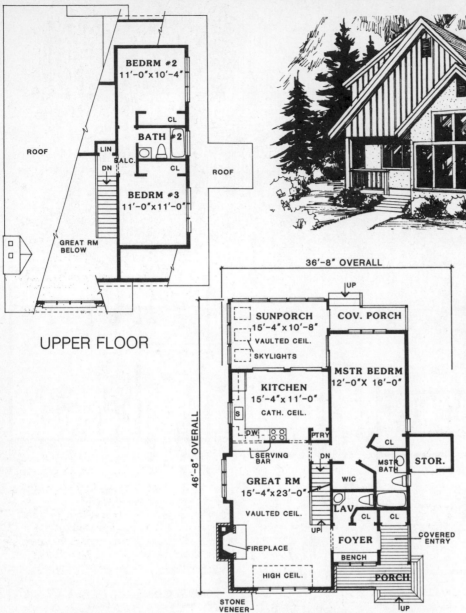

UPPER FLOOR

BEDRM #2
11'-0"x10'-4"

CL

BATH #2

LIN

BALC.

DN

CL

ROOF

BEDRM #3
11'-0"x11'-0"

ROOF

GREAT RM
BELOW

REAR VIEW

36'-8" OVERALL

UP

SUNPORCH
15'-4"x10'-8"
VAULTED CEIL.
SKYLIGHTS

COV. PORCH

46'-8" OVERALL

KITCHEN
15'-4"x11'-0"
CATH. CEIL.

S

MSTR BEDRM
12'-0"X 16'-0"

DW

PTRY

SERVING
BAR

DN

CL

MSTR
BATH

STOR.

GREAT RM
15'-4"x23'-0"

WIC

VAULTED CEIL.

LAV

CL

CL

UP

FIREPLACE

FOYER

COVERED
ENTRY

BENCH

HIGH CEIL.

PORCH

STONE
VENEER

UP

MAIN FLOOR

Perfect for Year-Round Fun

- Whether it's used as a ski house, a cabin or a year-round residence, this delightful rustic home will be a pleasure to come home to.
- Steeply pitched rooflines and plenty of windows make it picturesque from any angle.
- The main entrance stems from a porch with a covered entry and leads to a large vaulted Great Room with fireplace.
- The spacious eat-in kitchen, also with a dramatic high ceiling, offers a serving bar and a pantry.
- The vaulted rear sun porch has private access from the master bedroom.
- Two extra bedrooms share the upper level.

Plan AX-91317

Bedrooms: 3	Baths: 2 ½
Space:	
Upper floor	411 sq. ft.
Main floor	1,008 sq. ft.
Sun porch	173 sq. ft.
Total Living Area	**1,592 sq. ft.**
Basement	1,008 sq. ft.
Storage	42 sq. ft.
Exterior Wall Framing	2x4
Foundation options:	
Standard Basement	
Slab	
(Foundation & framing conversion diagram	
available—see order form.)	
Blueprint Price Code	**B**

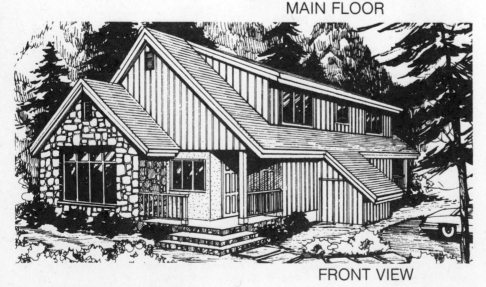

FRONT VIEW

Plan AX-91317

Lakeside Retreat Sleeps Eight

- Four bedrooms border the exterior walls of this lakeside retreat, affording a fair amount of privacy.
- A deck and a vaulted screened-in porch surround the spectacular cathedral-ceilinged Great Room and dining area. The large living space is also loaded with glass so you can enjoy your favorite scenic site.
- The adjoining kitchen features an oversized eating bar and work counter combination.
- Two full baths sit back-to-back, conveniently serving both bedroom wings. A handy main-floor laundry room is also included.

Plan PH-1600	
Bedrooms: 4	**Baths:** 2
Space:	
Main floor	1,600 sq. ft.
Total Living Area	**1,600 sq. ft.**
Exterior Wall Framing	2x6
Foundation options:	
Crawlspace	
Pole	
Slab	
(Foundation & framing conversion diagram available—see order form.)	
Blueprint Price Code	**B**

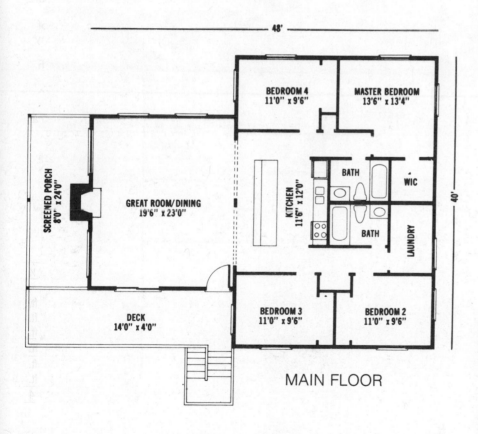

MAIN FLOOR

Plan PH-1600

TO ORDER THIS BLUEPRINT,
CALL TOLL-FREE 1-800-547-5570
(prices and details on pp. 12-15.)

Solarium Adds Excitement

- Modest and unassuming from the street side, this home blossoms on a site with a view to the rear.
- A sunny solarium/spa room adjoins a spacious, vaulted Great Room with a wall of windows facing the scenery. A massive fireplace is another prominent feature.
- A deluxe, double-doored master suite includes a private bath and a large closet, plus double-door access to the solarium and spa.
- A second bedroom is adjacent to another full bath, and a den or third bedroom would also make an attractive studio or office.
- A roomy kitchen includes a bay-windowed breakfast nook.

Plans P-6566-3A & -3D

Bedrooms: 2-3		**Baths:** 2
Space:		
Main floor (basement version)		1,642 sq. ft.
Main floor (crawlspace)		1,635 sq. ft.
Total Living Area		**1,642/1,635 sq. ft.**
Basement		1,642 sq. ft.
Garage		438 sq. ft.
Exterior Wall Framing		2x4
Foundation options:		**Plan #**
Daylight Basement		P-6566-3D
Crawlspace		P-6566-3A
(Foundation & framing conversion diagram available—see order form.)		
Blueprint Price Code		**B**

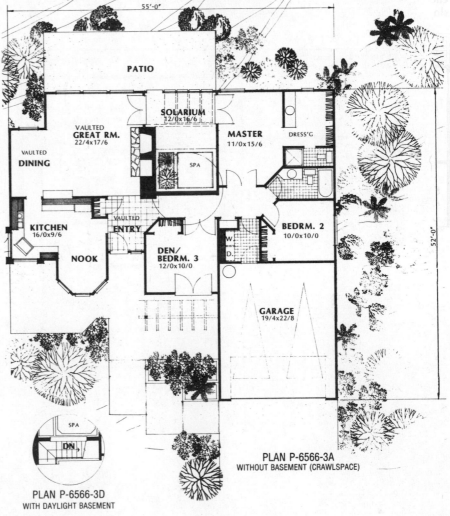

PLAN P-6566-3D
WITH DAYLIGHT BASEMENT

PLAN P-6566-3A
WITHOUT BASEMENT (CRAWLSPACE)

Plans P-6566-3A & -3D

Year-Round Fun

- Whether you are looking for a vacation home nestled in the slopes of ski country or a lakeside retreat, this design has just the right look and features.
- A woodsy contemporary exterior incorporates angles, clerestory windows, skylights and varied rooflines to give a vacation air.
- The interior dramatically continues the retreat feeling with a high-sloped living room ceiling with fireplace and open loft and stair railings.
- The kitchen/dining room is spacious enough to accommodate plenty of friends and family.
- The main floor bedroom has a large walk-in closet and private patio, while the upper bedrooms each feature private balconies and sloped ceilings with clerestory glass.

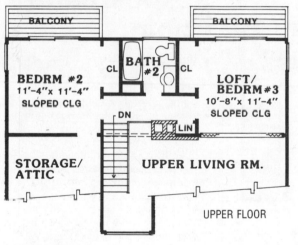

UPPER FLOOR

CLERESTORY WINDOW LOCATIONS

47'-0" OVERALL

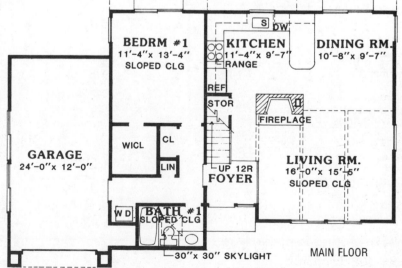

MAIN FLOOR

31'-0" OVERALL

Plan AX-98815

Bedrooms: 3	Baths: 2

Space:	
Upper floor:	531 sq. ft.
Main floor:	1,131 sq. ft.
Total living area:	**1,662 sq. ft.**
Basement:	1,112 sq. ft.
Garage:	288 sq. ft.
Exterior Wall Framing:	**2x4**

Foundation options:
Standard basement.
Slab.
(Foundation & framing conversion diagram available — see order form.)

Blueprint Price Code:	**B**

Plan AX-98815

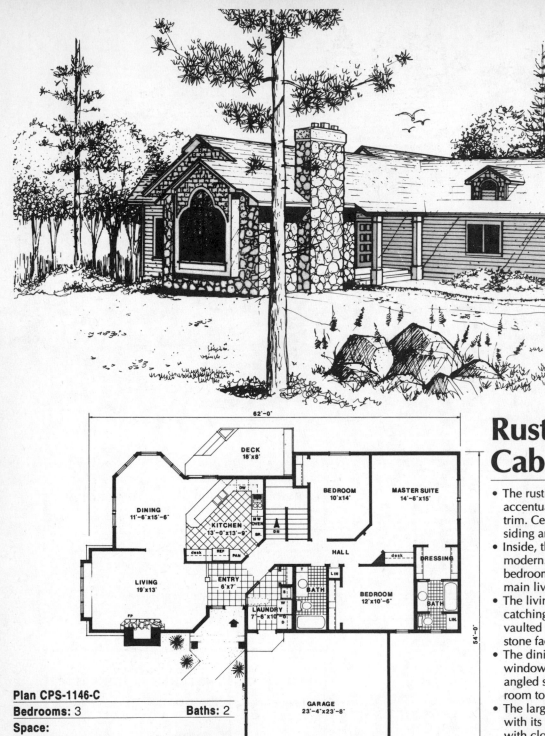

Rustic Country Cabin

- The rustic look of this country cabin is accentuated by a stone fireplace and trim. Cedar shakes and narrow lap siding are other traditional features.
- Inside, the floor plan is thoroughly modern. The covered entry leads to the bedroom wing on the right and the main living areas on the left.
- The living room features an eye-catching window set into an alcove. A vaulted ceiling and a fireplace with stone facing add to the room's impact.
- The dining room includes a large bay window and access to a deck. An angled snack bar connects the dining room to the ultra-modern kitchen.
- The large master suite is far from rustic, with its built-in desk, dressing room with closet space, and private bath with spa tub.
- Two more bedrooms share a full bath. A large laundry room is cleverly positioned to allow easy access from the kitchen, the bedrooms and the garage.

MAIN FLOOR

Plan CPS-1146-C	
Bedrooms: 3	**Baths:** 2
Space:	
Main floor	1,684 sq. ft.
Total Living Area	**1,684 sq. ft.**
Basement	1,684 sq. ft.
Garage	552 sq. ft.
Exterior Wall Framing	2x6
Foundation options:	
Standard Basement	
Crawlspace	
Slab	
(Foundation & framing conversion diagram available—see order form.)	
Blueprint Price Code	B

Plan CPS-1146-C

Lower-Level Expansion Space

- This modest Colonial bi-level design offers expansion space on the lower level as time and budget allow.
- The main level features a combined living room and formal dining area off the kitchen.
- The kitchen has its own casual dining corner and access to the raised rear deck.
- Two nice-sized bedrooms and a larger master bedroom share a full bath that has an isolated dressing area.
- Room for a future family room and bedroom is provided on the lower level, along with a half-bath, laundry facilities and a two-car garage.

Plan N-126-SB

Bedrooms: 3-4	**Baths:** 1½
Living Area:	
Main floor	1,166 sq. ft.
Total Living Area:	**1,166 sq. ft.**
Daylight basement	572 sq. ft.
Garage	479 sq. ft.
Exterior Wall Framing:	2x4

Foundation Options:
Daylight basement
(Typical foundation & framing conversion diagram available—see order form.)

BLUEPRINT PRICE CODE: A

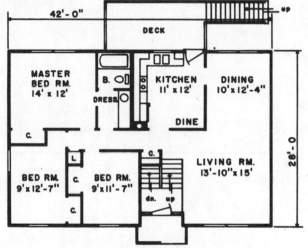

MAIN FLOOR

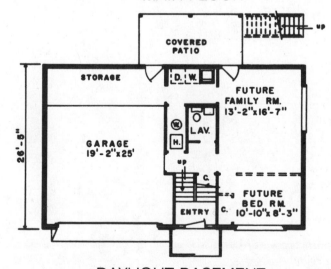

DAYLIGHT BASEMENT

Plan N-126-SB

FRONT VIEW

Sun Lovers' Hideaway

- Attractive, cozy and sunny are only three adjectives that come immediately to mind as one looks at this plan. Energy efficiency is also a major element.
- An air-lock entry helps seal heated or cooled air inside, and the home is well-insulated in walls, ceilings and floors for tight control of energy bills.
- The major portion of the main floor is devoted to a spacious living/dining/kitchen area with easy access to the large sun room.
- Two downstairs bedrooms share a full bath and include large double-glazed windows.
- Upstairs, the master suite features a private bath and large closet, plus a balcony overlook into the living room.
- An optional daylight basement offers potential for an additional bedroom as well as a large recreation room and general use area. In this version, the sun room is on the lower level, and a dramatic spiral staircase ascends to the main floor.

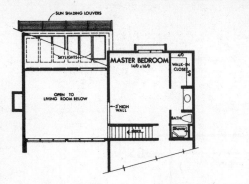

UPPER FLOOR

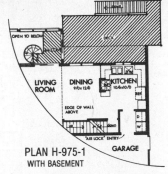

PLAN H-975-1
WITH BASEMENT

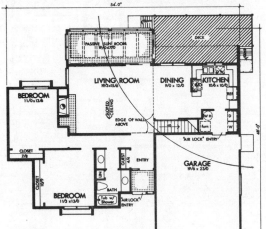

MAIN FLOOR
PLAN H-975-1A
WITHOUT BASEMENT

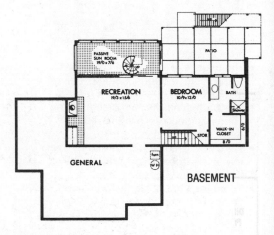

BASEMENT

Plans H-975-1 & -1A

Bedrooms: 3	Baths: 2

Space:	
Upper floor	370 sq. ft.
Main floor (including sun room)	1,394 sq. ft.
Optional daylight basement	1,394 sq. ft.
Finished (including sun room)	782 sq. ft.
Unfinished	612 sq. ft.
Total Living Area	**1,764/2,546 sq. ft.**
Garage	448 sq. ft.
Exterior Wall Framing	2x6

Foundation options:	Plan #
Daylight Basement	H-975-1
Crawlspace	H-975-1A

(Foundation & framing conversion diagram available—see order form.)

Blueprint Price Code	B/D

REAR VIEW

Plans H-975-1 & -1A

Unique Peaks

- This beautiful A-frame home offers spectacular sloped ceilings and window treatments that accent its unique design.
- Sun-worshipers will appreciate the spacious wraparound deck and the covered dining patio.
- Inside you'll find an entry hall with seat, a commodious kitchen with informal dining area and a dramatic family/living area with fireplace.
- Two bedrooms and a bath complete the main level.
- The fabulous master bedroom on the upper floor offers a private sitting area with a cozy fireplace. Windows on both ends bring in plenty of natural light.. A closet and a private bath are also featured.

Plan N-Lakepoint

Bedrooms: 3	Baths: 2
Living Area:	
Upper floor	624 sq. ft.
Main floor	1,126 sq. ft.
Total Living Area:	**1,750 sq. ft.**
Daylight basement	1,126 sq. ft.
Exterior Wall Framing:	2x4

Foundation Options:
Daylight basement
Slab

(Typical foundation & framing conversion diagram available—see order form.)

BLUEPRINT PRICE CODE:	**B**

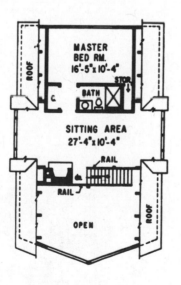

MAIN FLOOR

UPPER FLOOR

Plan N-Lakepoint

Master Bedroom Loft

- For a country design with rustic charm, consider this spacious two-story.
- The focal point of the home is a two-story-high Great Room with a sloped ceiling.
- The adjoining L-shaped kitchen features a built-in grill and a sliding door to the patio.
- Two bedrooms are located on the main level, serviced by a full bath.
- For privacy and quiet, the oversized master bedroom is housed on the upper level. It offers its own bath, double closets and a private balcony. The balcony on the opposite side of the stairway looks into the Great Room below and may be used as a library.

Plan N-1200

Bedrooms: 2-3	Baths: 2
Living Area:	
Upper floor	444 sq. ft.
Main floor	1,320 sq. ft.
Total Living Area:	**1,764 sq. ft.**
Standard basement	1,320 sq. ft.
Garage	498 sq. ft.
Exterior Wall Framing:	2x4

Foundation Options:

Standard basement

Crawlspace

(Typical foundation & framing conversion diagram available—see order form.)

BLUEPRINT PRICE CODE: B

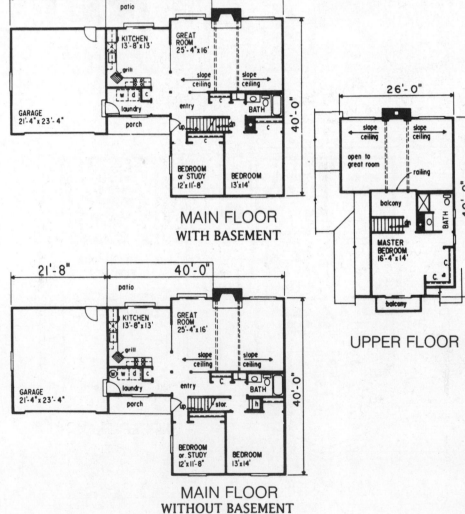

MAIN FLOOR
WITH BASEMENT

MAIN FLOOR
WITHOUT BASEMENT

UPPER FLOOR

Plan N-1200

Contemporary Blends with Site

The striking contemporary silhouette of this home paradoxically blends with the rustic setting. Perhaps it is the way the shed rooflines repeat the spreading limbs of the surrounding evergreens, or the way the foundation conforms to the grade much as do the rocks in the foreground. Whatever the reason, the home "belongs."

Aesthetics aside, one must examine the floor plan to determine genuine livability. From the weather-protected entry there is access to any part of the house without annoying cross traffic. Kitchen, dining and living room, the active "waking-hours" section of the residence, are enlarged and enhanced by the convenient outdoor deck. Laundry and bath are located inconspicuously along the hall leading to the main floor bedroom. A huge linen closet is convenient to this area. The additional bedrooms are located upstairs on the 517 sq. ft. second level. A romantic feature of the second floor is the balcony overlooking the living area.

Plans including a full basement are available at your option. A large double garage completes the plan and is an important adjunct, especially if the home is built without a basement, because it can provide much needed storage space.

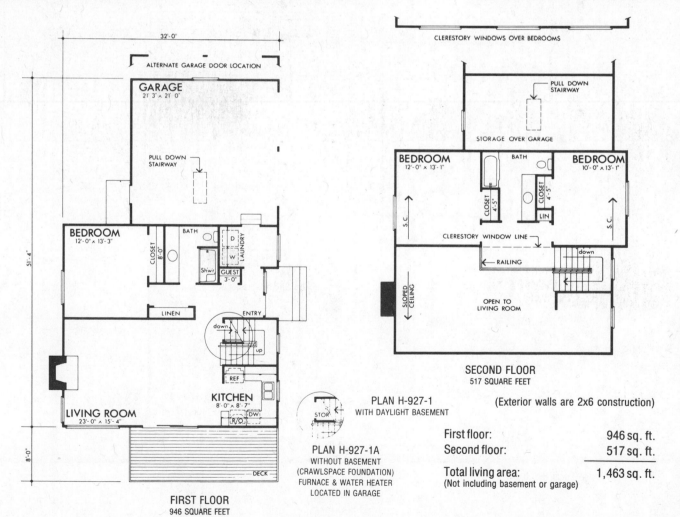

PLAN H-927-1
WITH DAYLIGHT BASEMENT

PLAN H-927-1A
WITHOUT BASEMENT
(CRAWLSPACE FOUNDATION)
FURNACE & WATER HEATER
LOCATED IN GARAGE

FIRST FLOOR
946 SQUARE FEET

SECOND FLOOR
517 SQUARE FEET

(Exterior walls are 2x6 construction)

First floor:	946 sq. ft.
Second floor:	517 sq. ft.
Total living area: (Not including basement or garage)	1,463 sq. ft.

Blueprint Price Code A

Plans H-927-1 & H-927-1A

Spacious Deck for Easy Living

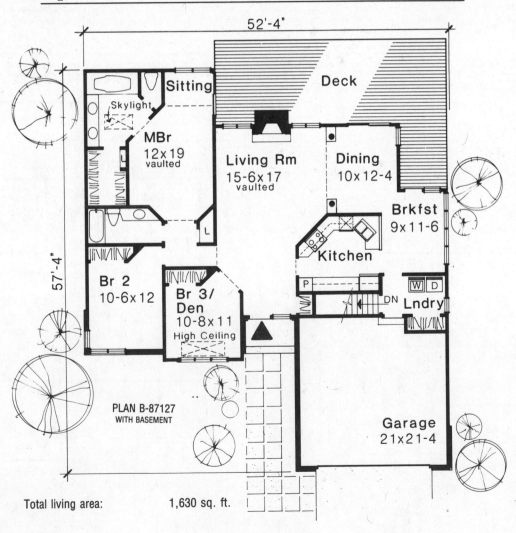

Sitting

Skylight

Deck

MBr
12 x 19
vaulted

Living Rm
15-6 x 17
vaulted

Dining
10 x 12-4

Brkfst
9 x 11-6

Kitchen

Br 2
10-6 x 12

Br 3/
Den
10-8 x 11
High Ceiling

P

DN

W D

Lndry

PLAN B-87127
WITH BASEMENT

Garage
21 x 21-4

52'-4"

57'-4"

Total living area: 1,630 sq. ft.

Blueprint Price Code B
Plan B-87127

Compact & Cozy

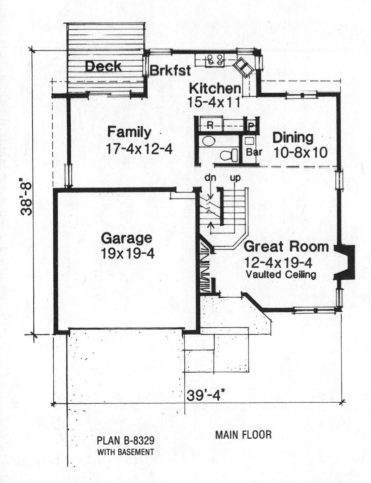

Deck

Brkfst

Kitchen
15-4x11

Family
17-4x12-4

R   P
Bar

Dining
10-8x10

dn   up

Garage
19x19-4

Great Room
12-4x19-4
Vaulted Ceiling

38'-8"

39'-4"

PLAN B-8329
WITH BASEMENT

MAIN FLOOR

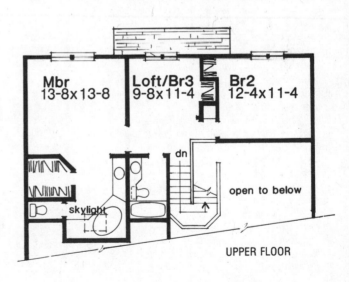

Mbr
13-8x13-8

Loft/Br3
9-8x11-4

Br2
12-4x11-4

dn

open to below

skylight

UPPER FLOOR

First floor:	904 sq. ft.
Second floor:	756 sq. ft.
Total living area:	1,660 sq. ft.

(Not counting basement or garage)

Blueprint Price Code B

Plan B-8329

Soaring Wings Accent Cross-Shaped Plan

- The soaring wing-like roof of this plan is a striking eye-catcher, and the cross-shaped floor plan offers abundant window space and efficient traffic patterns.
- The central sunken ''conversation pit'' is defined by a massive stone fireplace and is open to the dining area at the right and the living room which opens to a huge deck.
- The rear arm of the cross is devoted to an efficient arrangement of kitchen, bath and laundry area.
- A bedroom with two closets completes the downstairs.
- The second floor includes another bedroom and a second full bath, plus a balcony area which can be used for additional sleeping space as well as for a library, sitting room, hobby room or studio overlooking the living room below.

UPPER FLOOR

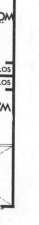

MAIN FLOOR

Plan H-805-4 & -4A

Bedrooms: 2-3	Baths: 2
Space:	
Upper floor	513 sq. ft.
Main floor	1,028 sq. ft.
Total Living Area	**1,541 sq. ft.**
Basement (approx)	1,028 sq. ft.

Exterior Wall Framing	2x4
Foundation options:	**Plan #**
Standard Basement	H-805-4
Crawlspace	H-805-4A
(Foundation & framing conversion diagram available—see order form.)	
Blueprint Price Code	B

TO ORDER THIS BLUEPRINT, CALL TOLL-FREE 1-800-547-5570

(prices and details on pp. 12-15.)

Plans H-805-4 & -4A

Bedrooms on Walkout Level

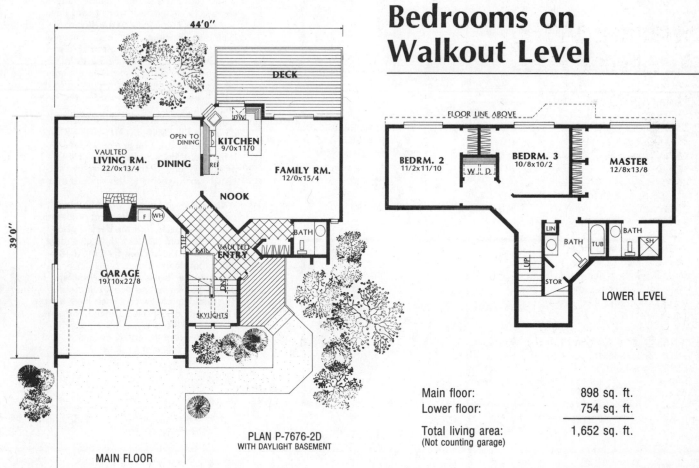

44'0"

DECK

VAULTED
LIVING RM.
22/0x13/4

DINING

OPEN TO
DINING

DW

KITCHEN
9/0x11/0

REF

FAMILY RM.
12/0x15/4

NOOK

39'0"

F WH

STEP

VAULTED
ENTRY

RAIL

BATH

GARAGE
19/10x22/8

DN

SKYLIGHTS

MAIN FLOOR

PLAN P-7676-2D
WITH DAYLIGHT BASEMENT

FLOOR LINE ABOVE

BEDRM. 2
11/2x11/10

W D

BEDRM. 3
10/8x10/2

MASTER
12/8x13/8

LIN

BATH

UP

STOR

BATH TUB BATH SH

LOWER LEVEL

Main floor: 898 sq. ft.
Lower floor: 754 sq. ft.

Total living area: 1,652 sq. ft.
(Not counting garage)

Blueprint Price Code B

Plan P-7676-2D

TO ORDER THIS BLUEPRINT, CALL TOLL-FREE 1-800-547-5570
(prices and details on pp. 12-15.) **133**

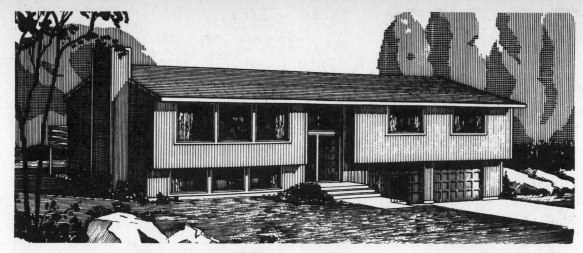

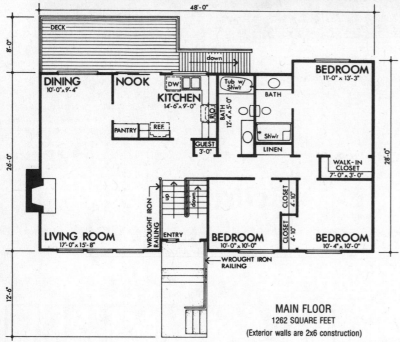

48'-0"

DECK

DINING
10'-0" x 9'-4"

NOOK

KITCHEN
14'-6" x 9'-0"

DW

down

PANTRY   REF.

Tub w/
Sh'wr

BATH
12'-4" x 5'-0"

BATH

BEDROOM
11'-0" x 13'-3"

GUEST
3'-0"

Sh'wr

LINEN

WALK-IN
CLOSET
7'-0" x 3'-0"

LIVING ROOM
17'-0" x 15'-8"

WROUGHT IRON RAILING

up   down

ENTRY

BEDROOM
10'-0" x 10'-0"

CLOSET
4'-10"

CLOSET
4'-10"

BEDROOM
10'-4" x 10'-0"

← WROUGHT IRON
RAILING

MAIN FLOOR
1262 SQUARE FEET
(Exterior walls are 2x6 construction)

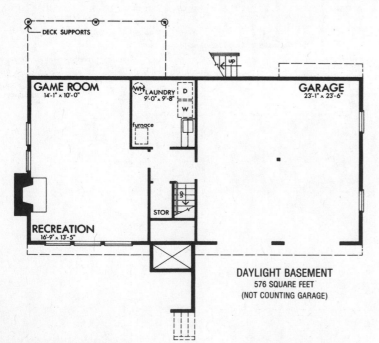

DECK SUPPORTS

up

GAME ROOM
14'-1" x 10'-0"

WH   LAUNDRY
9'-0" x 9'-8"

D
W

GARAGE
23'-1" x 23'-6"

furnace

up

STOR

RECREATION
16'-9" x 13'-5"

DAYLIGHT BASEMENT
576 SQUARE FEET
(NOT COUNTING GARAGE)

Economical Hillside Design

The solid, expansive, well-to-do appearance of this home plan belies the fact that it contains only 1,262 sq. ft. on the main floor and 1,152 sq. ft. on the lower level, including garage space.

This plan has a simple framing pattern, rectangular shape and straight roof line, and it lacks complicated embellishments. Even the excavation, only half as deep as usual, helps make this an affordable and relatively quick and easy house to build.

A split-level entry opens onto a landing between floors, providing access up to the main living room or down to the recreation and work areas.

The living space is large and open. The dining and living rooms combine with the stairwell to form a large visual space. A large 8'x20' deck, visible through the picture window in the dining room, adds visual expansiveness to this multi-purpose space.

The L-shaped kitchen and adjoining nook are perfect for daily food preparation and family meals, and the deck is also accessible from this area through sliding glass doors. The kitchen features a 48 cubic foot pantry closet.

The master bedroom has a complete private bathroom and oversized closet. The remaining bedrooms each have a large closet and access to a full-size bathroom.

A huge rec and game room is easily accessible from the entry, making it ideal for a home office or business.

Main floor:	1,262 sq. ft.
Lower level:	576 sq. ft.
Total living area: (Not counting garage)	1,838 sq. ft.

Blueprint Price Code B
Plan H-1332-5

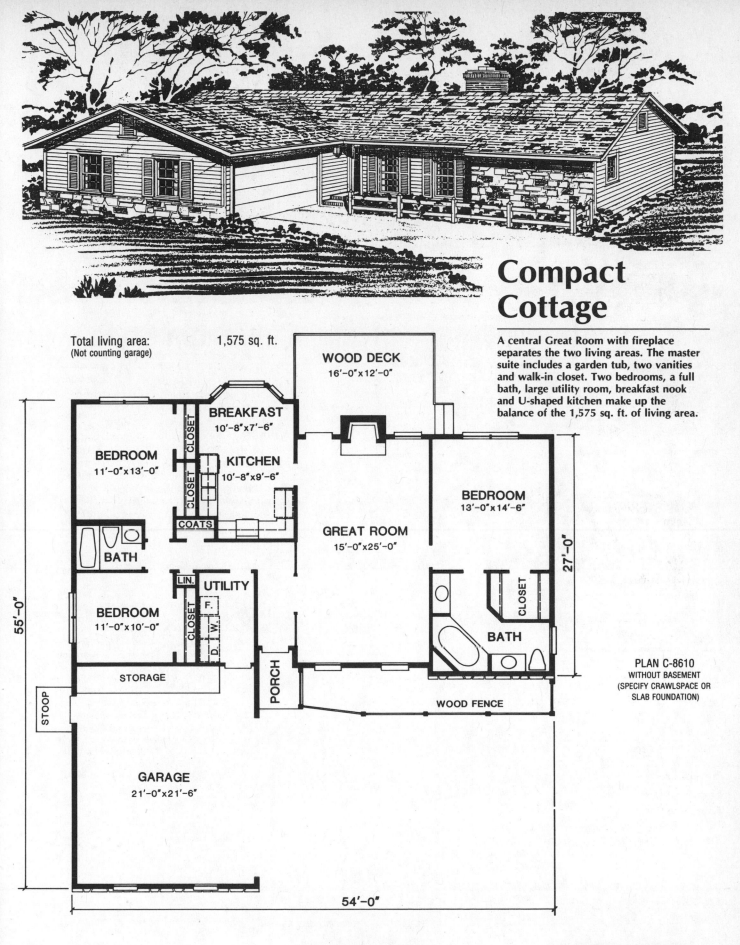

Compact Cottage

A central Great Room with fireplace separates the two living areas. The master suite includes a garden tub, two vanities and walk-in closet. Two bedrooms, a full bath, large utility room, breakfast nook and U-shaped kitchen make up the balance of the 1,575 sq. ft. of living area.

Total living area:
(Not counting garage)   1,575 sq. ft.

WOOD DECK
16'-0" x 12'-0"

BREAKFAST
10'-8" x 7'-6"

CLOSET

CLOSET

BEDROOM
11'-0" x 13'-0"

KITCHEN
10'-8" x 9'-6"

COATS

BATH

BEDROOM
13'-0" x 14'-6"

GREAT ROOM
15'-0" x 25'-0"

27'-0"

LIN.

UTILITY

CLOSET

F.

D.   W.

BEDROOM
11'-0" x 10'-0"

CLOSET

BATH

55'-0"

STOOP

STORAGE

PORCH

WOOD FENCE

PLAN C-8610
WITHOUT BASEMENT
(SPECIFY CRAWLSPACE OR
SLAB FOUNDATION)

GARAGE
21'-0" x 21'-6"

54'-0"

Blueprint Price Code B
Plan C-8610

TO ORDER THIS BLUEPRINT,
CALL TOLL-FREE 1-800-547-5570
(prices and details on pp. 12-15.) **135**

California Style

- Open, versatile living is the key to this California styled two-story.
- The high, spacious foyer reveals the massive Great Room which spans almost the entire length of the home; it features a dramatic vaulted ceiling open to the master bedroom balcony and skylights.
- A counter bar separates the Great Room from the adjoining kitchen.
- Laundry facilities are conveniently located near the sleeping rooms on the upper level, along with storage space and two full baths.

SKYLIGHTS

BEDRM #2 10'0" x 12'6"

BEDRM #3 10'0" x 13'6"

9' CL

OPEN TO LIVING

W D

6' CL

BATH

MASTER 14'0" x 15'0"

DN

OPEN TO FOYER

BATH

UPPER FLOOR

WALK-IN CLOSET

LOW STORAGE

LIVING 15'8" x 15'8" VAULTED

DINING 12'0" x 11'0"

KITCHEN 11'0" x 15'8"

DECK

CL

P

FOYER

PR

GARAGE 19'4" x 23'0"

DN

UP

MAIN FLOOR

40'

40'

Plan PH-1839	
Bedrooms: 3	Baths: 2 ½
Space:	
Upper floor	970 sq. ft.
Main floor	869 sq. ft.
Total Living Area	**1,839 sq. ft.**
Basement	869 sq. ft.
Garage	437 sq. ft.
Exterior Wall Framing	2x6

Foundation options:
Daylight Basement
Standard Basement
Crawlspace
Slab
(Foundation & framing conversion diagram available—see order form.)

Blueprint Price Code   B

*TO ORDER THIS BLUEPRINT,
CALL TOLL-FREE 1-800-547-5570*

(prices and details on pp. 12-15.)

Plan PH-1839

FRONT VIEW

REAR VIEW

Popular Plan for Any Setting

- City, country, or casual living is possible in this versatile two-story design.
- A spa room and sunning area lie between the master suite and Great Room, all encased in an extended eating and viewing deck.
- U-shaped kitchen, nook, and dining area fulfill your entertaining and dining needs.
- Two additional bedrooms and a balcony hall are located on the second level.
- Daylight basement option provides a fourth bedroom, shop, and recreation area.

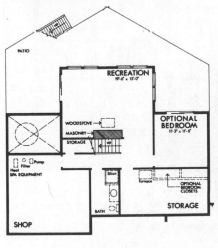

BASEMENT

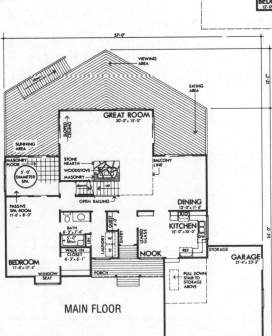

MAIN FLOOR

UPPER FLOOR

Plans H-952-1A &-1B

Bedrooms: 3-4	Baths: 2-3

Space:	
Upper floor:	470 sq. ft.
Main floor:	1,207 sq. ft.
Passive spa room:	102 sq. ft.
Total living area:	**1,779 sq. ft.**
Basement:	1,105 sq. ft.
Garage:	496 sq. ft.

Exterior Wall Framing:	2x6

Foundation options:
Daylight Basement (Plan H-952-1B).
Crawlspace (Plan H-952-1A).
(Foundation & framing conversion diagram available — see order form.)

Blueprint Price Code:

H-952-1A:	B
H-952-1B:	D

TO ORDER THIS BLUEPRINT,
CALL TOLL-FREE 1-800-547-5570
(prices and details on pp. 12-15.) **137**

Plans H-952-1A & -1B

Compact Contemporary With Clerestory

This 1,457 square foot contemporary design features a large family room with a stone fireplace, double doors to the rear patio, dining area, open stairwell to the full basement and a vaulted ceiling with exposed wood beams and triple clerestory windows. The master suite includes two walk-in closets and a private bath. Both front bedrooms have a walk-in closet and share a second full bath. The eat-in kitchen includes access from the dining area as well as the front opening garage. Additional features include a coat closet off the foyer, vertical wood siding with stone, and a recessed entry with a front porch.

Total living area: 1,457 sq. ft.
(Not counting basement or garage)

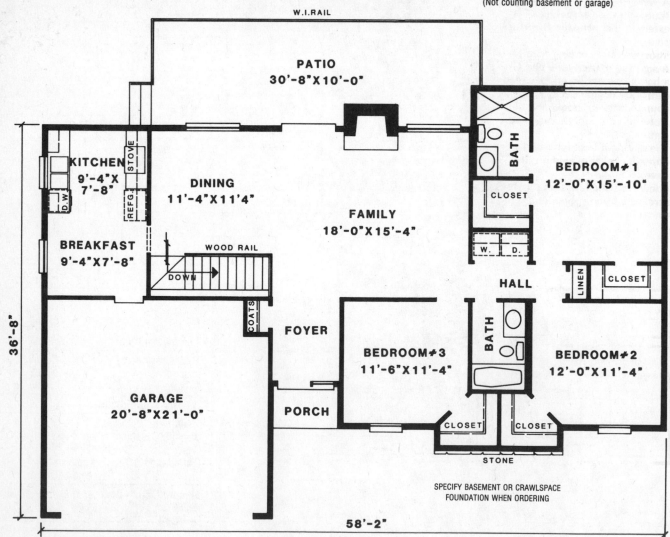

SPECIFY BASEMENT OR CRAWLSPACE FOUNDATION WHEN ORDERING

TO ORDER THIS BLUEPRINT, CALL TOLL-FREE 1-800-547-5570

Blueprint Price Code A
Plan C-8356

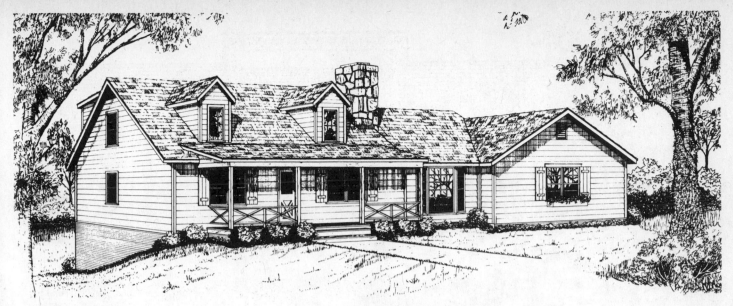

Rustic Country Design

- A welcoming front porch, window shutters and a bay window on the exterior of this rustic design are complemented by a comfortable, informal interior.
- A spacious country kitchen includes a bay-windowed breakfast area, center work island and abundant counter and cabinet space.
- Note the large utility room in the garage entry area.
- The large Great Room includes an impressive fireplace and another informal eating area with double doors opening to a deck, patio or screened porch. Also note the half-bath.

- The main floor master suite features a walk-in closet and compartmentalized private bath.
- Upstairs, you will find two more bedrooms, another full bath and a large storage area.

UPPER FLOOR

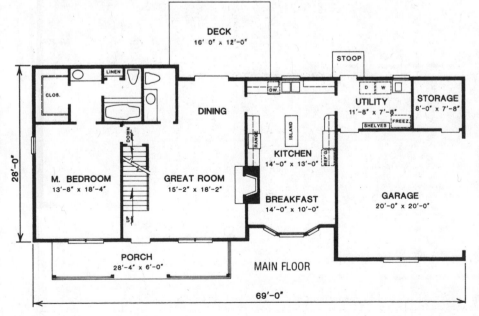

MAIN FLOOR

Plan C-8476

Bedrooms: 3	Baths: 2½

Space:

Upper floor:	720 sq. ft.
Main floor:	1,277 sq. ft.

Total living area:	**1,997 sq. ft.**
Basement:	approx. 1,200 sq. ft.
Garage:	400 sq. ft.
Storage:	(in garage) 61 sq. ft.

Exterior Wall Framing:	2x4

Foundation options:
Daylight basement.
Standard basement.
Crawlspace.
Slab.
(Foundation & framing conversion diagram available — see order form.)

Blueprint Price Code:	B

Plan C-8476

Great Room Featured

- In this rustic design, the centrally located Great Room features a cathedral ceiling with exposed wood beams. Living and dining areas are separated by a massive fireplace.
- The isolated master suite features a walk-in closet and compartmentalized bath.
- The gallery type kitchen is between the breakfast room and formal dining area. A large utility room and storage room complete the garage area.
- On the opposite side of the Great Room are two additional bedrooms and a second full bath.

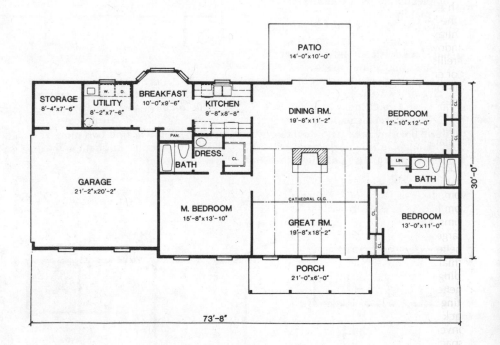

Plan C-8460

Bedrooms: 3	Baths: 2

Space:

Total living area:	1,670 sq. ft.
Basement:	approx. 1,600 sq. ft.
Garage:	427 sq. ft.
Storage:	63 sq. ft.
Exterior Wall Framing:	2x4

Foundation options:
Standard basement.
Crawlspace.
Slab.
(Foundation & framing conversion diagram available — see order form)

Blueprint Price Code: B

Plan C-8460

Distinctive One-Story Design

- Angles and curves define the exterior of this distinctive home. A hipped roof with deep overhangs caps the main part of the house. A gabled roof provides contrast and emphasizes the picture window with charming planter box.
- A trellised walkway leads to the double-door entry. The foyer is brightened by a half-round roof window that accentuates the semi-circular ceiling.
- The living room, straight ahead, is highlighted by a cathedral ceiling and a fireplace framed by angled glass walls. A French door opens to a large backyard terrace.
- The dining room is open to the living room, but a lower ceiling in the dining room helps visually separate the two rooms.
- A large combination family room, dinette and kitchen is adjacent to the formal living areas. The family room has sliding glass doors to the terrace, the dinette is distinguished by a bayed eating alcove, and the kitchen has a snack bar.
- Convenient to the family living areas are a spacious laundry room, a mud room and a utility area with a pantry closet plus two additional closets.
- The sleeping wing is well isolated from the activity areas. The spacious master bedroom includes twin closets plus a large walk-in closet. The private bath features an oversized whirlpool tub and double-bowl vanity.
- The two smaller bedrooms also have double closets and share a second bath with dual sinks.

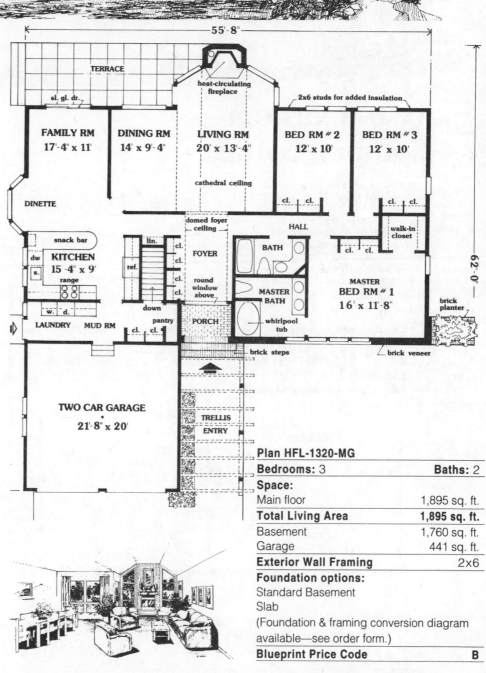

Plan HFL-1320-MG

Plan HFL-1320-MG	
Bedrooms: 3	Baths: 2
Space:	
Main floor	1,895 sq. ft.
Total Living Area	**1,895 sq. ft.**
Basement	1,760 sq. ft.
Garage	441 sq. ft.
Exterior Wall Framing	2x6

Foundation options:
Standard Basement
Slab
(Foundation & framing conversion diagram available—see order form.)

| **Blueprint Price Code** | **B** |

Two-Bedroom Country Cottage

A covered veranda and screened rear porch provide extra living spaces in this modest-sized ranch design. The large all-purpose family room has a built-in fireplace and bright dining corner.

Two roomy bedrooms and two full baths make up the sleeping wing.

An efficient galley kitchen is adjacent to utility room (with pantry) and side-entry garage.

Total living area: 1,420 sq. ft.
(Not counting basement or garage)

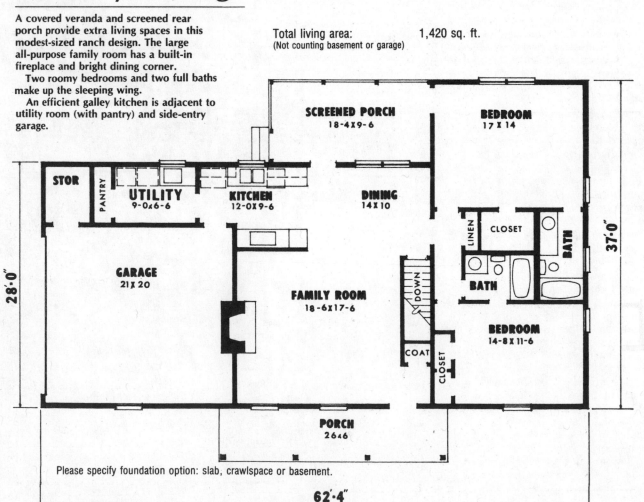

STOR

PANTRY

UTILITY
9-0x6-6

KITCHEN
12-0x9-6

SCREENED PORCH
18-4X9-6

DINING
14X10

BEDROOM
17 X 14

LINEN

CLOSET

BATH

GARAGE
21 X 20

FAMILY ROOM
18-6X17-6

DOWN

BATH

COAT

CLOSET

BEDROOM
14-8X11-6

28'-0"

37'-0"

PORCH
26x6

62'-4"

Please specify foundation option: slab, crawlspace or basement.

TO ORDER THIS BLUEPRINT, CALL TOLL-FREE 1-800-547-5570

Blueprint Price Code A

Plan C-7520

(prices and details on pp. 12-15.)

Cozy Three-Bedroom with Solar Features

In this design, a large stone fireplace doubles as a heat-storing thermal mass when sunlight passes through tall living room windows.

The surrounding floor can be surfaced with tile to enhance heat storage.

Living-family room boasts cathedral ceilings; built-in cabinet serves as room divider to dining room. The master bedroom has sliding glass doors to front wood deck.

PLAN C-1454
WITHOUT BASEMENT
(Specify Crawlspace or Slab Foundation)

Total living area: 1,454 sq. ft.
(Excluding carport)

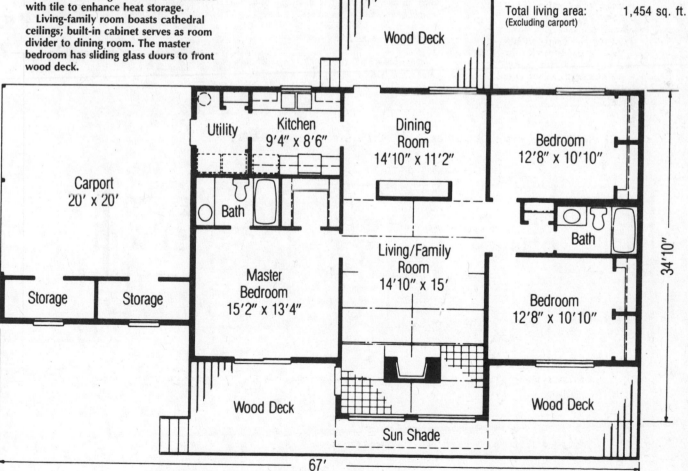

Blueprint Price Code A
Plan C-1454

TO ORDER THIS BLUEPRINT,
CALL TOLL-FREE 1-800-547-5570
(prices and details on pp. 12-15.) **143**

Modern Country Cottage for Small Lot

This drive-under garage design is great for smaller lots. But even though the home is relatively compact, it's still loaded with modern features. The deluxe master bedroom has a large bath with garden tub and shower. The country kitchen/dining room combination has access to a deck out back. The large living room with fireplace is accessible from the two story foyer.

The upper floor has two large bedrooms and a full bath, and the large basement has room for two cars and expandable living areas.

This plan is available with basement foundation only.

Main floor:	1,100 sq. ft.
Second floor:	664 sq. ft.
Total living area:	1,764 sq. ft.
(Not counting basement or garage)	
Basement:	1,100 sq. ft.

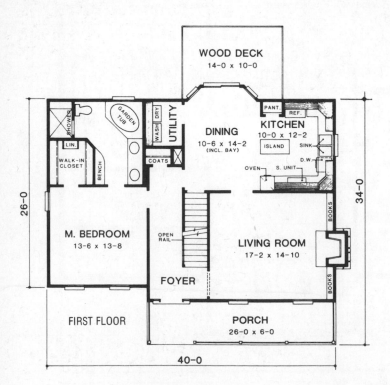

PLAN C-8870
WITH BASEMENT

TO ORDER THIS BLUEPRINT, CALL TOLL-FREE 1-800-547-5570

Blueprint Price Code B
Plan C-8870

Quality Design for a Narrow, Sloping Lot

Multi-pitched rooflines, custom window treatments and beveled board siding add a distinctive facade to this two-level home of only 1,516 sq. ft. Its slim 34' width allows it to fit nicely on a narrow lot while offering ample indoor and outdoor living areas.

The enclosed entry courtyard is a pleasant area for al fresco breakfasts or spill-over entertaining. The wide, high-ceilinged entry hall opens directly into the sweeping Great Room and dining area. This room is warmed by a large fireplace and has a door to a large wood deck. Also off the entry hall is the morning room with a vaulted ceiling and a matching arched window overlooking the courtyard. A half-bath and utility room is on the other side of the entry.

An open-railed stairway leads from the entry to the bedrooms on the second level. The master suite has a high dormer with peaked windows, a walk-in closet and a private bathroom. The larger of the other bedrooms could be used as a den, and it also overlooks the morning room and entry hall. If additional room is required, this plan is available with a daylight basement.

**NOTE: The above photographed home may have been modified by the homeowner. Please refer to floor plan and/or drawn elevation shown for actual blueprint details.

PATIO

KITCHEN 9/0 x 10/0

DINING AREA

GREAT RM. 24/0 x 17/6

VAULTED MORNING RM. 8/0x8/0

ENTRY

BREAKFAST PATIO

W. D. W H

UTILITY RM.

GARAGE 19/4 x 21/8

34'-0"

48'-0"

PLAN P-6563-4A WITHOUT BASEMENT

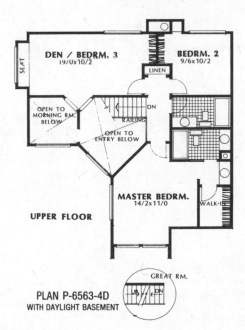

DEN / BEDRM. 3 19/0x10/2

BEDRM. 2 9/6x10/2

LINEN

SEAT

OPEN TO MORNING RM. BELOW

RAILING

DN

OPEN TO ENTRY BELOW

MASTER BEDRM. 14/2x11/0

WALK-IN

UPPER FLOOR

GREAT RM.

PLAN P-6563-4D WITH DAYLIGHT BASEMENT

Main floor:	750 sq. ft.
Upper floor:	766 sq. ft.
Total living area:	1,516 sq. ft.
Basement level:	809 sq. ft.

Blueprint Price Code B

Plans P-6563-4A & P-6563-4D

TO ORDER THIS BLUEPRINT, CALL TOLL-FREE 1-800-547-5570 (prices and details on pp. 12-15.)

Split-Level Vacation Home

By opting for a smaller than average lot, a family choosing a split-level design such as this will benefit from the space-savings and their attending cost savings. Notice, for example, the overall width of 68' includes the projection of the double-sized garage on one side and the location of a sun deck that flanks the sliding doors of the den. Since most leisure home building sites have some slope, the three-level design of this dwelling will fit many situations.

This plan is an example of a design for seclusion, with all the primary living areas oriented to the rear of the home. Notice how the living room, dining area and U-shaped kitchen face the rear wall and have access to the spacious raised deck. The recreation room at the basement level and a third bedroom also face the rear garden.

The main floor area of 1,200 sq. ft. is actually on two elevations. The entry hall is on the same level as the adjacent den and bedroom with bath. A dramatic effect is achieved by the placement of the living room four steps below. The soaring height

of the vaulted ceiling, with exposed beams extending from the central ridge to the exterior wall, adds to the feeling of openness to the outdoors, framed by the window wall and sliding glass doors.

The kitchen itself is convenient to both the dining area and informal portions of the home, and has a work-saving U-shaped design.

The spacious master bedroom suite offers the unencumbered view of an eagle's nest, and also boasts a walk-in

closet and private bath with shower stall. Another added luxury is the 4' cantilevered sun deck, accessible through sliding glass doors. This raised portion of the home that includes the master bedroom contains 320 additional sq. ft.

Other features which should be pointed out include the two massive fireplaces. One is located in the recreation room and the other is the focal point of the end wall of the living room. A third full bath is also placed at the basement level.

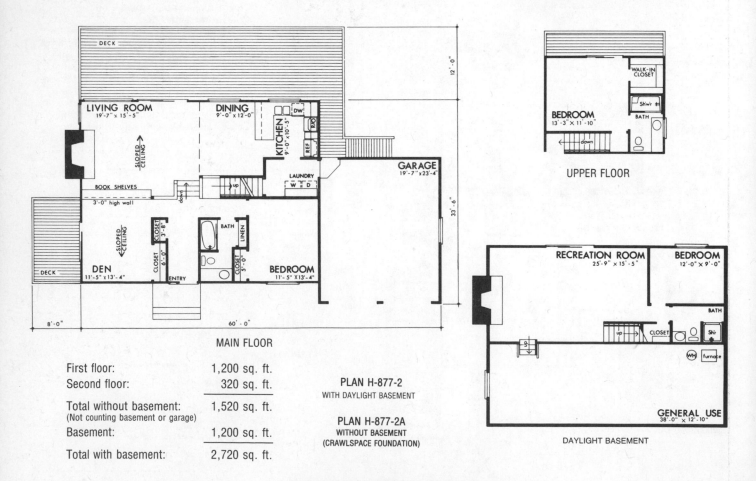

MAIN FLOOR

UPPER FLOOR

DAYLIGHT BASEMENT

First floor:	1,200 sq. ft.
Second floor:	320 sq. ft.
Total without basement: (Not counting basement or garage)	1,520 sq. ft.
Basement:	1,200 sq. ft.
Total with basement:	2,720 sq. ft.

PLAN H-877-2
WITH DAYLIGHT BASEMENT

PLAN H-877-2A
WITHOUT BASEMENT
(CRAWLSPACE FOUNDATION)

Blueprint Price Code D With Basement
Blueprint Price Code B Without Basement

Plans H-877-2 & -2A

Ideal Home for a Narrow Lot

- This design features a room arrangement that is wide-open, yet confined to an economical width of only 28'.
- The entryway greets you with a balconied staircase and lovely bay window.
- The Great Room, dining area, and kitchen are arranged so no one is excluded from conversation or on-going activities.
- Other highlights include a woodstove/stone hearth in the Great Room, a large outdoor deck off the dining area, and a spacious U-shaped kitchen with breakfast bar.
- Second level features a master suite with walk-through closet and private bath.

UPPER FLOOR

PLAN H-1427-3B
WITH DAYLIGHT BASEMENT

CLERESTORY WINDOWS
OVER STAIRWAY

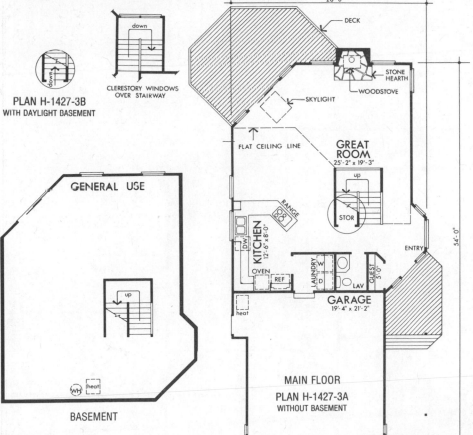

GENERAL USE

BASEMENT

MAIN FLOOR
PLAN H-1427-3A
WITHOUT BASEMENT

Plans H-1427-3A & -3B

Bedrooms: 3	Baths: 2½
Space:	
Upper floor:	880 sq. ft.
Main floor:	810 sq. ft.
Total without basement:	1,690 sq. ft.
Basement:	810 sq. ft.
Total with basement:	2,500 sq. ft.
Garage:	443 sq. ft.
Exterior Wall Framing:	2x4

Foundation options:
Daylight basement.
Crawlspace.
Foundation & framing conversion diagram available — see order form.)

Blueprint Price Code:
Without basement: B
With basement: D

Plans H-1427-3A & -3B

Rustic Home Offers Comfort, Economy

- Rustic and compact, this home offers economy of construction and good looks.
- The homey front porch, multi-paned windows, shutters and horizontal siding combine to create a rustic exterior.
- An L-shaped kitchen is open to the dining room and also to the living room to create a Great Room feel to the floor plan.
- The living room includes a raised-hearth fireplace.
- The main-floor master suite features a large walk-in closet and a double vanity in the master bath.
- An open two-story-high foyer leads to the second floor, which includes two bedrooms with walk-in closets and a full bath with two linen closets.

Plan C-8339

Bedrooms: 3	Baths: 2

Space:

Upper floor:	660 sq.ft.
Main floor:	1,100 sq.ft.

Total living area:	1,760 sq.ft.
Basement:	Approx. 1,100 sq.ft.
Garage:	Included in basement.

Exterior Wall Framing:	2x4

Foundation options:
Standard basement only.
(Foundation & framing conversion diagram available — see order form.)

Blueprint Price Code:	B

BEDROOM 13'-6" X 13'-4"

BATH

BEDROOM 12'-4" X 15'-4"

STORAGE

SLOPED CEILING

WALK-IN CLOSET

LINEN

HALL

RAIL

OPEN

DOWN

LINEN

WALK-IN CLOSET

STORAGE

STORAGE

UPPER FLOOR

WOOD DECK 14'-0" X 10'-0"

MASTER BEDROOM 13'-6" X 13'-6"

WALK-IN CLOSET

BATH

H W H

W/SH | DRY

COATS

UTILITY

HALL

DOWN TO GARAGE

RAIL

DINING ROOM 10'-0" X 12'-0"

KITCHEN 10'-6" X 12'-0"

PANTRY

LIVING ROOM 17'-0" X 14'-8"

FOYER

26' - 0"

28' - 0"

PORCH 26'-2" X 6'-0"

MAIN FLOOR

40' - 0"

Plan C-8339

DECK

DINING
17'-0" x 12'-0"

KITCHEN

SLOPED CEILING

LIVING ROOM
19'-8" x 15'-4"

STOR

LAUNDRY
W D

down

GUEST

LINEN

BATH
10'-3" x 8'-9"

CLOSET
8'-4"

BEDROOM
11'-6" x 13'-7"

ENTRY

BEDROOM
11'-6" x 13'-7"

STORAGE

CLOSET
6'-6"

GARAGE
12'-10" x 23'-8"

MAIN FLOOR
1217 SQUARE FEET

PLAN H-925-2
WITH DAYLIGHT BASEMENT

DECK

SLOPED C. CEILING

WALK-IN CLOSET
7'-5" x 5'-0"

Sh'w'r

BEDROOM
14'-0" x 14'-0"

BATH

down

SECOND FLOOR
360 SQUARE FEET

STOR
heat

PLAN H-925-2A
WITHOUT BASEMENT
(CRAWLSPACE FOUNDATION)

First floor:	1,217 sq. ft.
Second floor:	360 sq. ft.
Total living area: (Not counting basement or garage)	1,577 sq. ft.

Economical and Convenient

In an effort to merge the financial possibilities and the space requirements of the greatest number of families, the designers of this home restricted themselves to just over 1,200 sq. ft. of ground cover (exclusive of garage), and still managed to develop a superior three-bedroom design.

From a covered walkway, one approaches a centralized entry hall which effectively distributes traffic throughout the home without causing interruptions. Two main floor bedrooms and bath as well as the stairway to the second floor master suite are immediately accessible to the entry. Directly forward and four steps down finds one in the main living area, consisting of a large living room with vaulted ceiling and a dining-kitchen combination with conventional ceiling height. All these rooms have direct access to an outdoor living deck of over 400 sq. ft. Thus, though modest and unassuming from the street side, this home evolves into eye-popping expansion and luxury toward the rear.

To ease homemaking chores, whether this is to be a permanent or vacation home, the working equipment, including laundry space, is all on the main floor. Yet the homemaker remains part of the family scene because there is only a breakfast counter separating the work space from the living area.

Tucked away upstairs, in complete privacy, one finds a master bedroom suite equipped with separate bath, walk-in wardrobe and a romantic private deck.

The plan is available with or without a basement and is best suited to a lot that slopes gently down from the road.

Economical Design

FRONT VIEW

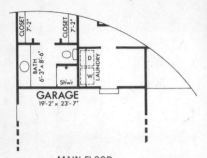

MAIN FLOOR
PLAN H-868-1A
WITHOUT BASEMENT

- Uninterrupted glass and a full, rear deck afford a sweeping view of the outdoors.
- Rear orientation provides a seclusion from street and neighbors.

- Open, flexible family living areas allow for efficient traffic flow.
- Optional daylight basement plan offers recreation room, additional bedroom and third bath.

Plans H-868-1 & -1A	
Bedrooms: 3-4	**Baths:** 2-3
Space:	
Main floor:	1,525 sq. ft.
Total living area:	1,525 sq. ft.
Basement:	1,420 sq. ft.
Garage:	426 sq. ft.
Exterior Wall Framing:	2x4

Foundation options:
Daylight basement (Plan H-868-1).
Crawlspace (Plan H-868-1A).
(Foundation & framing conversion diagram available — see order form.)

Blueprint Price Code:
Without basement	B
With basement	D

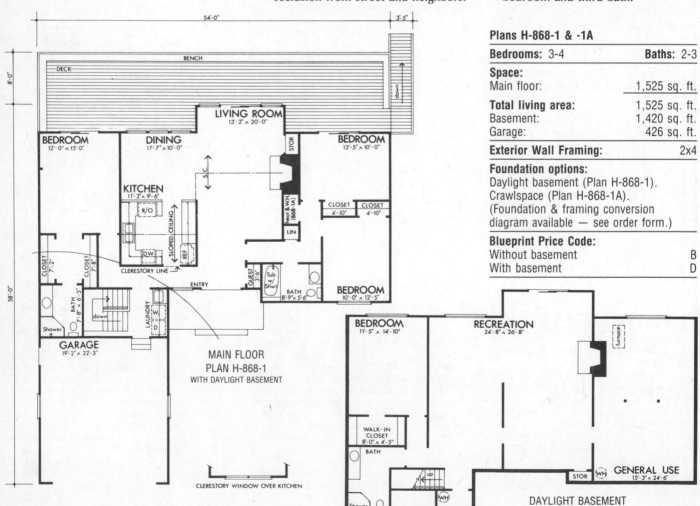

MAIN FLOOR
PLAN H-868-1
WITH DAYLIGHT BASEMENT

CLERESTORY WINDOW OVER KITCHEN

DAYLIGHT BASEMENT

Plans H-868-1 & -1A

For Full-Time Living or Part-Time Fun

This is one of several plans in this book that can serve as either a recreation home or a permanent year-round dwelling. A large, formal entry hall introduces you to several options. You can turn right into the kitchen, left into your bedroom or the main floor bath, up the stairway to a second floor suite or, crossing the balcony type family room, go down a few steps to the living room. Huge deck areas surround the house. A private outdoor dining deck is immediately off the kitchen-family room complex. On this level you will also find a handy laundry room and access to the garage.

Besides the two good-sized main floor bedrooms, there is a suite upstairs consisting of a 13' by almost 17' master bedroom, closet space and a totally private bath. This suite is designed to take full advantage of whatever view you have.

To preserve the possibility of usage as a permanent home, we kept the street side of this plan as conventional as possible, but we designed the rear as a vacation home. The two level house-spanning deck, the cantilevered overhang of the upstairs bedroom and the numerous sliding glass doors all combine to make this a desirable vacation home.

One final note. Space does not permit us to include a picture to show the dramatic openness of the living room-family room-kitchen complex. In reality, this group of rooms forms one large area almost 20' x 40' in size, broken only by the floor level difference between living room and family room.

First floor: 1,342 sq. ft.
Second floor: 429 sq. ft.

Total living area: 1,771 sq. ft.
(Not counting garage)

FRONT VIEW

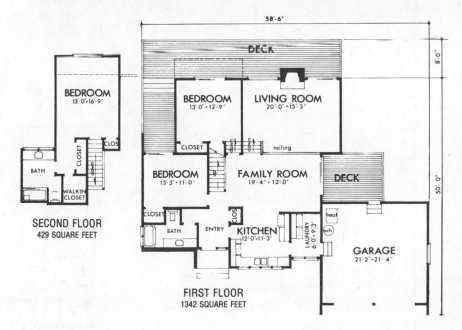

SECOND FLOOR
429 SQUARE FEET

FIRST FLOOR
1342 SQUARE FEET

Blueprint Price Code B
Plan H-911-1A

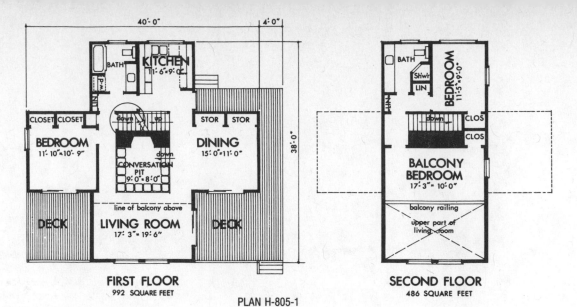

FIRST FLOOR
992 SQUARE FEET

40'-0" / 4'-0"

38'-0"

KITCHEN 11'-6"×9'-0"
BATH
P.w.
CLOSET CLOSET
BEDROOM 11'-10"×10'-9"
down UP
CONVERSATION PIT 9'-0"×8'-0"
down
STOR STOR
DINING 15'-0"×11'-0"
line of balcony above
DECK
LIVING ROOM 17'-3"×19'-6"
DECK

SECOND FLOOR
486 SQUARE FEET

BATH
Shwr
LIN
BEDROOM 11'-5"×9'-0"
down
CLOS
CLOS
BALCONY BEDROOM 17'-3"×10'-0"
balcony railing
upper part of living room

PLAN H-805-1
WITH BASEMENT

PLAN H-805-1A
WITHOUT BASEMENT
(CRAWLSPACE FOUNDATION)

STOR

First floor:	992 sq. ft.
Second floor:	486 sq. ft.
Total living area: (Not counting basement)	1,478 sq. ft.

Coziness and Charm in Unique Plan

This rustic design is keynoted by a cathedral window wall. Handsome from inside or outside, the windows assure that both levels are well lighted.

The focal point of the lower living level is a 9' x 8' sunken conversation area in front of the fireplace. Both living and dining rooms are warmed by this fireplace.

During the summer the home is cooled by breezes coming through the sliding glass doors that serve the decks. The fireplace divides the living area from the master bedroom and bath.

Upstairs a sleeping loft and additional bedroom are served by a second full bath. Other features include the washer-dryer in the bath and the abundant storage throughout.

TO ORDER THIS BLUEPRINT, CALL TOLL-FREE 1-800-547-5570

Blueprint Price Code A

Plans H-805-1 & -1A

Photo by James Erickson

Rustic Styling, Comfortable Interior

- Front-to-back split level with large decks lends itself to steep sloping site, particularly in a scenic area.
- Compact, space-efficient design makes for economical construction.
- Great Room design concept utilizes the entire 36' width of home for the kitchen/dining/living area.
- Two bedrooms and a bath are up three steps, on the entry level.
- Upper level bedroom includes a compact bath and a private deck.

NOTE:
The above photographed home may have been modified by the homeowner. Please refer to floor plan and/or drawn elevation shown for actual blueprint details.

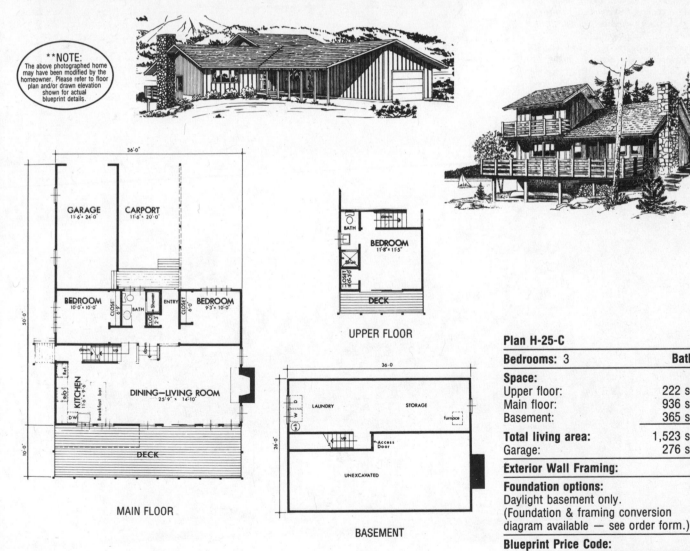

MAIN FLOOR

36'-0"

| GARAGE 11'-6" x 24'-0" | CARPORT 11'-6" x 20'-0" |

50'-0"

BEDROOM 10'-0" x 10'-0"

CLOSET 6'-0"

BATH

CLOS. 2'-3"

Shower

ENTRY

CLOSET 6'-0"

BEDROOM 9'-3" x 10'-0"

down / up

down

KITCHEN 11'-6" x 9'-6"

Ref.

DW

Breakfast bar

DINING—LIVING ROOM 25'-9" x 14'-10"

10'-0"

DECK

UPPER FLOOR

BATH

BEDROOM 11'-8" x 11'-5"

CLOSET 5'-3"

SINK

DECK

BASEMENT

36'-0"

LAUNDRY

D

W

STORAGE

furnace

26'-0"

Access Door

UNEXCAVATED

Plan H-25-C

Bedrooms: 3	Baths: 2
Space:	
Upper floor:	222 sq. ft.
Main floor:	936 sq. ft.
Basement:	365 sq. ft.
Total living area:	1,523 sq. ft.
Garage:	276 sq. ft.
Exterior Wall Framing:	2x4

Foundation options:
Daylight basement only.
(Foundation & framing conversion diagram available — see order form.)

| **Blueprint Price Code:** | B |

Plan H-25-C

Block Masonry Home Offers Economy and Easy Maintenance

The designers have combined the ageless qualities of building block materials with an attractive contemporary concept of architecture. Note the clerestory windows that highlight the vaulted ceiling of the living room. Wing walls protect the entry and give relief to the front exterior.

A step-saving floor plan produces smooth circulation of traffic and good room sizes. An abundance of closets is found throughout the dwelling.

The theme of open planning for the kitchen, dining area and living room gives the home a feeling of spacious comfort. Sliding glass doors provide access from these rooms to the rear patio.

The second-floor bedroom has its own private bathroom and walk-in closet. An outdoor deck spans the length of the room. Note the skylights that are placed over the staircase landing and bathroom ceiling.

Main floor exterior walls are constructed of 8x4x16 concrete blocks with 2x4 wall furring. Upper floor exterior walls are wood siding over 2x6 studs.

First floor:	1,226 sq. ft.
Second floor:	343 sq. ft.
Total living area: (Not counting garage)	1,569 sq. ft.

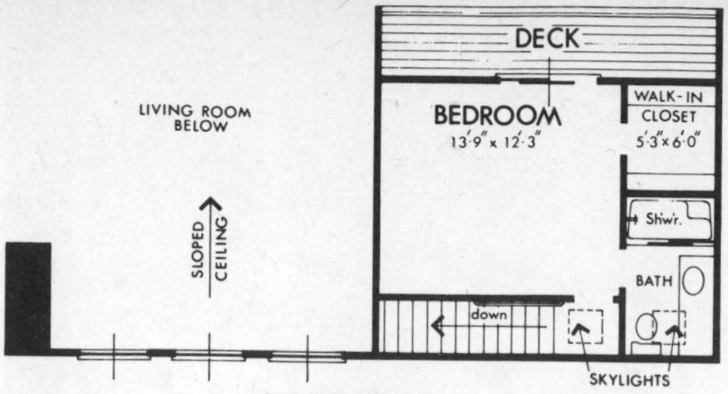

SECOND FLOOR
343 SQUARE FEET

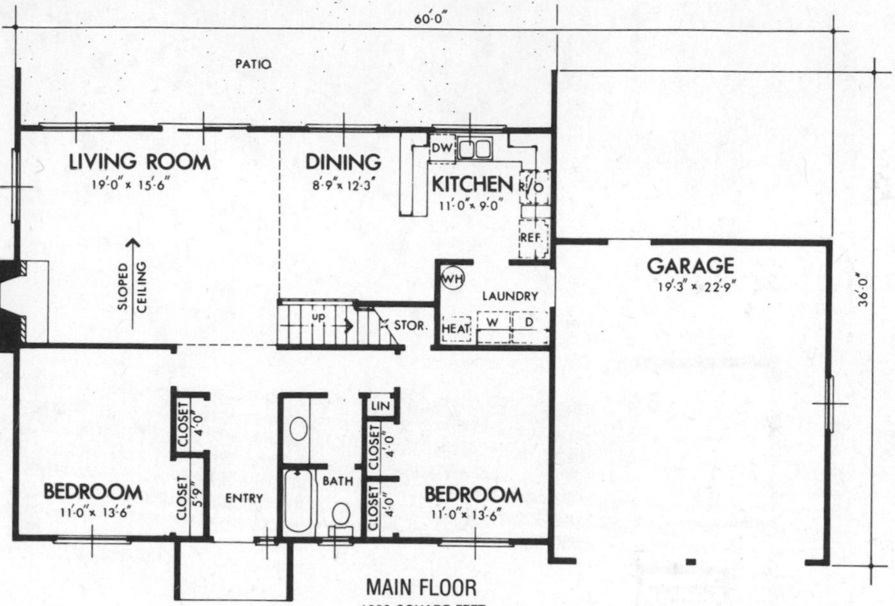

MAIN FLOOR
1226 SQUARE FEET

PLAN H-877-M4A
WITHOUT BASEMENT
(SLAB-ON-GRADE)

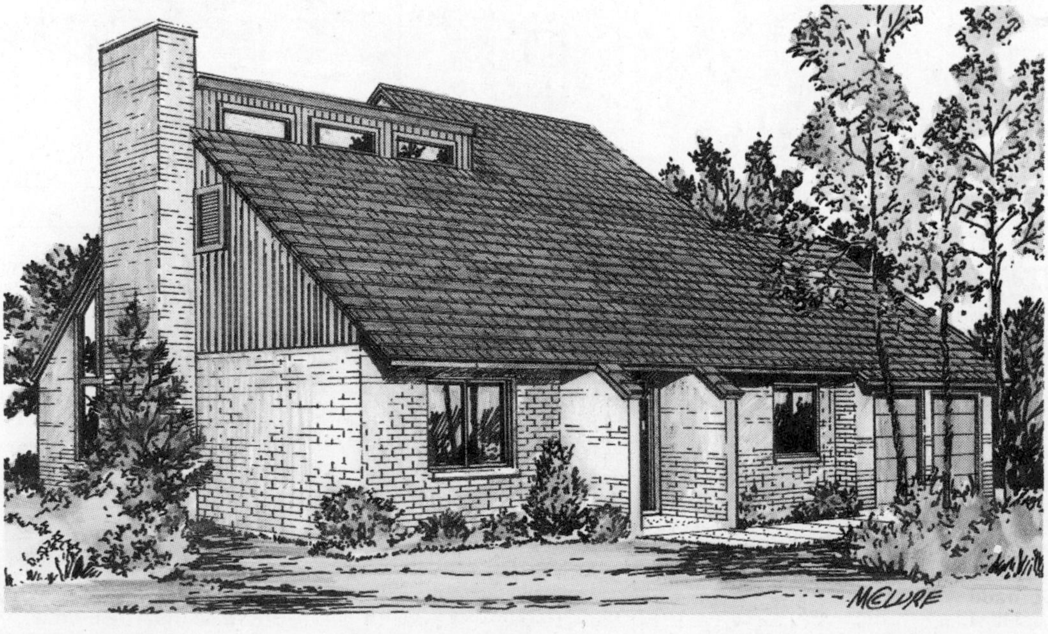

Blueprint Price Code B

Plan H-877-M4A

TO ORDER THIS BLUEPRINT, CALL TOLL-FREE 1-800-547-5570
(prices and details on pp. 12-15.)

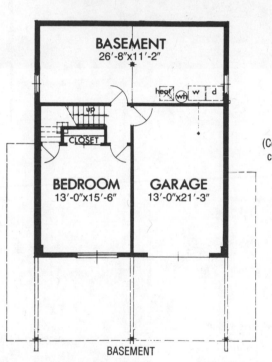

BASEMENT
26'-8"x11'-2"

heat wh w d

UP

CLOSET

BEDROOM
13'-0"x15'-6"

GARAGE
13'-0"x21'-3"

(Concrete block
construction)

BASEMENT

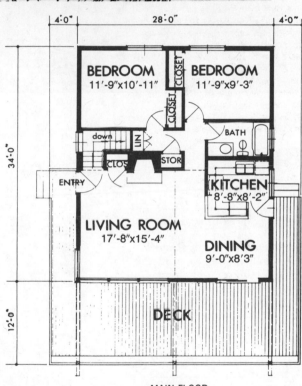

4'-0"   28'-0"   4'-0"

BEDROOM
11'-9"x10'-11"

BEDROOM
11'-9"x9'-3"

CLOSET

CLOSET

down

LIN

BATH

34'-0"

CLOS

STOR

KITCHEN
8'-8"x8'-2"

ENTRY

LIVING ROOM
17'-8"x15'-4"

DINING
9'-0"x8'3"

12'-0"

DECK

MAIN FLOOR

Economical Recreational Home

A huge wrap-around deck suggests recreational use for this compact two- or three-bedroom home. However, the completeness of detail affords the opportunity for use as a year around residence. As the illustration shows, it is best adapted to an uphill site.

A heavy "shake-style" concrete roof provides virtually carefree lifetime protection for both indoor and outdoor living areas. This is important in rural forested areas where the elements are especially destructive to conventional wood products. Solid block exterior walls laid in a distinctive 8x8 grid pattern are equally impervious to natural deterioration.

The floor plan is a model of efficiency and utility as evidenced by the small but completely adequate kitchen area. Dining and living combine to form a visual concept of much larger rooms. The central

fireplace is located in a convenient spot for refueling either from basement or outdoors. The downstairs room marked "bedroom" is admittedly a room with many other potential uses such as shop, hobby or recreational.

Main floor:	952 sq. ft.
Basement:	676 sq. ft.
Total living area: (Not counting garage)	1,628 sq. ft.
Garage:	276 sq. ft.

Blueprint Price Code B

Plan H-806-M3

Rustic Comfort for Rec Home

- This delightful plan offers striking design inside and out.
- A huge "Grand Room" is flanked by two equally impressive Master Suites, both with walk-in closets and private baths.
- The central kitchen offers easy access from any part of the home.
- Upstairs, a guest suite provides two bedrooms.

Plan EOF-13

Bedrooms: 4	Baths: 3

Space:	
Upper floor:	443 sq. ft.
Main floor:	1,411 sq. ft.

Total living area:	1,854 sq. ft.
Garage:	264 sq. ft.
Storage area:	50 sq. ft.

Exterior Wall Framing:	2x6

Foundation options:
Crawlspace.
(Foundation & framing conversion diagram available — see order form.)

Blueprint Price Code:	B

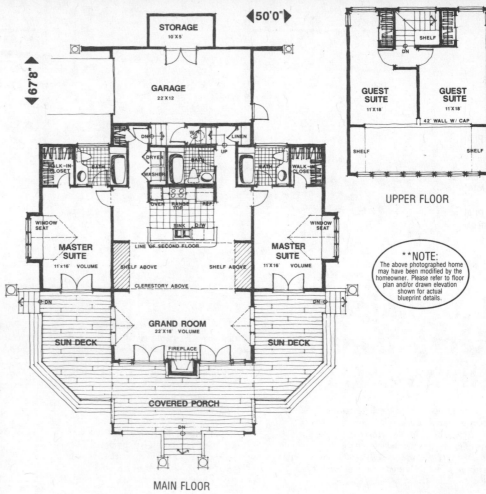

**NOTE:
The above photographed home may have been modified by the homeowner. Please refer to floor plan and/or drawn elevation shown for actual blueprint details.

UPPER FLOOR

MAIN FLOOR

TO ORDER THIS BLUEPRINT, CALL TOLL-FREE 1-800-547-5570

Plan EOF-13

REAR VIEW

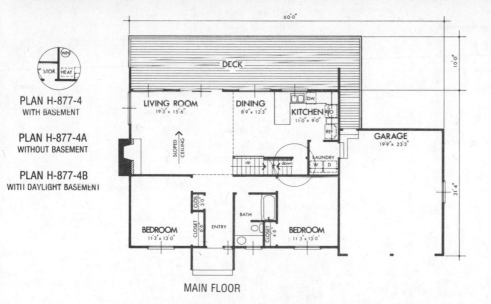

Hillside Design
Fits Contours

- Split-level design perfect for hillside lot.
- Excellent separation of living and sleeping areas.
- Corner kitchen features eating counter and handy laundry facilities.
- Rear wrap-around deck is seen from spacious living room and adjoining dining room; living room features sloped ceiling and corner fireplace.
- Upstairs master suite offers walk-in closet, private bath, and sun deck accessible through sliding glass doors.

PLAN H-877-4
WITH BASEMENT

PLAN H-877-4A
WITHOUT BASEMENT

PLAN H-877-4B
WITH DAYLIGHT BASEMENT

MAIN FLOOR

UPPER FLOOR

Plans H-877-4, -4A & -4B

Bedrooms: 3	Baths: 2

Space:

Upper floor:	333 sq. ft.
Main floor:	1,200 sq. ft.
Total living area:	**1,533 sq. ft.**
Basement:	741 sq. ft.
Garage:	459 sq. ft.

Exterior Wall Framing: 2x6

Foundation options:
Daylight basement (Plan H-877-4B).
Standard basement (Plan H-877-4).
Crawlspace (Plan H-877-4A).
(Foundation & framing conversion diagram available — see order form.)

Blueprint Price Code: B

TO ORDER THIS BLUEPRINT,
CALL TOLL-FREE 1-800-547-5570
(prices and details on pp. 12-15.)

Plans H-877-4, -4A & -4B

BEDROOM 11'-0" × 11'-0"

BATH

Shower

BEDR'M 8'-6" × 13'-5"

DOWN

CLOS CLOS

LIN

BALCONY

UPPER PART OF LIVING ROOM

UPPER FLOOR

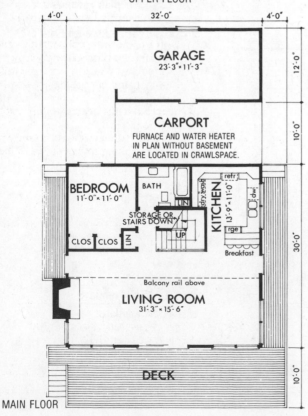

4'-0"   32'-0"   4'-0"

GARAGE 23'-3" × 11'-3"

12'-0"

CARPORT

FURNACE AND WATER HEATER IN PLAN WITHOUT BASEMENT ARE LOCATED IN CRAWLSPACE.

10'-0"

BEDROOM 11'-0" × 11'-0"

BATH

dry/wash

KITCHEN 13'-9" × 11'-0"

refr

dw

STORAGE OR STAIRS DOWN

LIN

UP

rge

Breakfast

CLOS CLOS

30'-0"

Balcony rail above

LIVING ROOM 31'-3" × 15'-6"

DECK

10'-0"

MAIN FLOOR

Surprising Spaces via Beamed Ceilings

- Open and spacious floor plan allows for uninhibited movement.
- Bordering decks beckon you to the outdoors.
- Expansive living room features beamed ceiling open to second level and front window wall at an attractive angle.
- Large, versatile kitchen and breakfast bar make dining a pleasure and laundry an easy chore.
- Inviting balcony adjoins second level bedrooms.

Plans H-876-1 & -1A

Bedrooms: 3	Baths: 2
Space:	
Upper floor:	592 sq. ft.
Main floor:	960 sq. ft.
Total living area:	1,552 sq. ft.
Basement:	approx. 960 sq. ft.
Garage:	262 sq. ft.
Exterior Wall Framing:	2x4

Foundation options:
Standard basement (Plan H-876-1).
Crawlspace (Plan H-876-1A).
(Foundation & framing conversion diagram available — see order form.)

Blueprint Price Code:	B

Plans H-876-1 & -1A

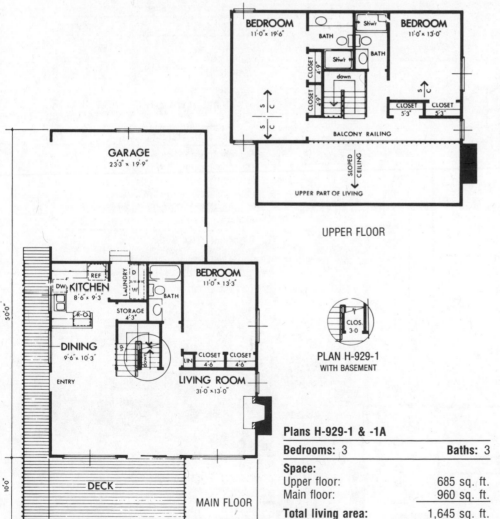

GARAGE
23'-3" x 19'-9"

KITCHEN
8'-6" x 9'-3"

REF

DW

LAUNDRY

D

W

BATH

BEDROOM
11'-0" x 13'-3"

STORAGE
4'-3"

R-O

DINING
9'-6" x 10'-3"

UP

down

ENTRY

LIN

CLOSET
4'-6"

CLOSET
4'-6"

LIVING ROOM
31'-0" x 13'-0"

DECK

50'-0"

10'-0"

4'-0"

32'-0"

MAIN FLOOR

BEDROOM
11'-0" x 19'-6"

BATH

Sh'w'r

BATH

BEDROOM
11'-0" x 13'-0"

CLOSET
4'-9"

CLOSET
4'-9"

Sh'w'r

down

CLOSET
5'-3"

CLOSET
5'-3"

S
C

S
C

S
C

BALCONY RAILING

SLOPED CEILING

UPPER PART OF LIVING

UPPER FLOOR

CLOS.
3'-0"

PLAN H-929-1
WITH BASEMENT

Contemporary Retreat

- Main floor plan revolves around an open, centrally located stairway.
- Spaciousness prevails throughout entire home with open kitchen and combination dining/living room.
- Living room features a great-sized fireplace and access to two-sided deck.
- Separate baths accommodate each bedroom.
- Upstairs hallway reveals an open balcony railing to oversee activities below.

Plans H-929-1 & -1A

Bedrooms: 3	Baths: 3

Space:

Upper floor:	685 sq. ft.
Main floor:	960 sq. ft.

Total living area:	1,645 sq. ft.
Basement:	approx. 960 sq. ft.
Garage:	459 sq. ft.

Exterior Wall Framing:	2x6

Foundation options:
Daylight basement (Plan H-929-1).
Crawlspace (Plan H-929-1A).
(Foundation & framing conversion diagram available — see order form.)

Blueprint Price Code:	B

Plans H-929-1 & -1A

Surrounded by Decks

- Wrap-around deck offers a panoramic view of the surroundings as well as space for outdoor living and relaxation.
- Angular arrangement of garage, breezeway, and home provides front-yard privacy and a visual barrier to front bedrooms from street traffic.
- Exciting L-shaped dining room, attached sunken living room, and deck create a perfect atmosphere for entertaining.
- Basement is available with either a concrete floor (Plan H-2083), a framed floor for steep sloping sites (Plan H-2083-B), or on a crawlspace (Plan H-2083-A).

DECK

BEDROOM 12'-0" x 15'-10"

BATH

NOOK 7'-0" x 12'-6"

KITCHEN 9'-0" x 9'-2"

DW

WALK-IN CLOSET

Shower

DINING 10'-0" x 12'-6"

Ref

R-O

wh furnace

STOR.

6'-0" high wall

HALL

down 2 risers

BEDROOM 11'-0" x 11'-0"

CLOSET

LINEN

BATH

LAUNDRY

D W

BEDROOM 10'-0" x 11'-0"

CLOSET 4'-0"

ENTRY

CLOSET 6'-0"

SUNKEN LIVING ROOM 14'-3" x 27'-3"

ENTRY ROOF

down

GARAGE 23'-3" x 23'-3"

MAIN FLOOR

PLAN H-2083-A
WITH CRAWLSPACE

GENERAL USE

RECREATION ROOM 14'-3" x 26'-6"

furnace

BATH

wh

BASEMENT

Plans H-2083, -A & -B

Bedrooms: 3	Baths: 2-3
Space:	
Main floor:	1,660 sq. ft.
Basement:	1,660 sq. ft.
Total living area with basement:	3,320 sq. ft.
Garage:	541 sq. ft.
Exterior Wall Framing:	2x4

Foundation options:
Daylight basement (Plans H-2083 & H-2083-B).
Crawlspace (Plan H-2083-A).
(Foundation & framing conversion diagram available — see order form.)

Blueprint Price Code:

Without basement:	B
With basement:	E

(Seeing facing page for alternate floor plan).

PLAN H-2083-B
WITH BASEMENT
WOOD-FRAMED
LOWER LEVEL

PLAN H-2083
WITH CONCRETE BASEMENT

Plans H-2083, -A & -B

FRONT VIEW

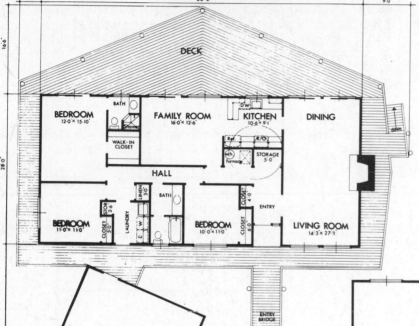

DECK

BEDROOM
12'-0" x 15'-10"

BATH

Shower

WALK-IN CLOSET

FAMILY ROOM
16'-0" x 12'-6"

KITCHEN
10'-6" x 9'-1"

D.W.

Ref.

DINING

HALL

BEDROOM
11'-0" x 11'-0"

CLOSET 5'-0"

STOR 2'-6"

LAUNDRY

LINEN 3'-0"

BATH

furnace

STORAGE 5'-0"

W.H.

BEDROOM
10'-0" x 11'-0"

CLOSET 4'-0"

ENTRY

down

LIVING ROOM
14'-3" x 27'-3"

ENTRY BRIDGE

GARAGE
23'-3" x 23'-3"

MAIN FLOOR

Gracious Indoor/ Outdoor Living

- A clean design makes this plan adaptable to almost any climate or setting.
- Perfect for a scenic, hillside lot, the structure and wrap-around deck offers a spanning view.
- Kitchen is flanked by family and dining rooms, allowing easy entrance from both.
- Foundation options include a daylight basement on concrete slab (H-2083-1), a wood-framed lower level (H-2083-1B), and a crawlspace (H-2083-1A).

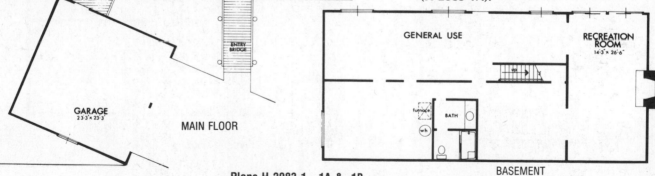

GENERAL USE

RECREATION ROOM
14'-3" x 26'-6"

UP

furnace

wh

BATH

BASEMENT

PLAN H-2083-1
WITH DAYLIGHT BASEMENT
(ON CONCRETE SLAB)

PLAN H-2083-1B
(WITH WOOD-FRAMED LOWER LEVEL)

(See facing page for both rear view and alternate floor plan.)

Plans H-2083-1, -1A & -1B

Bedrooms: 3	Baths: 2-3

Space:

Main floor:	1,660 sq. ft.
Basement:	1,660 sq. ft.

Total living area:

with basement:	3,320 sq. ft.
Garage:	541 sq. ft.

Exterior Wall Framing: 2x4

Foundation options:
Daylight basement (Plan H-2083-1 or -1B).
Crawlspace (Plan H-2083-1A).
(Foundation & framing conversion diagram available — see order form.)

Blueprint Price Code:

Without basement:	B
With basement:	E

Plans H-2083-1, -1A & -1B

TO ORDER THIS BLUEPRINT,
CALL TOLL-FREE 1-800-547-5570
(prices and details on pp. 12-15.) **161**

Rustic Rec Plan with Rear Orientation

- Windows, sliding glass doors, and an expansive rear deck provide a scenic view of your backyard and beyond, in this two-level rustic home.
- The main level offers vaulted living areas, a dining area, and an open kitchen. A fireplace to the front of the living room and clerestory windows to the rear add a dramatic effect. Two bedrooms share a full main-floor bath.
- A spiral staircase takes you to the vaulted loft and bath on the upper level.

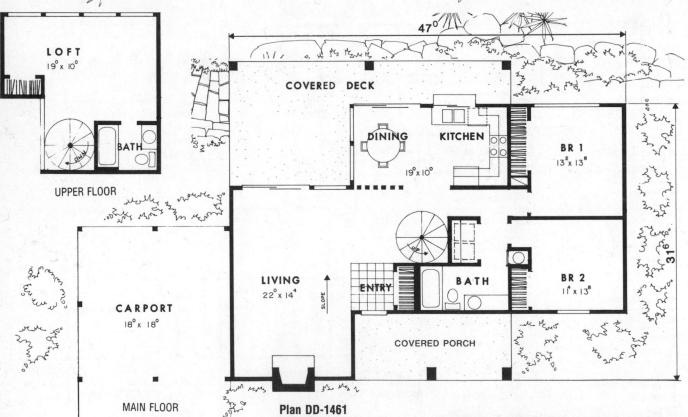

LOFT
19⁰ x 10⁰

BATH

UPPER FLOOR

COVERED DECK

DINING
19⁰ x 10⁰

KITCHEN

BR 1
13² x 13⁸

LIVING
22⁰ x 14⁴

SLOPE

ENTRY

BATH

BR 2
11⁴ x 13⁸

COVERED PORCH

47⁰

31⁶

CARPORT
18⁰ x 18⁰

MAIN FLOOR

Plan DD-1461

Bedrooms: 2-3	Baths: 2
Space:	
Upper floor:	294 sq. ft.
Main floor:	1,116 sq. ft.
Total living area:	**1,410 sq. ft.**
Basement:	1,116 sq. ft.
Exterior Wall Framing:	2x4

Foundation options:
Standard Basement
Crawlspace
Slab
(Foundation & framing conversion diagram available — see order form.)

Blueprint Price Code: A

TO ORDER THIS BLUEPRINT,
CALL TOLL-FREE 1-800-547-5570
(prices and details on pp. 12-15.)

Plan DD-1461

Woodland Retreat

- Ease of construction is offered in this woodland contemporary design with clean, simple lines.
- A spacious Great Room with vaulted ceiling and fireplace gives living and dining functions both front and rear views.
- The large kitchen offers a work island and plenty of room for a breakfast table.
- The main floor master bedroom has a walk-in closet and private deck access.
- Two additional bedrooms upstairs share a walk-through bath and loft/study area open to the Great Room below.

Plan CPS-1119-E

Bedrooms: 3	Baths: 2

Space:	
Upper floor:	635 sq. ft.
Main floor:	1,062 sq. ft.

Total living area:	1,697 sq. ft.
Basement:	1,062 sq. ft.
Garage:	588 sq. ft.

Exterior Wall Framing:	2x6

Foundation options:
Standard basement.
(Foundation & framing conversion diagram available — see order form.)

Blueprint Price Code:	B

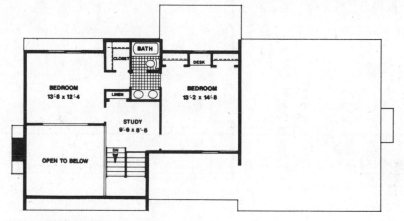

UPPER FLOOR

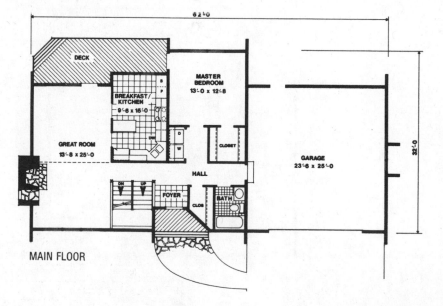

MAIN FLOOR

Plan CPS-1119-E

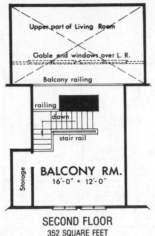

PLAN H-865-1
WITH BASEMENT

PLAN H-865-1A
WITHOUT BASEMENT
(CRAWLSPACE FOUNDATION)

Upper part of Living Room

Gable and windows over L. R.

Balcony railing

railing

down

stair rail

BALCONY RM.
16'-0" × 12'-0"

Storage

SECOND FLOOR
352 SQUARE FEET

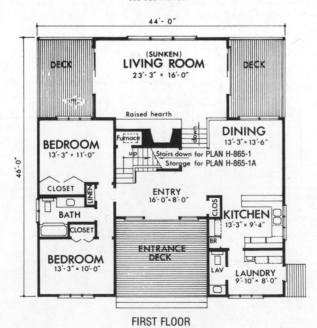

44'-0"

DECK

**(SUNKEN)
LIVING ROOM**
23'-3" × 16'-0"

DECK

Raised hearth

46'-0"

BEDROOM
13'-3" × 11'-0"

Furnace

up

Stairs down for PLAN H-865-1
Storage for PLAN H-865-1A

DINING
13'-3" × 13'-6"

down

CLOSET

LINEN

BATH

CLOSET

BEDROOM
13'-3" × 10'-0"

ENTRY
16'-0" × 8'-0"

CLOS

BR

KITCHEN
13'-3" × 9'-4"

**ENTRANCE
DECK**

LAV

LAUNDRY
9'-10" × 8'-0"

FIRST FLOOR
1520 SQUARE FEET

Compact but not Cramped

This dwelling is compact but made to seem larger through the effective use of windows and decks. A profusion of balconies, decks and a courtyard open the interior spaces to the outdoors. The principal rooms connect with little interruption yet maintain a maximum of privacy.

Entering the spacious entry hall, one is impressed by the massive stairway that ascends from one corner landing against the backdrop of the attractive masonry of the fireplace. Light spills dramatically down from a large clerestory at the top of the house and bathes the balcony and rooms beyond in light.

Plans include a detached 20x24 garage.

First floor:	1,520 sq. ft.
Second floor:	352 sq. ft.
Total living area: (Not counting basement)	**1,872 sq. ft.**

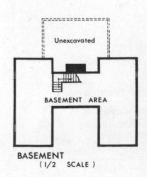

Unexcavated

BASEMENT AREA

BASEMENT
(1/2 SCALE)

Blueprint Price Code B

Plans H-865-1 & -1A

Contrasting Rustic and Contemporary

- In this design, contemporary styling is combined with the rustic atmosphere of a country lodge, for a home that will serve equally well for year-round or recreational living.
- A studio-type master bedroom is isolated upstairs, and includes a private bath, a balcony overlooking the living room below and a private outdoor deck.
- Interior touches include diagonal paneling, an open-beamed, cathedral ceiling and a massive stone fireplace with raised hearth.
- The main floor offers easy access to three large decks.
- Three foundation options include a daylight basement with recreation room, standard basement or crawlspace.

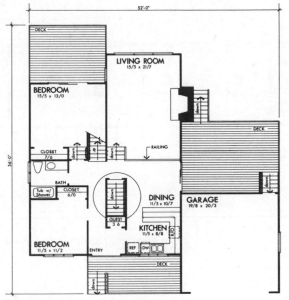

MAIN FLOOR

UPPER FLOOR

WITHOUT BASEMENT
(CRAWLSPACE FOUNDATION)

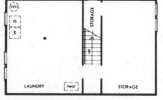

STANDARD BASEMENT

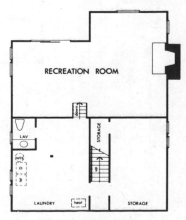

DAYLIGHT BASEMENT

Plans H-834-5, -5A & -5B

Bedrooms: 3	Baths: 2

Space:

Upper floor:	399 sq. ft.
Main floor:	1,249 sq. ft.
Total without basement:	**1,648 sq. ft.**
Daylight basement:	1,249 sq. ft.
Total with basement:	**2,897 sq. ft.**
Standard basement:	640 sq. ft.
Garage:	398 sq. ft.

Exterior Wall Framing: 2x4

Foundation options:
Daylight basement (H-834-5B).
Standard basement (H-834-5).
Crawlspace (H-834-5A).
(Foundation & framing conversion diagram available — see order form.)

Blueprint Price Code:

Without basement:	B
With standard basement:	C
With daylight basement:	D

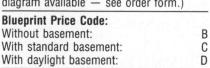

Plans H-834-5, -5A & -5B

UPPER FLOOR

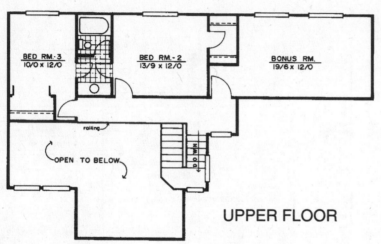

BED RM.-3
10/0 x 12/0

BED RM.-2
13/9 x 12/0

BONUS RM.
19/6 x 12/0

railing

OPEN TO BELOW

DN

Economical Energy Features

- The energy features in this home should meet most of its heating needs. A concrete slab floor, greenhouse enclosure vented into the home, a woodstove, and clerestory windows with insulated shutters are some of these features.
- The vaulted ceiling in the living/dining room and the open stairs and loft hallway above let heat flow naturally to all rooms.
- The master bedroom is privately positioned on the main level.
- A convenient washer and dryer are also on the main level, hidden behind the kitchen.

Plan I-1586-A

Bedrooms: 3-4	Baths: 2
Space:	
Upper floor	541 sq. ft.
Bonus Room	275 sq. ft.
Main floor	1,017 sq. ft.
Total Living Area	**1,833 sq. ft.**
Garage	439 sq. ft.
Exterior Wall Framing	2x6

Foundation options:

Crawlspace
(Foundation & framing conversion diagram available—see order form.)

Blueprint Price Code	B

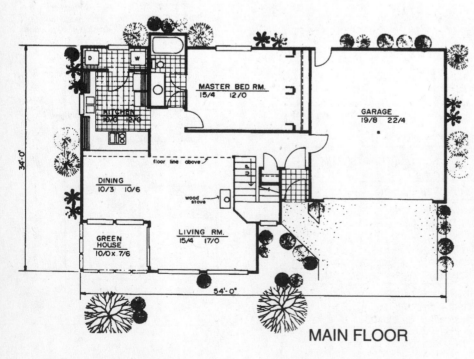

KITCHEN
10/0 12/0

MASTER BED RM.
15/4 12/0

GARAGE
19/8 22/4

floor line above

DINING
10/3 10/6

wood stove

GREEN HOUSE
10/0 x 7/6

LIVING RM.
15/4 17/0

34'-0"

54'-0"

MAIN FLOOR

Plan I-1586-A

A Dramatic Entrance

- This striking contemporary design borrows classic Doric columns to add traditional grace and charm to its roomy foyer.
- The ceiling of the large living room soars to clerestory windows above the foyer.
- The living and dining areas combine to form a huge space for entertaining for both formal and casual gatherings.
- The bay-windowed family room is separated from the kitchen by a large breakfast counter. A pantry is included in the adjoining utility area.
- The roomy master suite includes a deluxe bath and a whole wall of closets, not to mention easy access to a terrace or deck.
- Two secondary bedrooms share another full bath and complete the sleeping area of the home.

Plan HFL-1100-SH

Bedrooms: 3	Baths: 2
Space:	
Main floor	1,655 sq. ft.
Total Living Area	**1,655 sq. ft.**
Basement	1,510 sq. ft.
Garage	420 sq. ft.
Exterior Wall Framing	2x6

Foundation options:
Standard Basement
Slab
(Foundation & framing conversion diagram available—see order form.)

Blueprint Price Code	B

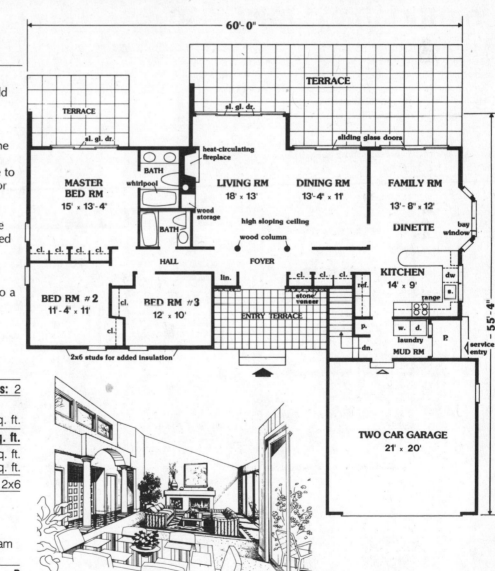

Plan HFL-1100-SH

Comfortable, Open Plan

- A central Great Room features a cathedral ceiling and is visually separated from the dining area by a huge fireplace.
- A wing on the left includes two secondary bedrooms which share a bath.
- In the right wing, you'll find a spacious master bedroom with private bath and walk-in closet.
- The kitchen is roomy and well-planned,

with a utility room in the garage entry area.
- A house-spanning front deck adds an extra welcoming touch to the plan.

Plan C-8160		
Bedrooms: 3		**Baths:** 2
Space:		
Main floor		1,669 sq. ft.
Total Living Area		**1,669 sq. ft.**
Basement	(approx.)	1,660 sq. ft.
Carport		413 sq. ft.
Storage	(approx.)	85 sq. ft.
Exterior Wall Framing		2x4
Foundation options:		
Standard Basement		
Crawlspace		
Slab		
(Foundation & framing conversion diagram available—see order form.)		
Blueprint Price Code		**B**

TO ORDER THIS BLUEPRINT,
CALL TOLL-FREE 1-800-547-5570

Plan C-8160

Cathedral Ceiling Featured

The open floor plan of this modified A-Frame design virtually eliminates wasted hall space. The centrally located Great Room features a 15'4" cathedral ceiling with exposed wood beams and large areas of fixed glass on both front and rear. Living and dining areas are visually separated by a massive stone fireplace.

The isolated master suite features a walk-in closet and sliding glass doors opening onto the front deck.

A walk-thru utility room provides easy access from the carport and outside storage area to the compact kitchen. On the opposite side of the Great Room are two additional bedrooms and a second full

bath. All this takes up only 1,454 square feet of heated living area. A full length deck and vertical wood siding with stone accents on the corners provide a rustic yet contemporary exterior.

Total living area: 1,454 sq. ft.
(Not counting basement or garage)

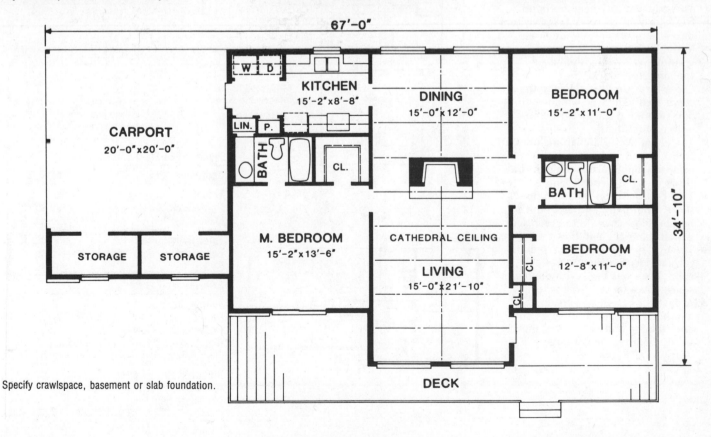

Specify crawlspace, basement or slab foundation.

Blueprint Price Code A

Plan C-7360

169

Excellent Family Design

- Long sloping rooflines and bold design features make this home attractive for any neighborhood.
- Inside, a vaulted entry takes visitors into an impressive vaulted Great Room with a wood stove and window-wall facing the house-spanning rear deck.
- Clerestory windows flanking the stove area and large windows front and rear flood the Great Room with natural light.
- The magnificent kitchen includes a stylish island and opens to the informal dining area which in turn flows into the Great Room.
- Two bedrooms on the main floor share a full bath, and bedroom #2 boasts easy access to the rear deck which spans the width of the house.
- The upstairs comprises an "adult retreat," with a roomy master suite, luxurious bath with double sinks, and a large walk-in closet.
- A daylight basement version adds another 1,410 sq. ft. of space for entertaining and recreation, plus a fourth bedroom and a large shop/storage area.

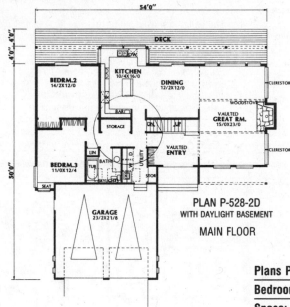

PLAN P-528-2D
WITH DAYLIGHT BASEMENT
MAIN FLOOR

UPPER FLOOR

PLAN P-528-2A
WITHOUT BASEMENT
(CRAWLSPACE FOUNDATION)

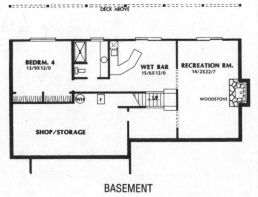

BASEMENT

Plans P-528-2A & -2D

Bedrooms: 3-4	Baths: 2-3
Space:	
Upper floor:	498 sq. ft.
Main floor:	1,456 sq. ft.
Total living area:	**1,954 sq. ft.**
Basement:	1,410 sq. ft.
Garage:	502 sq. ft.
Exterior Wall Framing:	2x4

Foundation options:
Daylight basement (Plan P-528-2D).
Crawlspace (Plan P-528-2A).
(Foundation & framing conversion diagram available — see order form.)

Blueprint Price Code:

Without basement:	B
With basement:	E

Plans P-528-2A & -2D

Decked Out for Fun

- Spacious deck surrounds this comfortable cabin/chalet.
- Sliding glass doors and windows blanket the living-dining area, indulged with raised hearth and a breathtaking view.
- Dining area and compact kitchen separated by breakfast bar.
- Master bedroom, laundry room and bath complete first floor; two additional bedrooms located on second floor.
- Upper level also features impressive balcony room with exposed beams.

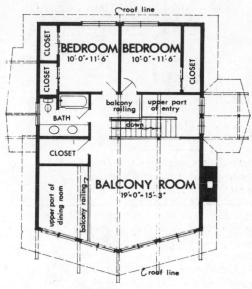

UPPER FLOOR

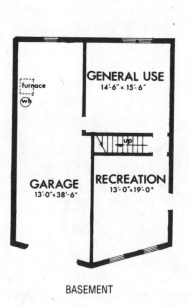

BASEMENT

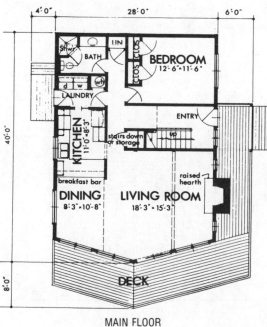

MAIN FLOOR

Plans H-919-1 & -1A

Bedrooms: 3	Baths: 2

Space:	
Upper floor:	869 sq. ft.
Main floor:	1,064 sq. ft.
Total living area:	**1,933 sq. ft.**
Basement:	475 sq. ft.
Garage:	501 sq. ft.

Exterior Wall Framing:	2x6

Foundation options:
Daylight basement (Plan H-919-1).
Crawlspace (Plan H-919-1A).
(Foundation & framing conversion diagram available — see order form.)

Blueprint Price Code:

Without basement:	B
With basement:	C

Plans H-919-1 & -1A

One-Bedroom Private Retreat

- The perfect solution for a private weekend — a one-bedroom retreat.
- This unique A-frame has the comforts you never had at home: a spacious, open, two-story living area with vaulted ceiling, two-story fireplace, relaxing wet bar, walls of windows and a spiral staircase that escalates to the upper-level master suite.
- A large island kitchen, dining area, bath and outdoor deck complete the first level.
- Upstairs, the exciting master suite has a private sitting area with attached deck, a walk-in closet, and a dramatic balcony that overlooks the living room below.

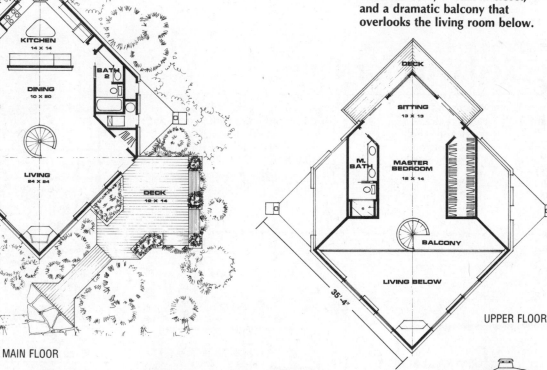

FRONT ELEVATION

MAIN FLOOR

UPPER FLOOR

SIDE ELEVATION

Plan DD-2194

Bedrooms: 1	Baths: 2

Space:

Upper floor:	658 sq. ft.
Main floor:	1,088 sq. ft.
Total living area:	**1,746 sq. ft.**
Basement:	1,088 sq. ft.

Exterior Wall Framing:	2x4

Foundation options:
Standard basement
Crawlspace
Slab
(Foundation & framing conversion diagram available — see order form.)

Blueprint Price Code:	B

Plan DD-2194

Covered Wrap-Around Deck Featured

- Covered deck spans home from main entrance to kitchen/side door.
- An over-sized fireplace is the focal point of the living room, which merges into an expandable dining area.
- Kitchen is tucked into one corner, but open counter space allows visual contact with living areas beyond.
- Good-sized main floor bedrooms furnished with sufficient closet space.
- Basement level adds a third bedroom and an additional 673 sq. ft. of living space.

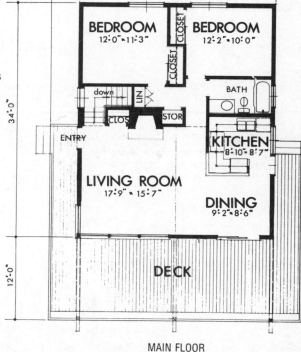

MAIN FLOOR

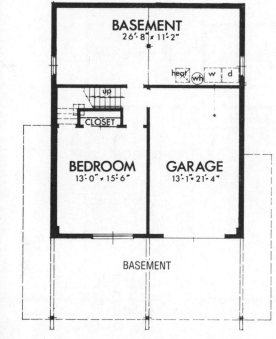

BASEMENT

Plan H-806-2

Bedrooms: 3	Baths: 1	Exterior Wall Framing:	2x6

Space:

		Foundation options:
Main floor:	952 sq. ft.	Daylight basement only.
Basement:	673 sq. ft.	(Foundation & framing conversion
Total living area:	1,625 sq. ft.	diagram available — see order form.)
Garage:	279 sq. ft.	**Blueprint Price Code:** B

Plan H-806-2

For Vacation or Year-Round Casual Living

- More than 500 square feet of deck area across the rear sets the theme of casual outdoor living for this compact plan.
- The living/dining/kitchen combination is included in one huge, 15' x 39' Great Room, which is several steps down from the entry level for even more dramatic effect.
- Two large downstairs bedrooms share a bath. Upstairs, a hideaway bedroom includes a private bath, walk-in closet and a romantic private deck.
- A utility room is conveniently placed in the garage entry area.

Plan H-877-1 & -1A	
Bedrooms: 3	**Baths:** 2
Space:	
Upper floor	320 sq. ft.
Main floor	1,200 sq. ft.
Total Living Area	**1,520 sq. ft.**
Basement	1,200 sq. ft.
Garage	155 sq. ft.
Exterior Wall Framing	2x6
Foundation options:	
Partial basement (under bedrooms)	
Crawlspace	
(Foundation & framing conversion diagram available—see order form.)	
Blueprint Price Code	B

UPPER FLOOR

STAIRWAY ARRANGEMENT
FOR PLAN WITH BASEMENT
(BASEMENT UNDER BEDROOMS)

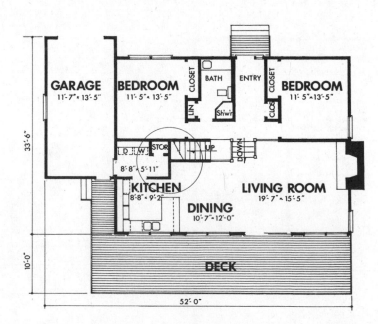

MAIN FLOOR

*TO ORDER THIS BLUEPRINT,
CALL TOLL-FREE 1-800-547-5570*

Plan H-877-1 & -1A

Private Decks Abound

- With two bedrooms opening to their own private deck, and another deck extending the full length of the living room, the scenic views can be fully enjoyed, both inside and out.
- The sunken living room features a fireplace, a dramatic 19-foot ceiling with skylights, and three sliding glass doors opening to the deck.
- The efficient kitchen overlooks the front yard and the rear view over the breakfast bar and dining room with opening to the living room.

Plan CAR-81007

Bedrooms: 3	Baths: 1½

Space:

Upper floor:	560 sq. ft.
Main floor:	911 sq. ft.

Total living area:	**1,471 sq. ft.**
Basement:	911 sq. ft.

Exterior Wall Framing:	2x6

Foundation options:
Standard basement.
(Foundation & framing conversion diagram available — see order form.)

Blueprint Price Code:	A

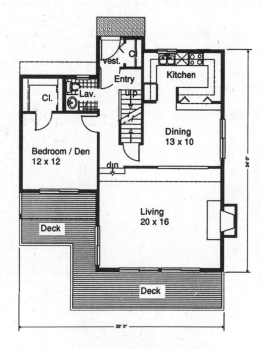

MAIN FLOOR

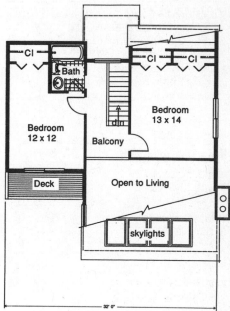

UPPER FLOOR

Plan CAR-81007

Spectacular Sloping Design

- For the lake or mountain-view sloping lot, this spectacular design hugs the hill and takes full advantage of the views.
- A three-sided wrap-around deck makes indoor-outdoor living a pleasure.

- The sunken living room, with cathedral ceiling, skylight, fireplace, and glass galore, is the heart of the plan.
- The formal dining room and the kitchen/breakfast room both overlook the living room and deck

views beyond.
- The main-floor master bedroom has private access to the deck and the bath.
- Two more bedrooms upstairs share a skylit bath and flank a dramatic balcony sitting area overlooking the living room below.

Plan AX-98607

Bedrooms: 3	Baths: 2

Space:	
Upper floor:	531 sq. ft.
Main floor:	1,098 sq. ft.
Total living area:	**1,629 sq. ft.**
Basement:	894 sq. ft.
Garage:	327 sq. ft.

Exterior Wall Framing:	2x4

Foundation options:
Standard basement.
Slab.
(Foundation & framing conversion diagram available — see order form.)

Blueprint Price Code:	B

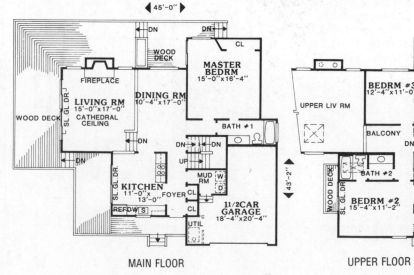

MAIN FLOOR

UPPER FLOOR

Plan AX-98607

Economical Plan for Narrow Lot

- Designed to accommodate a narrow lot, this economical plan still provides the amenities wanted by today's families.
- An efficient foyer distributes traffic in several directions, including the formal dining room on the right, living room on the left and the family room straight ahead.
- The kitchen is designed with efficiency in mind, and features an angled snack counter and a sunny breakfast nook.
- Upstairs, a deluxe master suite includes a private bath and large walk-in closet.
- Three secondary bedrooms and another full bath are also found upstairs.

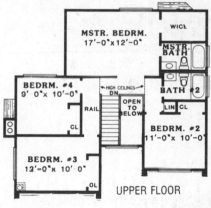

UPPER FLOOR

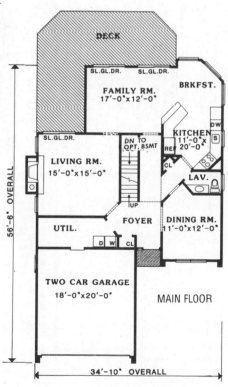

MAIN FLOOR

Plan AX-98821

Bedrooms: 4	**Baths:** 2½

Space:

Upper floor	886 sq. ft.
Main floor	1,104 sq. ft.
Total Living Area	**1,990 sq. ft.**
Basement	1,013 sq. ft.
Garage	383 sq. ft.
Exterior Wall Framing	2x4

Foundation options:

Standard Basement
Slab
(Foundation & framing conversion diagram available—see order form.)

Blueprint Price Code	**B**

Plan AX-98821

Raised Interest

- The raised living and deck areas of this design takes full advantage of surrounding views. A sloping lot can be accommodated with the shown lower level retaining wall.
- The lower level foyer feels high and is bright with a two-and-a-half-story opening lighting the stairwell.
- A two-car tuck-under garage and two bedroom suites complete the lower level.
- At the top of the stairs, guests are wowed with a view into the Grand room, with high vaulted ceiling, fireplace and atrium doors and windows overlooking the main deck.
- The kitchen incorporates a sunny good morning room.
- The master suite dazzles with a vaulted ceiling, plant shelves, a private deck and a splashy master bath.

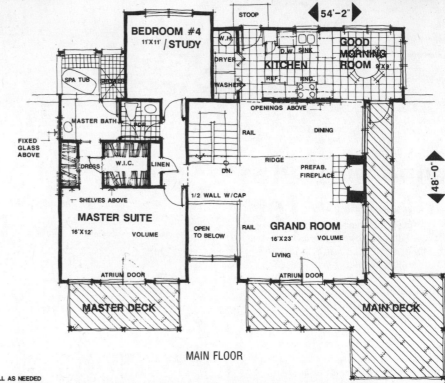

MAIN FLOOR

Plan EOF-44

Bedrooms: 4	Baths: 2
Space:	
Main floor:	1,256 sq. ft.
Lower floor:	541 sq. ft.
Total living area:	**1,797 sq. ft.**
Garage:	460 sq. ft.
Exterior Wall Framing:	2x4

Foundation options:
Daylight basement.
(Foundation & framing conversion diagram available — see order form.)

Blueprint Price Code:	B

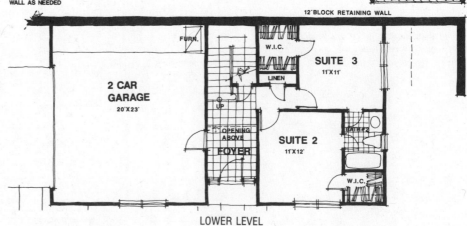

LOWER LEVEL

Plan EOF-44

TO ORDER THIS BLUEPRINT,
CALL TOLL-FREE 1-800-547-5570
178 (prices and details on pp. 12-15.)

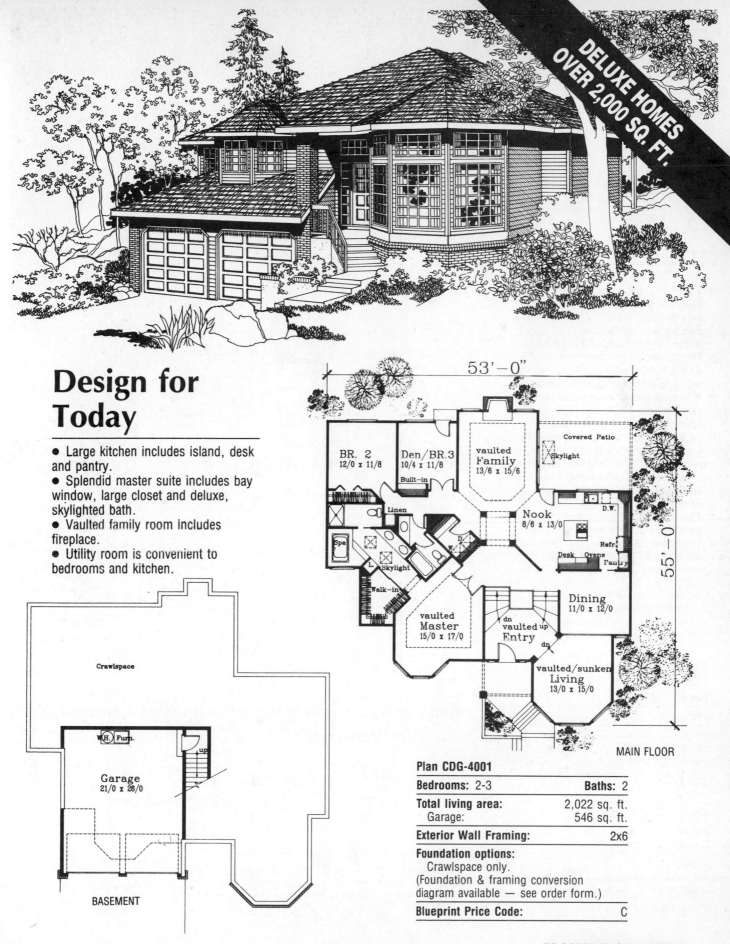

Design for Today

- Large kitchen includes island, desk and pantry.
- Splendid master suite includes bay window, large closet and deluxe, skylighted bath.
- Vaulted family room includes fireplace.
- Utility room is convenient to bedrooms and kitchen.

Crawlspace

W.H. Furn.
up

Garage
21/0 x 26/0

BASEMENT

53'-0"

55'-0"

BR. 2
12/0 x 11/8

Den/BR.3
10/4 x 11/8

vaulted Family
13/6 x 15/6

Covered Patio
Skylight

Built-in

Linen

D.W.

Nook
8/6 x 13/0

Refr

Spa

Desk   Ovens   Pantry

Skylight

Walk-in

vaulted Master
15/0 x 17/0

dn vaulted up
Entry

dn

Dining
11/0 x 12/0

vaulted/sunken Living
13/0 x 15/0

MAIN FLOOR

Plan CDG-4001

Bedrooms: 2-3		Baths: 2
Total living area:		2,022 sq. ft.
Garage:		546 sq. ft.
Exterior Wall Framing:		2x6

Foundation options:
Crawlspace only.
(Foundation & framing conversion diagram available — see order form.)

Blueprint Price Code: C

Plan CDG-4001

Rustic Home with Options

- This home is designed for either a level or a sloping site, with the option of placing the garage on the end or underneath.
- An impressive wood and stone facade greets visitors, and large front windows allow sunlight to penetrate both the front-facing kitchen and the dining room, as well as the loft area above.
- The large Great Room features an attention-getting fireplace that is flanked by windows and sliding glass doors to allow easy viewing of the outdoors.
- The master suite on the right includes a luxurious private bath and two large closets. Three bedrooms on the left share a compartmentalized bath.
- The loft area offers potential for many uses, such as hobbies, exercise, a studio or overflow sleeping area.

Plan N-1144-1 & -2

Bedrooms: 4	Baths: 2
Space:	
Loft	326 sq. ft.
Main floor	2,093 sq. ft.
Total Living Area	**2,419 sq. ft.**
Partial daylight basement	680 sq. ft.
Tuck-under garage (N-1144-1)	592 sq. ft.
Above ground garage (N-1144-2)	505 sq. ft.
Exterior Wall Framing	2x4
Foundation options:	**Plan #**
Partial Daylight Basement	N-1144-1
Crawlspace	N-1144-2
(Foundation & framing conversion diagram available—see order form.)	
Blueprint Price Code	C

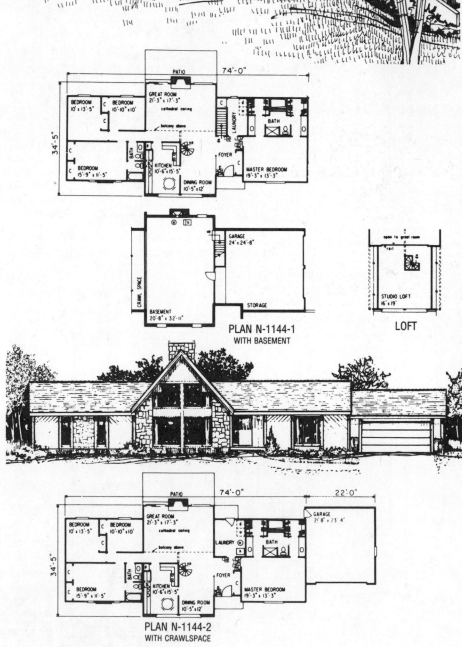

PLAN N-1144-1
WITH BASEMENT

LOFT

PLAN N-1144-2
WITH CRAWLSPACE

TO ORDER THIS BLUEPRINT,
CALL TOLL-FREE 1-800-547-5570
180 (prices and details on pp. 12-15.)

Plans N-1144-1 & -2

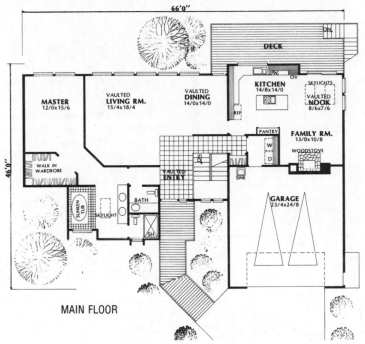

MAIN FLOOR

66'0"

46'0"

DECK

DN

MASTER
12/0x15/6

VAULTED
LIVING RM.
15/4x18/4

VAULTED
DINING
14/0x14/0

KITCHEN
14/8x14/0

DW
OV

SKYLIGHTS

VAULTED
NOOK
8/6x7/6

REF

PANTRY

FAMILY RM.
13/0x10/8

W
D

WOODSTOVE

WALK IN
WARDROBE

VAULTED
ENTRY

SINK

SUNKEN
TUB

SKYLIGHT

BATH

SH

GARAGE
23/4x24/8

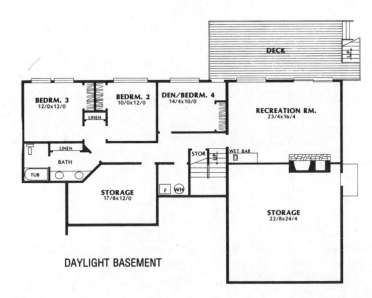

DAYLIGHT BASEMENT

DECK

BEDRM. 3
12/0x12/0

BEDRM. 2
10/0x12/0

DEN/BEDRM. 4
14/4x10/0

RECREATION RM.
23/4x16/4

LINEN

LINEN

BATH

TUB

STOR

UP

WET BAR

STORAGE
17/8x12/0

F
WH

STORAGE
22/8x24/4

Spacious Home for Sloping Scenic Site

- Designed to gain full advantage of a sloping site with a view to the rear, this plan looks great from either side.
- The front view offers strong, horizontal lines and a series of stepped-up gable roofs. The rear offers eye-catching decks and abundant windows.
- Virtually every part of the interior offers a view to the backyard. The garage, storage areas and bathrooms face the street, to buffer the living areas.
- The island kitchen, nook and family room flow together for a great informal living space with a full window wall facing the view.
- The family room provides for a cozy wood stove, and the rec room offers an impressive fireplace as well as a wet bar.
- Huge "storage" areas on the lower level are available for many other uses, such as woodworking, exercise, play rooms or for a "cottage industry" of some type.

Plan P-7637-2D

Bedrooms: 4	Baths: 2½
Space:	
Main floor	1,691 sq. ft.
Daylight basement	2,023 sq. ft.
Total Living Area	**3,714 sq. ft.**
Garage	575 sq. ft.
Exterior Wall Framing	2x4
Foundation options:	
Daylight Basement (Foundation & framing conversion diagram available—see order form.)	
Blueprint Price Code	F

Plan P-7637-2D

Well-Ordered Contemporary

- This attractive plan takes full advantage of a lot that slopes from side to side and that also offers a view to the rear.
- The active main-level areas are open and airy, with the living and dining rooms flowing together to create an enormous space for parties or family gatherings.
- The family room and kitchen face onto a large deck, and the family room provides for a cozy wood stove.
- The master suite also takes maximum advantage of the scenery, with large windows to the rear. The suite also features a large walk-in closet and a private bath.
- Two more bedrooms, another bath and an entry area complete the main floor.
- Downstairs, you'll note another bedroom, which could be used for an office or other purpose. Also, note the large recreation room, plus the bath, utility and storage areas.

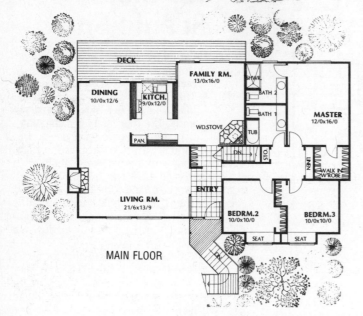

MAIN FLOOR

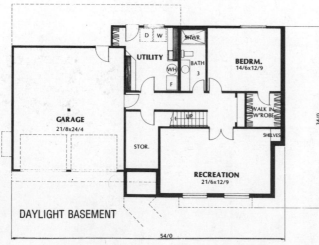

DAYLIGHT BASEMENT

Plan P-7673-2D

Bedrooms: 3-4	Baths: 3
Space:	
Main floor	1,652 sq. ft.
Daylight basement	1,124 sq. ft.
Total Living Area	**2,776 sq. ft.**
Garage	527 sq. ft.
Exterior Wall Framing	2x4

Foundation options:
Daylight Basement
(Foundation & framing conversion diagram available—see order form.)

Blueprint Price Code	D

Plan P-7673-2D

Simple Plan Lets You Enjoy the View

- This straightforward plan would be at home on any lot, but is especially attractive if you have a nice scenic view to the rear. Almost every room features abundant window area to the back of the house.
- The dining and living rooms together make a large space for gatherings of any kind, and the sunken living room features a fireplace and vaulted ceiling.
- The kitchen, nook and family room flow together for a wide range of family activities, and a convenient utility area offers handy access to the garage.
- The upper floor hosts four bedrooms, with the master suite including a private bath and large walk-in closet.
- An optional daylight basement adds another 1,200 square feet of living space.

Plans P-7492-2A & -2D

Bedrooms: 4	Baths: 2½
Space:	
Upper floor	1,048 sq. ft.
Main floor	1,200 sq. ft.
Total Living Area	**2,248 sq. ft.**
Basement	1,200 sq. ft.
Garage	532 sq. ft.
Exterior Wall Framing	2x4
Foundation options:	**Plan #**
Daylight Basement	P-7492-2D
Crawlspace	P-7492-2A
(Foundation & framing conversion diagram available—see order form.)	
Blueprint Price Code	**C**

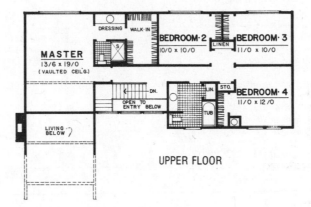

UPPER FLOOR

PLAN P-7492-2D
WITH DAYLIGHT BASEMENT

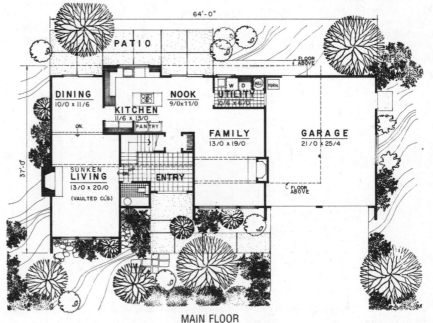

MAIN FLOOR
PLAN P-7492-2A
WITHOUT BASEMENT

Plans P-7492-2A & -2D

Rustic Four-Bedroom Home

This 2,467 sq. ft. rustic design includes a deluxe master suite with walk-in and walk-thru closets, linen closet, large double vanity and both a tub and separate shower stall.

The U-shaped kitchen features a counter bar open to the Great Room, which has a raised-hearth fireplace. A large utility room and a second bedroom and full bath with linen closet are located on the 1,694 sq. ft. main floor.

Two additional bedrooms and a third full bath with linen closet are located upstairs. A built-in bookcase, window seats and access to attic storage areas are also included on the 773 sq. ft. upper floor.

Front porch, dormers, shutters, multi-paned windows and a combination of wood and stone materials combine for a rustic exterior. The screened-in porch doubles as a covered breezeway connecting house and garage.

Specify crawlspace or basement foundation when ordering.

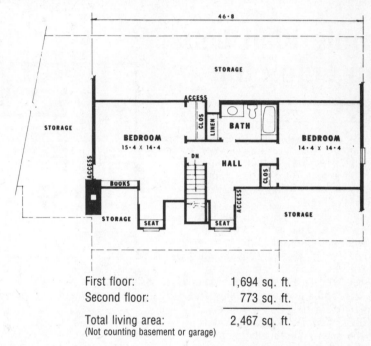

First floor: 1,694 sq. ft.

Second floor: 773 sq. ft.

Total living area: 2,467 sq. ft.
(Not counting basement or garage)

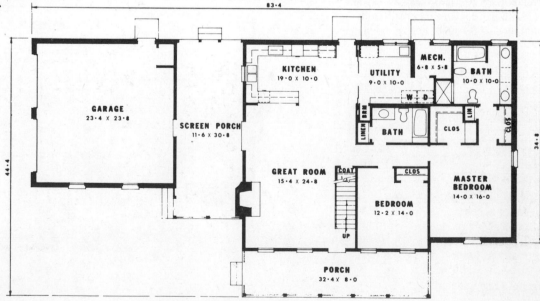

Blueprint Price Code C

Plan C-7746

Raised Living for Heightened Views

- Picture your new home nestled into an upsloping lot with an entire living room window wall looking back to your panoramic view.
- The raised main level gives a better view of the surroundings, without being blocked by a road, cars, or low trees. The resulting larger windows and walk-out on the lower level avoid a basement feeling in the rec room.
- The sunken living room, at the top of a half-flight of stairs, has a dramatic cathedral ceiling highlighted by angled transom windows.
- A see-through fireplace separates the living room from the formal dining room, also with a cathedral ceiling.
- The kitchen incorporates a spacious breakfast bay overlooking the rear deck.
- The main floor also houses three bedrooms and two full baths.

Plan AX-8486-A

Bedrooms: 3	Baths: 2

Space:

Main floor:	1,630 sq. ft.
Basement & rec room:	978 sq. ft.
Total living area:	**2,608 sq. ft.**
Garage:	400 sq. ft.
Storage area:	110 sq. ft.
Exterior Wall Framing:	**2x4**

Foundation options:
Daylight basement.
(Foundation & framing conversion diagram available — see order form.)

Blueprint Price Code:	**D**

MAIN FLOOR

BASEMENT

Plan AX-8486-A

Three-Bedroom Split-Entry

- This lovely split-entry combines contemporary and traditional styling in an affordable floor arrangement.
- The main/upper level houses the sleeping rooms, two baths, convenient laundry facilities, and the main living areas.
- A formal dining room is divided from the foyer by an open handrail; the room can also overlook the front yard through a large, boxed window wall.
- The adjacent living room boasts a handsome fireplace and sliders to the rear patio.
- A large, versatile bonus space and a garage are found on the lower level.

50'-0"

Patio

Master Br
12x17

Living Rm
14x14

Brkfst
11x7-6

Br 2
12x11-6

Br 3
11x12

W
D

DN   UP

Dining
12-2x12-8

34'-4"

MAIN FLOOR

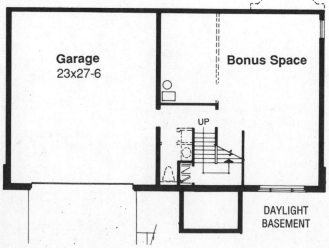

Garage
23x27-6

Bonus Space

UP

DAYLIGHT BASEMENT

Plan B-90014

Bedrooms: 3	Baths: 2-2½

Space:

Main/upper floor:	1,549 sq. ft.
Basement:	750 sq. ft.
Total living area:	**2,299 sq. ft.**
Garage:	633 sq. ft.

Exterior Wall Framing:	2x4

Foundation options:
Daylight basement.
(Foundation & framing conversion diagram available — see order form.)

Blueprint Price Code:	C

Plan B-90014

Design for Steep Terrain

- A railing separates the sunken living room from the vaulted dining room for a great visual flow of space.
- The kitchen is highlighted by a corner window sink, an island and a walk-in pantry.

- The master suite includes a luxury bath illuminated by a skylight and a spacious walk-in closet.
- The partial basement could be omitted for building on flat lots.

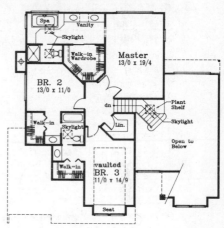

UPPER FLOOR

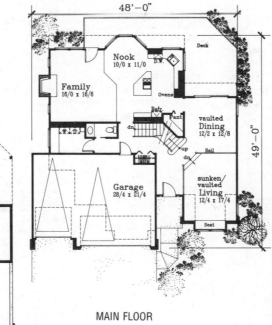

MAIN FLOOR

BASEMENT

Plan CDG-2009	
Bedrooms: 3	**Baths: 2½**
Space:	
Upper floor	1,113 sq. ft.
Main floor	1,230 sq. ft.
Total Living Area	**2,343 sq. ft.**
Basement	606 sq. ft.
Garage	604 sq. ft.
Exterior Wall Framing	2x4

Foundation options:
Partial Daylight Basement
(Foundation & framing conversion diagram available—see order form.)

Blueprint Price Code	**C**

TO ORDER THIS BLUEPRINT,
CALL TOLL-FREE 1-800-547-5570
(prices and details on pp. 12-15.)

Plan CDG-2009

Sprawling Contemporary

- Room to roam is what this sprawling contemporary ranch offers, plus plenty of surprises.
- A rustic wood exterior is highlighted by corner trapezoid windows which add dramatic curb appeal and interior enjoyment.
- From the double-doored entry, there is a panoramic view of the living spaces of the home.
- The sunken living room has a sloped ceiling accentuating the transom windows.
- The formal dining room overlooks the living room and the dramatic conversation pit nestled around the hearth.
- The family room also overlooks the conversation pit, and features a built-in wet bar and sliders to a covered porch.
- The sleeping wing includes a large master bedroom with sloped ceiling, sliders to the patio, a walk-in closet and private bath.

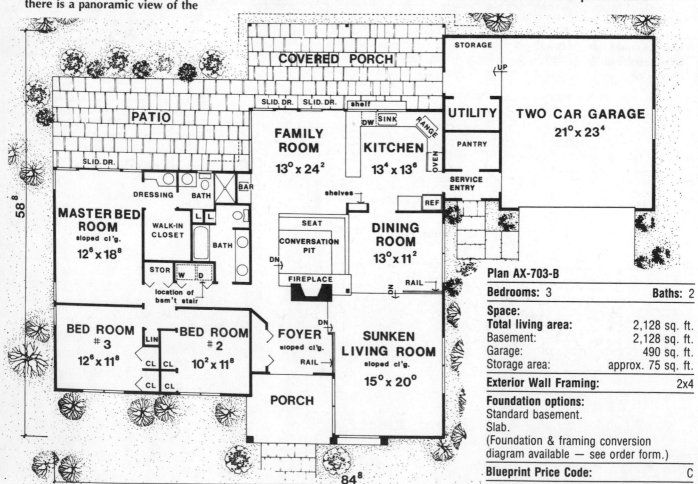

Plan AX-703-B

Bedrooms: 3	Baths: 2

Space:

Total living area:	2,128 sq. ft.
Basement:	2,128 sq. ft.
Garage:	490 sq. ft.
Storage area:	approx. 75 sq. ft.

Exterior Wall Framing:	2x4

Foundation options:
Standard basement.
Slab.
(Foundation & framing conversion diagram available — see order form.)

Blueprint Price Code:	C

Plan AX-703-B

Chalet Style for Town or Country

- The exterior features exposed beams, board siding and viewing decks with cut-out railings to give this home the look of a mountain chalet.
- Inside, the design lends itself equally well to year-round family living or part-time recreational enjoyment.
- An expansive Great Room features an impressive fireplace and includes a dining area next to the well-planned kitchen.
- The upstairs offers the possibility of an "adult retreat," with a fine master bedroom with private bath and large closets, plus a loft area available for many uses.
- Two secondary bedrooms are on the main floor, and share another bath.
- The daylight basement level provides space for a garage and large recreation room with fireplace.

Plan P-531-2D

Bedrooms: 3	Baths: 2
Space:	
Upper floor:	573 sq. ft.
Main floor:	1,120 sq. ft.
Lower level:	532 sq. ft.
Total living area:	2,225 sq. ft.
Garage:	approx. 588 sq. ft.

Exterior Wall Framing:	2x4
Foundation options:	
Daylight basement only.	
(Foundation & framing conversion diagram available — see order form.)	
Blueprint Price Code:	C

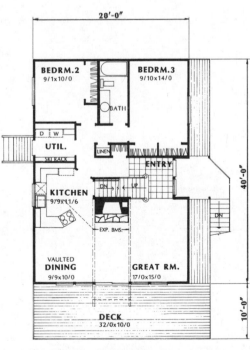

UPPER FLOOR

MAIN FLOOR

LOWER FLOOR

Plan P-531-2D

Panoramic View for Scenic Site

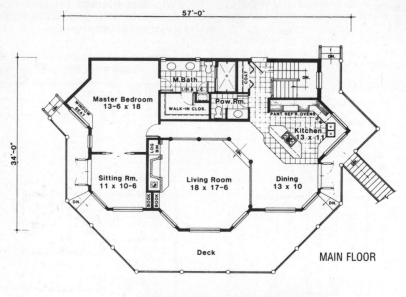

MAIN FLOOR

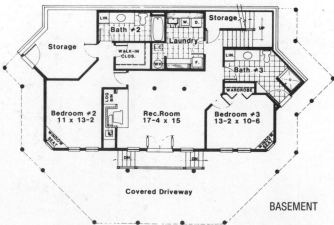

BASEMENT

- Large deck offers a panoramic view and plenty of space for outdoor living.
- Sunken living room features big windows and impressive fireplace.
- Living room is set off by railings, not walls, to create visual impact of big space.
- Master suite includes private bath, large closet, sitting area and access to deck.
- Lower level includes rec room with fireplace, two bedrooms, two baths and large utility area.

Plan NW-779

Bedrooms: 3	Baths: 3½

Space:

Main floor:	1,450 sq. ft.
Lower floor:	1,242 sq. ft.

Total living area: 2,692 sq. ft.

Exterior Wall Framing: 2x6

Foundation options:
Daylight basement only.
(Foundation & framing conversion diagram available — see order form.)

Blueprint Price Code: D

Plan NW-779

Simple, Spacious, Easy to Build

For a simple, spacious, easy-to-construct home away from home, you should definitely consider this plan.

Entrance to the home is by way of the lower level or the side door to the living room, or both, where grade levels permit. This has the advantage of elevating the second floor to take advantage of a view that otherwise may be blocked out by surrounding buildings.

The living area, consisting of the living room, dining room and kitchen, occupies 565 sq. ft. of the main floor. The open room arrangement allows the cook to remain part of the family even when occupied with necessary chores.

The design's basically simple rectangular shape allows for easy construction, and the home could be built by any moderately experienced do-it-yourselfer. All you have to do is order the plan that fits your setting.

Plan H-833-5 has the garage entry to the street side. H-833-6 puts the garage under the view-side deck.

Upper floor:	1,200 sq. ft.
Lower level:	876 sq. ft.
Total living area: (Not counting garage)	2,076 sq. ft.

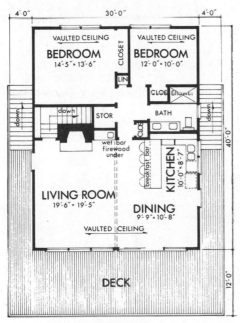

UPPER FLOOR
1200 SQUARE FEET

LOWER FLOOR
876 SQUARE FEET
PLAN H-833-5

LOWER FLOOR
876 SQUARE FEET
PLAN H-833-6

Blueprint Price Code C

Plans H-833-5 & -6

TO ORDER THIS BLUEPRINT,
CALL TOLL-FREE 1-800-547-5570
(prices and details on pp. 12-15.)

Country Kitchen and Great Room

Cozy front porch, dormers, shutters and multi-paned windows on the exterior of this Cape Code design are complemented by an informal interior. The 1,318 sq. ft. of heated living area on the main floor is divided into three sections. In the first section is an eat-in country kitchen with island counter and bay window and a large utility room which can be entered from either the kitchen or garage. The second section is the Great Room with inside fireplace, an informal dining nook and double doors opening onto the rear deck. The third section consists of a master suite, which features a walk-in closet and compartmentalized bath with linen closet.

An additional 718 sq. ft. of heated living area on the upper floor includes a second full bath and two bedrooms with ample closet space and window seats. A large storage area is provided over the garage. All or part of the basement can be used to supplement the main living area.

First floor:	1,318 sq. ft.
Second floor:	718 sq. ft.
Total living area:	2,036 sq. ft.
(Not counting basement or garage)	
Basement:	1,221 sq. ft.
Garage:	436 sq. ft.

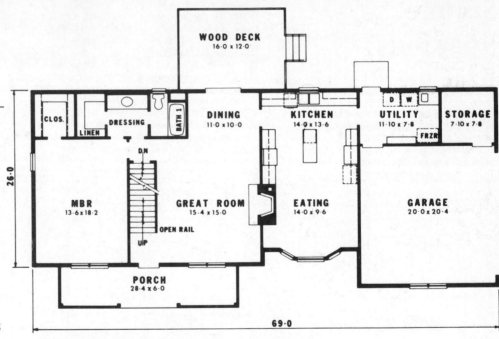

Specify basement, crawlspace or slab foundation when ordering.

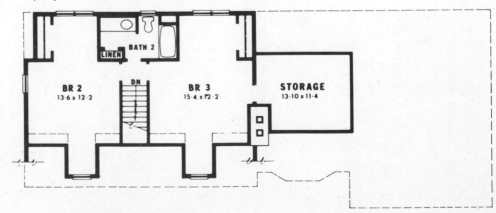

TO ORDER THIS BLUEPRINT, CALL TOLL-FREE 1-800-547-5570

Blueprint Price Code C

Plan C-8040

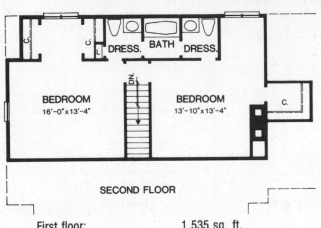

SECOND FLOOR

First floor: 1,535 sq. ft.
Second floor: 765 sq. ft.

Total living area: 2,300 sq. ft.
(Not counting basement or garage)

PLAN C-8535
WITH BASEMENT

Traditional Touches Dress Up a Country Cottage

Multipaned windows, shutters and a covered porch embellish the traditional exterior of this country cottage. The floor plan incorporates a central Great Room. A raised-hearth stone fireplace forms part of a wall separating the Great Room from the kitchen.

The large country kitchen features an island and abundant counter space. The breakfast room includes a bay window. A large dining room faces the front.

First-level master bedroom has its own super bath with separate shower, garden tub, twin vanities and walk in closets. Two large bedrooms, separate dressing areas and compartment tub occupy the second level.

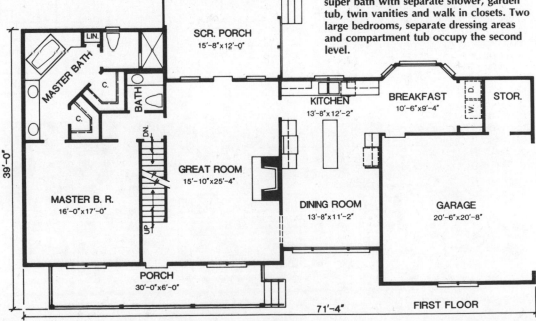

Blueprint Price Code C

Plan C-8535

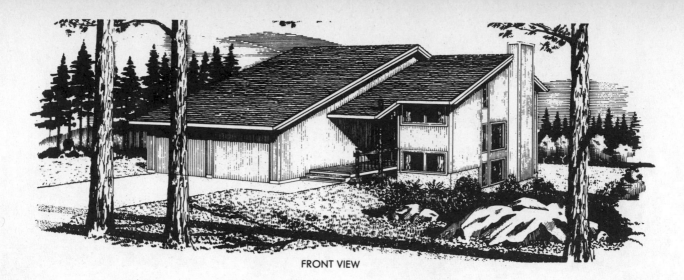

FRONT VIEW

Luxury on a Compact Foundation

Sky-lighted sloped ceilings, an intriguing stairway and overhead bridge and a carefully planned first floor arrangement combine to delight the senses as one explores this spacious 2737 sq. ft. home. A major element of the design is the luxurious master suite that is reached via the stairway and bridge. An abundance of closet space and an oversized bath are welcome features here.

Two bedrooms, generous bath facilities and a large family room provide lots of growing room for the younger members of the household.

All these features are available within a mere 36' width which allows the house to be built on a 50' wide lot — a real bonus these days.

Main floor:	1,044 sq. ft.
Upper level:	649 sq. ft.
Lower level:	1,044 sq. ft.
Total living area: (Not counting garage)	2,737 sq. ft.

(Exterior walls are 2x6 construction)

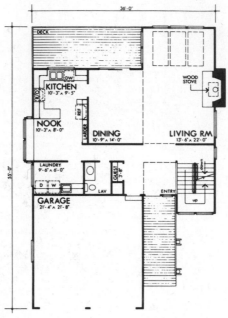

MAIN FLOOR
1044 SQUARE FEET

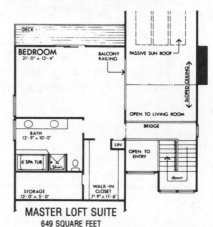

MASTER LOFT SUITE
649 SQUARE FEET

LOWER LEVEL
1044 SQUARE FEET

REAR VIEW

Blueprint Price Code D

Plan H-2110-1B

Upstairs Suite Creates Adult Retreat

- This multi-level design is ideal for a gently sloping site with a view to the rear.

- Upstairs master suite is a sumptuous "adult retreat" complete with magnificent bath, vaulted ceiling, walk-in closet, private deck and balcony loft.
- Living room includes wood stove area and large windows to the rear. Wood bin can be loaded from outside.
- Main floor also features roomy kitchen and large utility area.

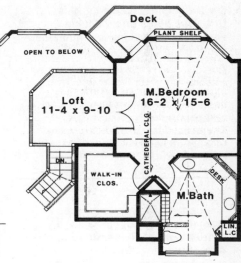

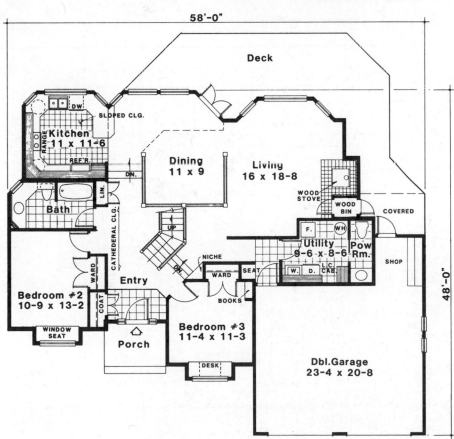

Plan NW-544-S

Plan NW-544-S	
Bedrooms: 3	Baths: 2½
Space:	
Upper floor:	638 sq. ft.
Main floor:	1,500 sq. ft.
Total living area:	2,138 sq. ft.
Garage:	545 sq. ft.
Exterior Wall Framing:	2x6
Foundation options: Crawlspace only. (Foundation & framing conversion diagram available — see order form.)	
Blueprint Price Code:	C

All Decked Out

- For the sloping, scenic lot, this rustic rec home offers double wrap-around decking and numerous windows to take advantage of the views.
- Corner glass walls in the sunken living room soar two stories in height for maximum visual impact and panoramic views.
- The main floor also has an open-feeling kitchen/breakfast room with sliders to the rear deck.
- A formal dining room, sewing room and full bath complete the main floor.
- The upper floor continues the dramatics via an open stairwell overlooking the living room.
- Three bedrooms and two full baths are oriented around a loft/study with sliders to the second-floor deck.
- The master bedroom also offers sliding-door access to the deck.

UPPER FLOOR

MAIN FLOOR

Plan DD-2178	
Bedrooms: 3	**Baths:** 3
Space:	
Upper floor:	994 sq. ft.
Main floor:	1,174 sq. ft.
Total living area:	2,168 sq. ft.
Basement:	1,174 sq. ft.
Exterior Wall Framing:	2x4

Foundation options:
Standard Basement
Crawlspace
Slab
(Foundation & framing conversion
diagram available — see order form.)

Blueprint Price Code:	C

Plan DD-2178

SECOND FLOOR

BEDROOM
10'-3''×13'-6''

CLOSET

DOWN

BATH

STORAGE

HALL

CLOSET

BEDROOM
13'-5''×14'-11''

WOOD DECK

BEDROOM
10'-3''×13'-7''

CLOSET

CLOSET

BATH

DRESSING

LINEN

CLOSET

Exciting Visual Design

Total living area: 2,168 sq. ft.

Specify basement, crawlspace or slab foundation.

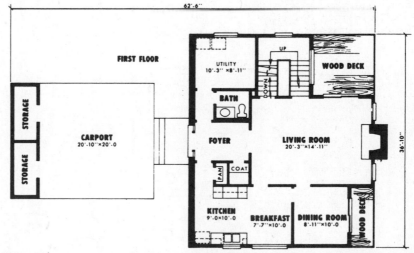

62'-6''

FIRST FLOOR

UTILITY
10'-3'' ×8'-11''

UP

WOOD DECK

DOWN

BATH

FOYER

LIVING ROOM
20'-3''×14'-11''

36'-10''

STORAGE

STORAGE

CARPORT
20'-10''×20'-0

PAN

COAT

KITCHEN
9'-0×10'-0

BREAKFAST
7'-7''×10'-0

DINING ROOM
8'-11''×10'-0

WOOD DECK

FIRST FLOOR

Blueprint Price Code C

Plan C-72110

TO ORDER THIS BLUEPRINT,
CALL TOLL-FREE 1-800-547-5570
(prices and details on pp. 12-15.) **197**

An Ever-Popular Floor Plan

PLAN H-2029-4
MAIN FLOOR
(DINING ROOM VERSION)
1664 SQUARE FEET

PLAN H-2029-5
MAIN FLOOR
(FAMILY ROOM VERSION)
1664 SQUARE FEET

The basic concept of this plan is to provide a simple straight-forward design for an uphill site. The plan is available with either a family room or dining room adjacent to the kitchen. Other features include a convenient laundry room, three bedrooms and two full baths. The living room features a fireplace and the wrap-around deck has access through the kitchen and laundry room. Total main floor area is 1,664 sq. ft.

Main floor:	1,664 sq. ft.
Lower level:	1,090 sq. ft.
Total living area:	2,754 sq. ft.
Garage:	573 sq. ft.

(Exterior walls are 2x6 construction)

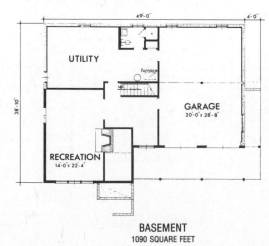

BASEMENT
1090 SQUARE FEET

TO ORDER THIS BLUEPRINT,
CALL TOLL-FREE 1-800-547-5570

Blueprint Price Code D

Plans H-2029-4 & H-2029-5

Dramatic Contemporary

- A dramatic roofline and a combination of vertical and horizontal siding give an interesting look to this contemporary.
- Drama continues to the large, sunken living room at the center of the home where you'll find a fireplace, cathedral ceiling open to the upper level, skylights and a rear attached deck accessed through sliding glass doors on three sides.
- The adjoining dining room also has a view of the fireplace and deck.
- A generous kitchen steps down to a utility area with handy washer/dryer and pantry before reaching the garage.
- Secluded to the rear is also a main-floor master bedroom with private access to the deck and a skylit bath with cathedral ceiling, dressing area and walk-in closet.

Plan AX-98712

Bedrooms: 4	Baths: 2 ½
Space:	
Upper floor	815 sq. ft.
Main floor	1,343 sq. ft.
Total Living Area	**2,158 sq. ft.**
Basement	1,298 sq. ft.
Garage	400 sq. ft.
Exterior Wall Framing	2x4
Foundation options:	
Standard Basement	
Slab	
(Foundation & framing conversion diagram available—see order form.)	
Blueprint Price Code	C

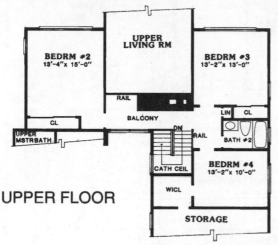

UPPER FLOOR

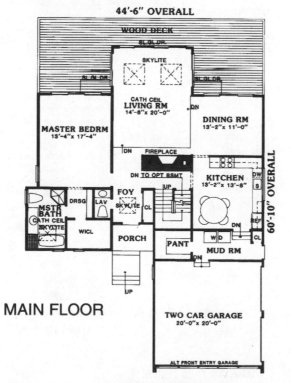

44'-6" OVERALL

MAIN FLOOR

Plan AX-98712

TO ORDER THIS BLUEPRINT,
CALL TOLL-FREE 1-800-547-5570
(prices and details on pp. 12-15.)

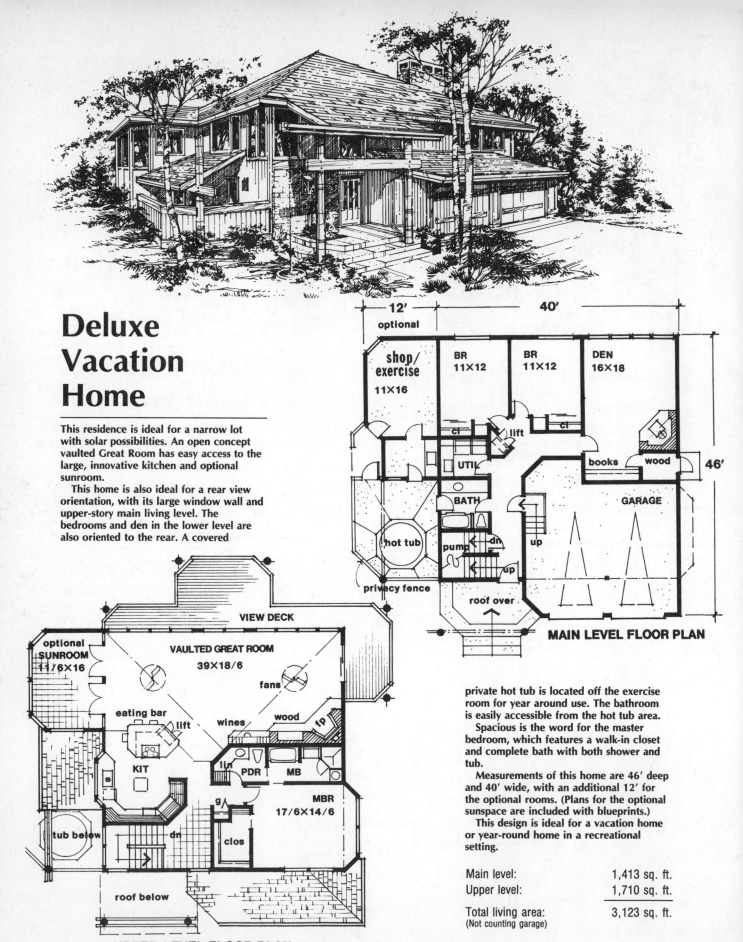

Deluxe Vacation Home

This residence is ideal for a narrow lot with solar possibilities. An open concept vaulted Great Room has easy access to the large, innovative kitchen and optional sunroom.

This home is also ideal for a rear view orientation, with its large window wall and upper-story main living level. The bedrooms and den in the lower level are also oriented to the rear. A covered

MAIN LEVEL FLOOR PLAN

- 12' optional
- 40'
- 46'

shop/exercise 11×16

BR 11×12

BR 11×12

DEN 16×18

cl

lift

cl

UTIL

books

wood

BATH

GARAGE

hot tub

pump

dn

up

up

privacy fence

roof over

UPPER LEVEL FLOOR PLAN

VIEW DECK

VAULTED GREAT ROOM 39×18/6

optional SUNROOM 11/6×16

fans

eating bar

lift

wines

wood

fp

KIT

lin

PDR

MB

tub below

g

MBR 17/6×14/6

dn

clos

roof below

private hot tub is located off the exercise room for year around use. The bathroom is easily accessible from the hot tub area.

Spacious is the word for the master bedroom, which features a walk-in closet and complete bath with both shower and tub.

Measurements of this home are 46' deep and 40' wide, with an additional 12' for the optional rooms. (Plans for the optional sunspace are included with blueprints.)

This design is ideal for a vacation home or year-round home in a recreational setting.

Main level:	1,413 sq. ft.
Upper level:	1,710 sq. ft.
Total living area: (Not counting garage)	3,123 sq. ft.

TO ORDER THIS BLUEPRINT, CALL TOLL-FREE 1-800-547-5570

Blueprint Price Code E

Plan S-60983

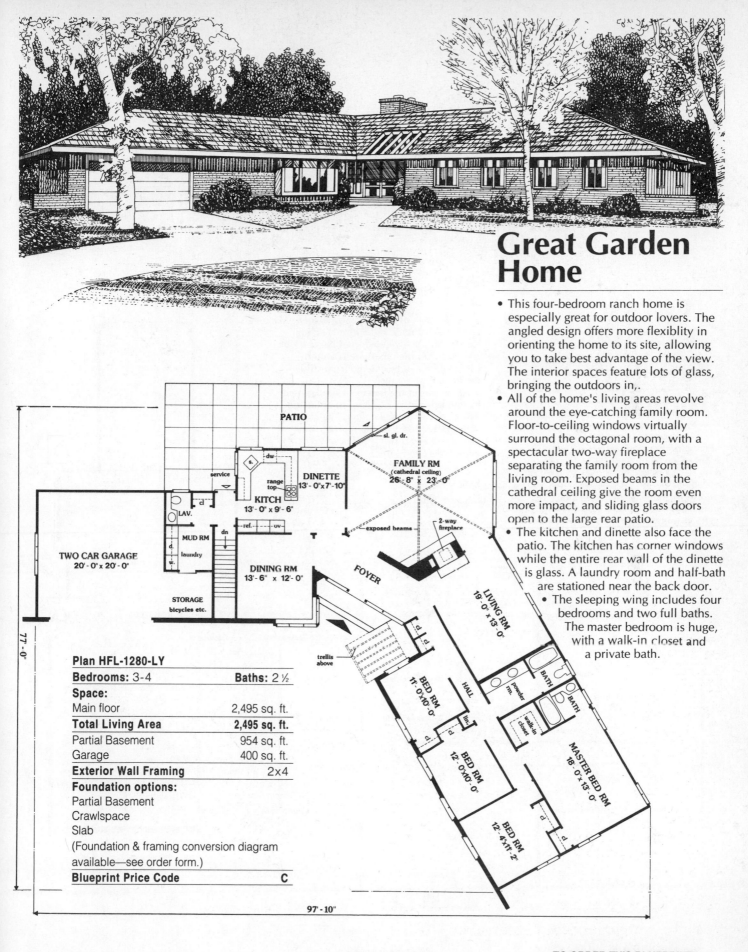

Great Garden Home

- This four-bedroom ranch home is especially great for outdoor lovers. The angled design offers more flexiblity in orienting the home to its site, allowing you to take best advantage of the view. The interior spaces feature lots of glass, bringing the outdoors in,.

- All of the home's living areas revolve around the eye-catching family room. Floor-to-ceiling windows virtually surround the octagonal room, with a spectacular two-way fireplace separating the family room from the living room. Exposed beams in the cathedral ceiling give the room even more impact, and sliding glass doors open to the large rear patio.

- The kitchen and dinette also face the patio. The kitchen has corner windows while the entire rear wall of the dinette is glass. A laundry room and half-bath are stationed near the back door.

- The sleeping wing includes four bedrooms and two full baths. The master bedroom is huge, with a walk-in closet and a private bath.

PATIO

sl. gl. dr.

FAMILY RM
(cathedral ceiling)
26'-8" x 23'-0"

DINETTE
13'-0"x7'-10"

dw

service

range top

KITCH
13'-0" x 9'-6"

LAV.

ref.

ov

exposed beams

2-way fireplace

TWO CAR GARAGE
20'-0" x 20'-0"

dn

MUD RM

laundry

DINING RM
13'-6" x 12'-0"

FOYER

STORAGE
bicycles etc.

trellis above

LIVING RM
19'-0" x 13'-0"

BED RM
11'-0"x10'-0"

HALL

powder rm.

BATH

BATH

walk-in closet

lin.

BED RM
12'-0"x10'-0"

MASTER BED RM
18'-0"x13'-0"

BED RM
12'-4"x11'-2"

77'-0"

97'-10"

Plan HFL-1280-LY

Bedrooms: 3-4	**Baths:** 2 ½

Space:

Main floor	2,495 sq. ft.
Total Living Area	**2,495 sq. ft.**
Partial Basement	954 sq. ft.
Garage	400 sq. ft.
Exterior Wall Framing	2x4

Foundation options:

Partial Basement
Crawlspace
Slab

(Foundation & framing conversion diagram available—see order form.)

Blueprint Price Code	C

Plan HFL-1280-LY

Cathedral Ceiling With Studio

This rustic/contemporary modified A-Frame design combines a 20' high cathedral ceiling over a sunken living room with a large studio over the two rear bedrooms. The isolated master suite features a walk-in closet and compartmentalized bath with double vanity and linen closet. The two rear bedrooms include ample closet space and share a unique bath-and-a-half arrangement.

On one side of the U-shaped kitchen and breakfast nook is the formal dining room which is separated from the entry by a planter. On the other side is a utility room which can be entered from either the kitchen or garage.

All or part of the basement can be used to supplement the 2,213 sq. ft. of heated living area on the main floor. The exterior features a massive stone fireplace, large glass areas and a combination of vertical wood siding and stone.

First floor:	2,213 sq. ft.
Second floor:	260 sq. ft.
Total living area:	2,473 sq. ft.

(Not counting basement or garage)

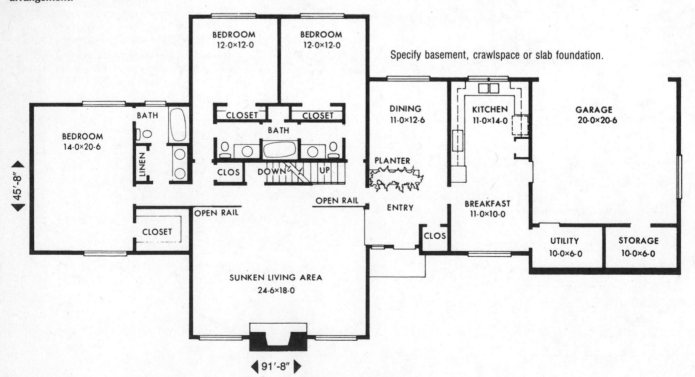

Specify basement, crawlspace or slab foundation.

Blueprint Price Code C
Plan C-7113

Loaded with Features

- A traditional feeling pervades this modern design, with its gabled roof, large front porch and two rear decks.
- Inside, you'll find an open-concept plan which lends a feeling of spaciousness throughout the home.
- The dining room off the entry can easily be converted to a den or even to a guest bedroom if formal dining isn't part of your family's routine.
- The large kitchen/nook/family room combination offers plenty of space for casual dining as well as for all sorts of family activities.
- The upper-level master suite features a double-door entry, luxurious bath, large closet and private balcony with an exterior spiral staircase.
- Two additional bedrooms share a second full bath, and a bonus room provides space for play, study, hobbies, exercise or for another sleeping room.

Plan S-62586

Bedrooms: 3-5	Baths: 2½

Space:

Upper floor	1,056 sq. ft.
Main floor	1,416 sq. ft.
Bonus area	144 sq. ft.

Total Living Area	**2,616 sq. ft.**
Basement (approx.)	1,416 sq. ft.
Garage (2-car version)	476 sq. ft.
(3-car version, approx.)	676 sq. ft.

Exterior Wall Framing	**2x6**

Foundation options:

Standard Basement
Crawlspace
(Foundation & framing conversion diagram available—see order form.)

Blueprint Price Code	**D**

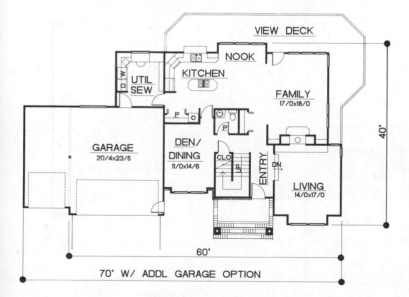

MAIN FLOOR

UPPER FLOOR

Plan S-62586

Rear of Home As Attractive As Front

The rear of this rustic/contemporary home features a massive stone fireplace and a full-length deck which make it ideal for mountain, golf course, lake or other locations where both the front and rear offer scenic views.

Sliding glass doors in the family room and breakfast nook open onto the deck. The modified A-Frame design combines a 20'6" cathedral ceiling over the sunken family room with a large studio over the two front bedrooms. An isolated master suite features a walk-in closet and compartmentalized bath with double vanity and linen closet. The front bedrooms include ample closet space and share a unique bath-and-a-half arrangement.

On one side of the U-shaped kitchen and breakfast nook is the formal dining room which opens onto the foyer. On the other side is a utility room which can be entered from either the kitchen or garage.

The exterior features a massive stone fireplace, large glass areas and a combination of vertical wood siding and stone.

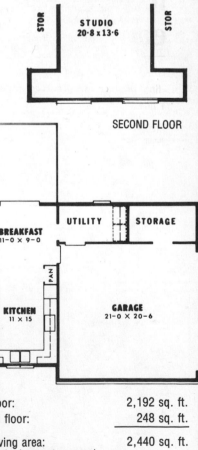

SECOND FLOOR

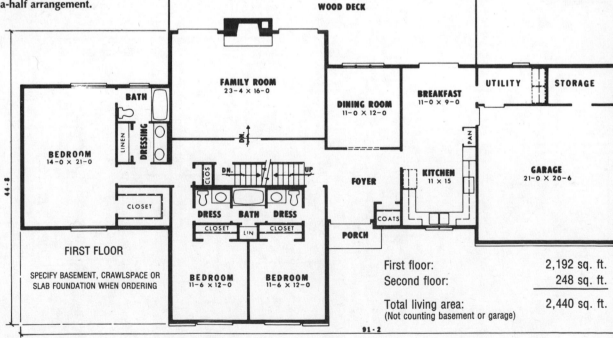

FIRST FLOOR

SPECIFY BASEMENT, CRAWLSPACE OR SLAB FOUNDATION WHEN ORDERING

First floor:	2,192 sq. ft.
Second floor:	248 sq. ft.
Total living area: (Not counting basement or garage)	2,440 sq. ft.

Blueprint Price Code C
Plan C-7710

"Adult Retreat" Includes Reading Loft

Main floor:	1,610 sq. ft.
Upper floor:	715 sq. ft.
Total living area: (Not counting basement or garage)	2,325 sq. ft.

READING LOFT
12/0x11/0

MASTER SUITE
13/0x17/2

BOOKS

LINEN

DN

SH

TUB
7/0x3/6

SKYLIGHTS

DRESSING

WALK IN WARDROBE

OPEN TO ENTRY

UPPER FLOOR

FAMILY ROOM

UP

PLAN P-7671-4D
WITH DAYLIGHT BASEMENT
BASEMENT LEVEL: 1634 sq. ft.

52'0"

49'0"

BEDRM.2
10/6x12/0

BEDRM.3
12/0x12/0

VAULTED FAMILY RM.
21/10x11/8

WOOD STOVE

BREAKFAST PATIO

LIN

TUB

BAR

KITCHEN
14/4x9/0

PAN

PLAN P-7671-4A
WITHOUT BASEMENT
(CRAWLSPACE FOUNDATION)

BEDRM.4
10/6x12/2

W D

VAULTED ENTRY

EXPOSED BEAMS

VAULTED DINING RM.
11/0x11/4

LAUNDRY CHUTE

WH

F

GARAGE
20/4x21/2

VAULTED LIVING RM.
14/4x19/4

MAIN FLOOR

Blueprint Price Code C

Plans P-7671-4A & P-7671-4D

Eye-Catching Hillside Design

Main floor:	1,010 sq. ft.
Upper floor:	958 sq. ft.
Lower level:	290 sq. ft.
Total living area:	2,258 sq. ft.

(Not counting garage)

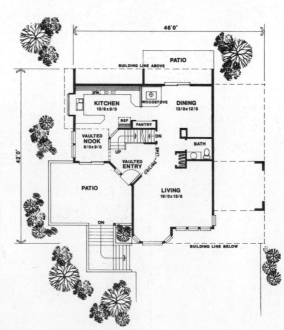

PLAN P-6604-4D

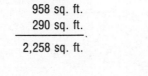

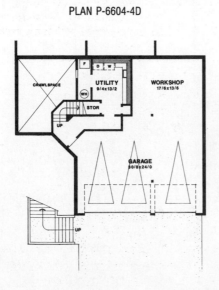

Blueprint Price Code C

Plan P-6604-4D

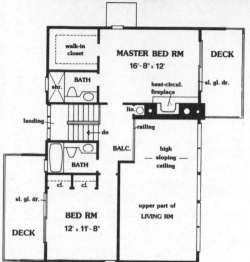

UPPER FLOOR

walk-in closet

MASTER BED RM
16'-8" x 12'

DECK

BATH

shr.

heat-circul. fireplace

lin.

landing

railing

dn

BALC.

BATH

high sloping ceiling

cl. cl.

sl. gl. dr.

BED RM
12' x 11'-8"

upper part of LIVING RM

DECK

LOWER FLOOR

up

DRESSING
8'-9" x 7'-2"

w.
d.

LAUNDRY
12'-1" x 11'-6"

BATH

shr.

laundry chute

cl.

UTILITY

up

stor.

FOYER

covered entry

storage

TWO CAR GARAGE
24' x 18'-8"

work shop

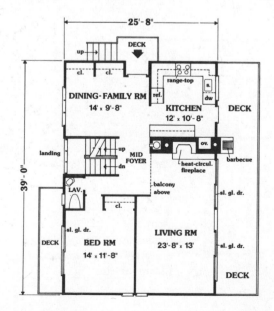

MAIN FLOOR

25'-8"

up

DECK

cl. cl.

range-top

s.

ref.

dw

DINING-FAMILY RM
14' x 9'-8"

KITCHEN
12' x 10'-8"

DECK

39'-0"

landing

up

MID FOYER

dn

heat-circul. fireplace

ov.

barbecue

balcony above

LAV.

sl. gl. dr.

cl.

sl. gl. dr.

DECK

BED RM
14' x 11'-8"

LIVING RM
23'-8" x 13'

sl. gl. dr.

DECK

Plan HFL-2176

A Deck for Each Room

- Exciting outdoor living is possible in this three-level contemporary design.
- The front entrance and garage are located on the lower level, along with a dressing room, full bath and laundry facilities.
- The main level offers a spectacular two-story living room overlooked by an upper-level balcony; highlights include a massive stone wall with heat-circulating fireplace and two sets of sliding glass doors that offer entrance to the front deck that stretches to the kitchen.
- Outdoor dining can take place off the kitchen deck with barbecue or off the formal dining/family area.
- The main-level bedroom and pair of upper-level bedrooms each offer private decks.

Plan HFL-2176

Bedrooms: 3	Baths: 3½
Space:	
Upper floor	712 sq. ft.
Main floor	1,001 sq. ft.
Lower floor	463 sq. ft.
Total Living Area	**2,176 sq. ft.**
Garage and storage	448 sq. ft.
Exterior Wall Framing	2x6
Foundation options:	
Slab (Foundation & framing conversion diagram available—see order form.)	
Blueprint Price Code	**C**

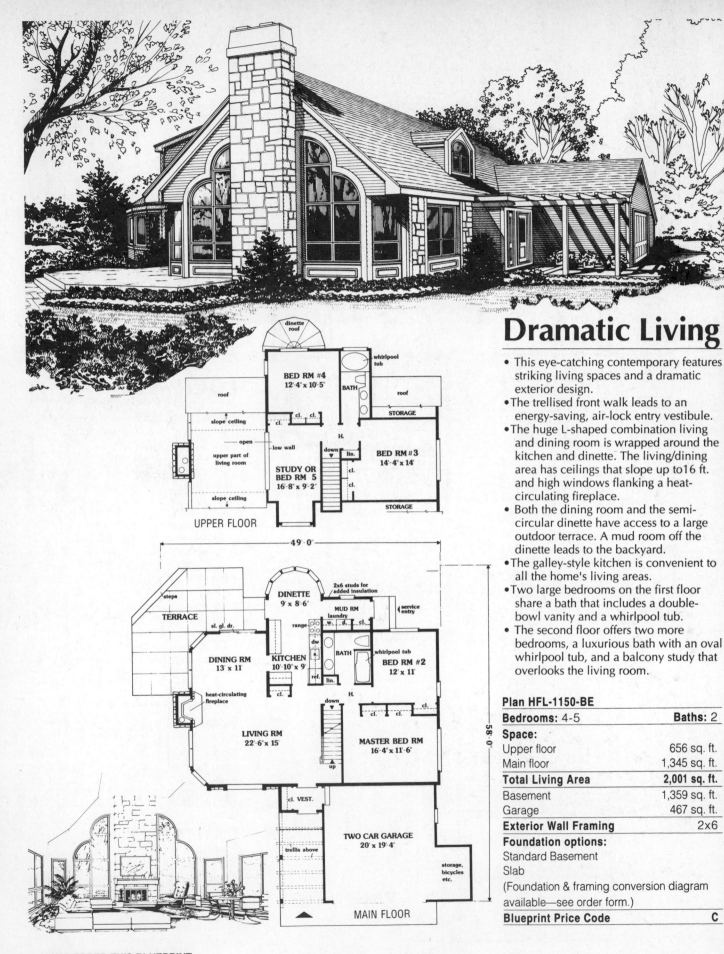

UPPER FLOOR

roof

slope ceiling

open — low wall

upper part of living room

slope ceiling

BED RM #4
12'-4" x 10'-5"

BATH

whirlpool tub

roof

STORAGE

cl. cl.

H.

down

lin.

STUDY OR BED RM 5
16'-8" x 9'-2"

cl.

cl.

BED RM #3
14'-4" x 14'

STORAGE

dinette roof

MAIN FLOOR

49'-0"

58'-0"

steps

TERRACE

sl. gl. dr.

DINETTE
9' x 8'-6"

2x6 studs for added insulation

service entry

MUD RM
laundry

w. d. cl.

range

DINING RM
13' x 11'

KITCHEN
10'-10" x 9'

dw

ref.

lin.

BATH

whirlpool tub

BED RM #2
12' x 11'

cl.

heat-circulating fireplace

LIVING RM
22'-6" x 15'

down

H.

cl. cl.

cl.

up

MASTER BED RM
16'-4" x 11'-6"

cl. VEST.

TWO CAR GARAGE
20' x 19'-4"

trellis above

storage, bicycles etc.

Dramatic Living

- This eye-catching contemporary features striking living spaces and a dramatic exterior design.
- The trellised front walk leads to an energy-saving, air-lock entry vestibule.
- The huge L-shaped combination living and dining room is wrapped around the kitchen and dinette. The living/dining area has ceilings that slope up to 16 ft. and high windows flanking a heat-circulating fireplace.
- Both the dining room and the semi-circular dinette have access to a large outdoor terrace. A mud room off the dinette leads to the backyard.
- The galley-style kitchen is convenient to all the home's living areas.
- Two large bedrooms on the first floor share a bath that includes a double-bowl vanity and a whirlpool tub.
- The second floor offers two more bedrooms, a luxurious bath with an oval whirlpool tub, and a balcony study that overlooks the living room.

Plan HFL-1150-BE

Bedrooms: 4-5	Baths: 2
Space:	
Upper floor	656 sq. ft.
Main floor	1,345 sq. ft.
Total Living Area	**2,001 sq. ft.**
Basement	1,359 sq. ft.
Garage	467 sq. ft.
Exterior Wall Framing	2x6

Foundation options:

Standard Basement

Slab

(Foundation & framing conversion diagram available—see order form.)

Blueprint Price Code	C

Plan HFL-1150-BE

REAR VIEW

A Striking Contemporary

A multiplicity of decks and outcroppings along with unusual window arrangements combine to establish this striking contemporary as a classic type of architecture. To adapt to the sloping terrain, the structure has three levels of living space on the downhill side. As one moves around the house from the entry to the various rooms and living areas, both the appearance and function of the different spaces change, as do the angular forms and cutouts that define the floor plan arrangement. Almost all the rooms are flooded with an abundance of daylight, yet are shielded by projections of wing walls and roof surfaces to assure privacy as well as to block undesirable direct rays of sunshine.

The design projects open planning of a spacious living room that connects with the dining and kitchen area. The home features four large bedrooms, two of which have walk-in closets and private baths. The remaining two bedrooms also have an abundance of wardrobe space, and the rooms are of generous proportions.

For energy efficiency, exterior walls are framed with 2x6 studs.

First floor:	1,216 sq. ft.
Second floor:	958 sq. ft.
Total living area: (Not counting basement or garage)	2,174 sq. ft.
Basement:	1,019 sq. ft.

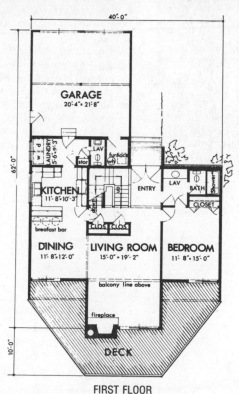

FIRST FLOOR
1216 SQUARE FEET

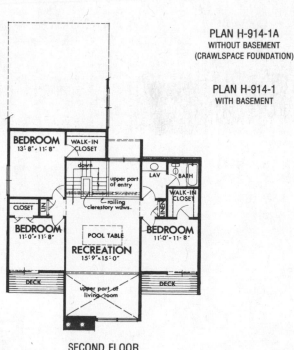

PLAN H-914-1A
WITHOUT BASEMENT
(CRAWLSPACE FOUNDATION)

PLAN H-914-1
WITH BASEMENT

SECOND FLOOR
958 SQUARE FEET

Blueprint Price Code C

Plans H-914-1 & H-914-1A

TO ORDER THIS BLUEPRINT, CALL TOLL-FREE 1-800-547-5570
(prices and details on pp. 12-15.)

Soaring Spaces under Vaulted Ceilings

- A dignified exterior and a gracious, spacious interior combine to make this an outstanding plan for today's families.
- The living, dining, family rooms and breakfast nook all feature soaring vaulted ceilings.
- An interior atrium provides an extra touch of elegance, with its sunny space for growing plants and sunbathing.
- The master suite is first class all the way, with a spacious sleeping area, opulent bath, large skylight and enormous walk-in closet.
- A gorgeous kitchen includes a large work/cooktop island, corner sink with large corner windows and plenty of counter space.

Plans P-7697-4A & -4D

Bedrooms: 3	Baths: 2

Space:	
Main floor (crawlspace version):	2,003 sq. ft.
Main floor (basement version):	2,030 sq. ft.
Basement:	2,015 sq. ft.
Garage:	647 sq. ft.

Exterior Wall Framing:	2x4

Foundation options:
Daylight basement (Plan P-7697-4D).
Crawlspace (Plan P-7697-4A).
(Foundation & framing conversion diagram available — see order form.)

Blueprint Price Code:	C

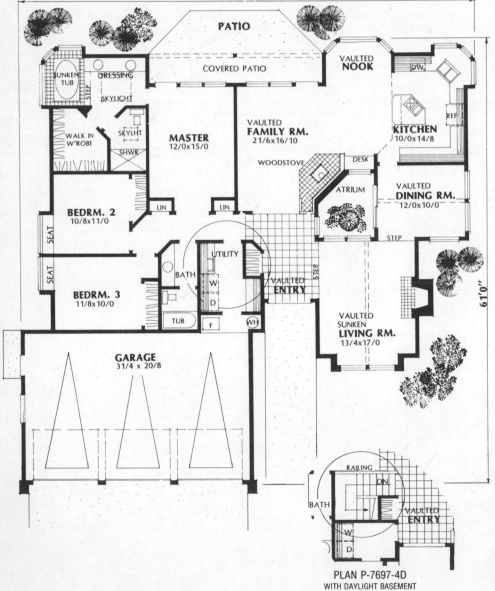

63'0''

PATIO

COVERED PATIO

SUNKEN TUB

DRESSING

SKYLIGHT

WALK IN W'ROBE

SKYLHT

SHWR

MASTER
12/0x15/0

VAULTED
FAMILY RM.
21/6x16/10

WOODSTOVE

VAULTED
NOOK

DW.

REF

KITCHEN
10/0x14/8

DESK

ATRIUM

VAULTED
DINING RM.
12/0x10/0

STEP

BEDRM. 2
10/8x11/0

LIN

LIN

SEAT

SEAT

BEDRM. 3
11/8x10/0

BATH

UTILITY

W

D

TUB

F

WH

VAULTED
ENTRY

VAULTED
SUNKEN
LIVING RM.
13/4x17/0

61'0''

GARAGE
31/4 x 20/8

RAILING

DN

BATH

VAULTED
ENTRY

W

D

PLAN P-7697-4D
WITH DAYLIGHT BASEMENT

Plans P-7697-4A & -4D

Dramatic Interior Makes a Best-Seller

- An incredible master suite takes up the entire 705 sq. ft. second floor, and includes deluxe bath, huge closet and skylighted balcony.
- Main floor design utilizes angles and shapes to create dramatic interior.
- Extra-spacious kitchen features large island, sunny windows and plenty of counter space.
- Sunken living room focuses on massive fireplace and stone hearth.
- Impressive two-level foyer is lit by skylights high above.
- Third bedroom or den with an adjacent bathroom makes an ideal home office or hobby room.

Photo by Karlis Grants

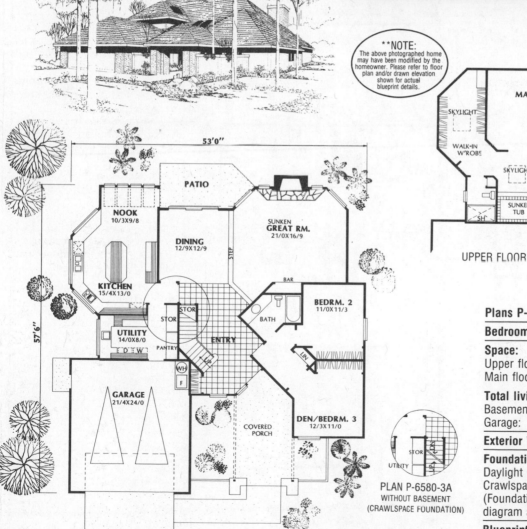

NOTE:
The above photographed home may have been modified by the homeowner. Please refer to floor plan and/or drawn elevation shown for actual blueprint details.

MASTER SUITE 20/0X15/0

SKYLIGHT

WALK-IN W'ROBE

SKYLIGHT

OPEN TO GREAT RM. BELOW

SKYLIGHTS

SUNKEN TUB

SH

ENTRY BELOW

UPPER FLOOR

53'0"

57'6"

PATIO

NOOK 10/3X9/8

DINING 12/9X12/9

SUNKEN GREAT RM. 21/0X16/9

STEP

KITCHEN 15/4X13/0

STOR

STOR

UTILITY 14/0X8/0

PANTRY

ENTRY

BAR

BATH

BEDRM. 2 11/0X11/3

LIN

DFW

WH F

GARAGE 21/4X24/0

COVERED PORCH

DEN/BEDRM. 3 12/3X11/0

MAIN FLOOR

STOR

UTILITY

PLAN P-6580-3A
WITHOUT BASEMENT
(CRAWLSPACE FOUNDATION)

Plans P-6580-3A & -3D

Bedrooms: 2-3	Baths: 2

Space:

Upper floor:	705 sq. ft.
Main floor:	1,738 sq. ft.

Total living area:	2,443 sq. ft.
Basement:	1,738 sq. ft.
Garage:	512 sq. ft.

Exterior Wall Framing:	2x4

Foundation options:
Daylight basement (Plan P-6580-3D).
Crawlspace (Plan P-6580-3A).
(Foundation & framing conversion diagram available — see order form.)

Blueprint Price Code:	C

Plans P-6580-3A & -3D

Contemporary Hillside Home

This three-level recreation home is designed to fit comfortably on a slope of approximately 20 degrees, with a fall of 15 to 17 feet for the depth of the building. Naturally the stability of the ground must be taken into consideration, and local professional advice should be sought. Otherwise, this home is designed to meet the requirements of the Uniform Building Code.

The pleasing contemporary nature of the exterior is calculated to blend into the surroundings as unobtrusively as possible, following the natural contours.

The modest roadside facade consisting of garage doors and a wooden entrance deck conceals the spacious luxury that lies beyond. Proceeding from the rustic deck into the skylighted entry hall, one is struck by the immensity of the living-dining room and the huge deck extending beyond. A massive masonry backdrop provides a setting for the pre-fab fireplace of your choice (this same structure incorporates the flue for a similar unit on the lower level).

Before descending from the entry hall, one must take notice of the balcony-type den, library, hobby or office room on this level — a private retreat from the activities below.

The efficient U-shaped kitchen has an adjoining attached breakfast bar for casual dining whenever the roomy dining room facilities are not required. A convenient laundry room is an important part of this housekeeping section.

The master bedroom suite occupies the remainder of the 1,256 sq. ft. contained on this level. The room itself, 12' x 16' in size, is served by a private full bathroom and two huge wardrobe closets. Direct access to the large deck provides opportunity for morning sit-ups or evening conversation under the stars. A final convenience on this level is the small lavatory for general use.

The focal point of the lower level is the spacious recreation room which is a duplicate size of the living room above. Flanking this room at either end are additional large bedrooms, one having a walk-in closet and the other a huge wall-spanning wardrobe. Another full bathroom serves this level. A small work shop or storage room completes this arrangement.

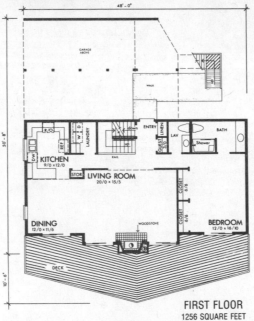

FIRST FLOOR
1256 SQUARE FEET

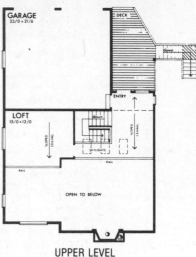

UPPER LEVEL
372 SQUARE FEET
528 SQUARE FEET - GARAGE

PLAN H-966-1B
WITH DAYLIGHT BASEMENT

(Exterior walls framed in 2x6 studs)

Upper level:	372 sq. ft.
Main floor:	1,256 sq. ft.
Basement:	1,256 sq. ft.
Total living area:	2,884 sq. ft.
(Not counting garage)	

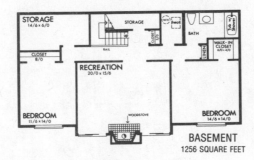

BASEMENT
1256 SQUARE FEET

Blueprint Price Code D
Plan H-966-1B

High Style in A Moderate Design

Sweeping roof lines amplify the clean exterior of this wood-finished contemporary home.

Majority of glass is positioned at rear of home for maximum solar benefit. A sunspace may also be added if desired.

Interior of home is designed around the "open plan concept," allowing free movement of air while visually borrowing space from the adjacent areas.

The vaulted entry features a clerestory located over the second-floor balcony, which overlooks the first floor spaces.

Kitchen, family and breakfast nook areas may be zoned off from the more formal areas of the home.

A large master bedroom features a walk-in closet, master bath, shower, tub and a deck to the rear of the home.

Living room of home is vaulted to the balcony level.

Total square footage of this residence is 2,139. Building dimensions are 50' wide by 52' deep. Please specify type of basement version desired.

Total living area: 2,139 sq. ft.
(Not counting basement or garage)

Exterior walls are 2x6 construction.

SECOND LEVEL

PLAN S-2001
WITHOUT BASEMENT
(CRAWLSPACE FOUNDATION)

PLAN S-2001-FB
FULL BASEMENT VERSION

PLAN S-2001-DB
DAYLIGHT BASEMENT VERSION

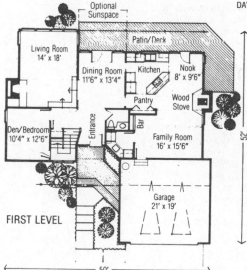

FIRST LEVEL

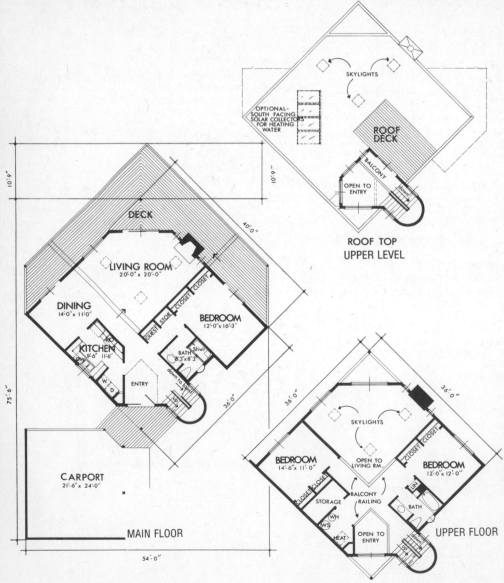

DECK

LIVING ROOM
20'-0" x 20'-0"

DINING
14'-0" x 11'-0"

BEDROOM
12'-0" x 16'-3"

KITCHEN
9'-6" x 11'-6"

BATH
8'.3" x 8'-3"

ENTRY

CARPORT
21'-6" x 24'-0"

MAIN FLOOR

54'-0"

75'-6"

10'-9"

40'-0"

36'-0"

SKYLIGHTS

OPTIONAL-
SOUTH FACING
SOLAR COLLECTORS
FOR HEATING
WATER

ROOF
DECK

BALCONY

OPEN TO
ENTRY

down

**ROOF TOP
UPPER LEVEL**

10'-9"

SKYLIGHTS

OPEN TO
LIVING RM.

BEDROOM
14'-6" x 11'-0"

BEDROOM
12'-0" x 12'-0"

BALCONY
RAILING

STORAGE

OPEN TO
ENTRY

BATH

UPPER FLOOR

36'-0"

36'-0"

Striking Vertical Design

- Unique roof deck and massive wrap-around main level deck harbor an equally exciting interior.
- Large sunken living room is brightened by a three-window skylight and also features a log-sized fireplace.
- U-shaped kitchen is just off the entry, adjacent to handy laundry area.
- Second-story balcony overlooks the large living room and entryway below.

Plans H-935-1 & -1A

Bedrooms: 3	Baths: 2
Space:	
Upper floor:	844 sq. ft.
Main floor:	1,323 sq. ft.
Total living area:	2,167 sq. ft.
Basement:	approx. 1,323 sq. ft.
Carport:	516 sq. ft.
Exterior Wall Framing:	2x6

Foundation options:
Standard basement (Plan H-935-1).
Crawlspace (Plan H-935-1A).
(Foundation & framing conversion diagram available — see order form.)

Blueprint Price Code: C

Plans H-935-1 & -1A

Simple Exterior, Luxurious Interior

- Modest and unassuming on the exterior, this design provides an elegant and spacious interior.
- Highlight of the home is undoubtedly the vast Great Room/Dining area, with its vaulted ceiling, massive hearth and big bay windows.
- An exceptionally fine master suite is also included, with a large sleeping area, luxurious bath and big walk-in closet.
- A beautiful kitchen is joined by a bright bay-windowed breakfast nook; also note the large pantry.
- The lower level encompasses two more bedrooms and a generously sized game room and bar.

49'3"

RAILING

DECK

HOT TUB

MASTER
19/0x14/0

VAULTED
GREAT RM.
21/6x17/6

PLNTR.

SUNKEN TUB

DRESSING

VAULTED
DINING
14/4x10/6

LIN

WALK IN
WARDROBE

BATH

PANTRY

SKYLIGHT

VAULTED
ENTRY

REF.

KITCHEN
13/6x10/6

GARAGE
21/4x21/8

DW

NOOK
10/0x10/0

50'8"

MAIN FLOOR

PATIO

FLOOR LINE ABOVE

BEDRM. 2
12/8x10/8

TUB

WOODSTOVE

BATH

GAME RM.
21/6x17/0

LINEN

BEDRM. 3
12/0x11/4

UP

WH

UTILITY

F

W
D

BAR

BASEMENT

Plan P-6595-3D

Bedrooms: 3	**Baths:** 2½	
Space:		
Main floor:	1,530 sq. ft.	
Lower level:	1,145 sq. ft.	
Total living area:	2,675 sq. ft.	
Garage:	462 sq. ft.	

Exterior Wall Framing:	2x6
Foundation options:	
Daylight basement only.	
(Foundation & framing conversion diagram available — see order form.)	
Blueprint Price Code:	D

Plan P-6595-3D

Photo by Mark Englund/HomeStyles

**NOTE:
The above photographed home may have been modified by the homeowner. Please refer to floor plan and/or drawn elevation shown for actual blueprint details.

Four-Bedroom Contemporary Style

Steeply pitched, multi-level gable rooflines accented by diagonal board siding and tall windows add imposing height to this contemporary, 2,289 sq. ft. home. With most of the 1,389 sq. ft. main floor devoted to the living, dining and family rooms, and a long patio or wood deck accessible off the nook, the home lends itself ideally to family activities and gracious entertaining.

Directly off the spacious foyer is the vaulted-ceiling living room and dining area, brightened with high windows and warmed by a log-sized fireplace. The wide U-shaped kitchen, nook and family room, with wood stove, join and extend across the back half of the main floor. With doors off the nook and utility room leading to a large patio, this area combines for large, informal activities. Also off the front entry hall is a full bathroom, a den or fourth bedroom, and the open stairway, brightened by a skylight, leading to the upper floor.

The master bedroom suite, occupying about half of the upper floor, has a wide picture window, walk-in dressing room/ wardrobe, and a skylighted bathroom with sunken tub and separate shower. The other two bedrooms share the hall bathroom. A daylight basement version of the plan further expands the family living and recreation areas of this home.

Main floor:	1,389 sq. ft.
Upper floor:	900 sq. ft.
Total living area:	2,289 sq. ft.
(Not counting basement or garage)	
Basement level:	1,389 sq. ft.

46'6"

47'6"

FAMILY RM.
17/0X12/6

WOODSTOVE

NOOK
10/0X12/6

KITCHEN
12/4X 14/0

D
W

PANT.

UTILITY

BEDRM.4
/DEN
10/6X11/0

SH

STOR.

BATH

DESK

UP

VAULTED
DINING
10/2X10/6

GARAGE
22/4X20/8

ENTRY

F

WH

VAULTED
LIVING RM.
16/10X13/0

MAIN FLOOR

PLAN P-7627-4A
WITHOUT BASEMENT

DESK

SH

BATH

DN

UP

ENTRY

LIVING RM.

PLAN P-7627-4D
WITH DAYLIGHT BASEMENT

MASTER
15/2X12/6

SUNKEN
TUB

SH

DRESSING

SKYLIGHT

BATH

LIN

DN

SKYLIGHT

TUB

L

BEDRM. 2
10/0X11/3

BEDRM. 3
10/0X13/4

UPPER FLOOR

TO ORDER THIS BLUEPRINT,
CALL TOLL-FREE 1-800-547-5570

216 (prices and details on pp. 12-15.)

Blueprint Price Code C

Plans P-7627-4A & -4D

Solar Features Add to Striking Design

The passive sun room in this plan has a full window wall and glass roof oriented to the south for gathering the sun's energy, and a plank hardwood floor and large stone fireplace which store the heat for later release.

Because this area also is the living room, the windows should be equipped with moveable screens to make the room comfortable when the sun needs muting.

The master bedroom suite, in an upper-level loft of 757 sq. ft., also is warmed by a window wall aligned with the glass roof. An adjoining bath, closets and skylighted den make this a complete adult retreat, with a balcony overlooking the living room.

The main floor is zoned carefully for easy traffic flow, with family living areas and the kitchen off to the right of the entry and the bedroom wing on the left. Stairs to the loft and the basement are located at the center of the home.

Exterior walls feature 2x6 construction.

MAIN FLOOR
PLAN H-3721-1
WITH BASEMENT

PLAN H-3721-1A
WITHOUT BASEMENT
(CRAWLSPACE FOUNDATION)

First floor: 1,888 sq. ft.
Second floor: 757 sq. ft.

Total living area: 2,645 sq. ft.
(Not counting basement or garage)

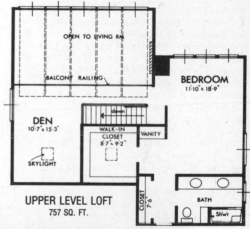

UPPER LEVEL LOFT
757 SQ. FT.

Blueprint Price Code D

Plans H-3721-1 & -1A

Gracious Living on a Grand Scale

Well suited to either a gently sloping or flat building site, this home is also geared to a conservative building budget. First, it saves money through the partial enclosure of the lower level with foundation walls. A portion of the lower level that is surrounded by concrete walls is devoted to a 15'-10" x 13'-0" bedroom or optional den with wardrobe closet, a spacious recreation room with fireplace, and a third complete bathroom along with an abundance of storage space.

The balance of the area at this level is devoted to a two-car garage. Access from this portion of the home to the floor directly above is via a central staircase.

In Plan H-2082-2, a formal dining room and large kitchen provide two places for family eating.

Plan H-2082-1 includes a combination family room and U-shaped kitchen in one open area. Spatial continuity is further extended into the cantilevered deck that projects over the garage driveway below and is accessible through sliding glass doors off the family room.

This system of multi-level planning offers economy in building where grading would otherwise be required.

PLAN H-2082-2
MAIN FLOOR
1500 SQUARE FEET

PLAN H-2082-1
MAIN FLOOR
1500 SQUARE FEET

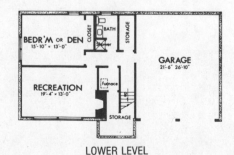

LOWER LEVEL
923 SQUARE FEET

Main floor:	1,500 sq. ft.
Lower level:	923 sq. ft.
Total living area: (Not counting garage)	2,423 sq. ft.

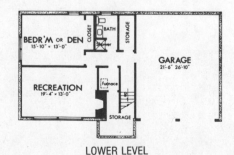

TO ORDER THIS BLUEPRINT, CALL TOLL-FREE 1-800-547-5570

Blueprint Price Code C
Plans H-2082-1 & -2

Sun Room Adds Warmth

At first glance this seems like just another very nice home, with crisp contemporary lines, a carefully conceived traffic flow and generous bedroom and living areas. What sets this home apart from most other houses is its passive sun room, a 13' x 11'6" solarium that collects, stores and distributes solar energy to warm the home, conserving fossil fuel and cutting energy costs. Adding to the energy efficiency of the design are 2x6 stud walls, allowing use of R-19 insulation batts, R-30 insulation in the ceiling, and an air-tight wood stove in the family room.

The passive sun room has glazing on three walls as it juts out from the home, and has a fully glazed ceiling to capture the maximum solar energy. A masonry tile floor stores the collected heat which is distributed to the family and living rooms through sliding glass doors. The wall adjoining the dining area also is glazed. With hanging plants, the sun room can be a visually stunning greenhouse extension of the vaulted-ceilinged living room. A French door from the sun room and sliding glass doors from the family room open onto a wood deck, for outdoor entertaining and relaxing.

First floor: 2,034 sq. ft.
Sun room: 159 sq. ft.

Total living area: 2,193 sq. ft.
(Not counting basement or garage)

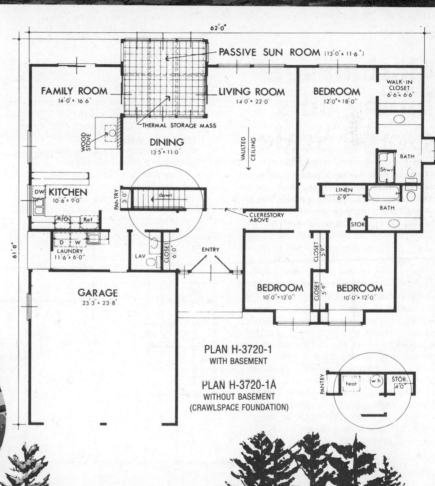

PASSIVE SUN ROOM (13'0" x 11'6")

FAMILY ROOM 14'0" x 16'6"

LIVING ROOM 14'0" x 22'0"

BEDROOM 12'0" x 18'0"

WALK-IN CLOSET 6'6" x 6'6"

THERMAL STORAGE MASS

WOOD STOVE

DINING 13'5" x 11'0"

VAULTED CEILING

BATH

Shwr

LINEN 6'9"

BATH

KITCHEN 10'6" x 9'0"

PANTRY 3'0"

down

STOR

CLERESTORY ABOVE

R/O

Ref

CLOSET 6'0"

ENTRY

CLOSET 5'9"

BEDROOM 10'0" x 12'0"

D   W

LAUNDRY 11'6" x 6'0"

LAV

CLOSET 5'9"

BEDROOM 10'0" x 12'0"

GARAGE 23'3" x 23'8"

62'0"

61'0"

PLAN H-3720-1
WITH BASEMENT

PLAN H-3720-1A
WITHOUT BASEMENT
(CRAWLSPACE FOUNDATION)

PANTRY   heat   w h   STOR. 4'0"

PLAN H-2107-1B

Solarium for Sloping Lots

PLAN H-2107-1

This plan is available in two versions. Plan H-2107-1B, shown above, is most suitable for a lot sloping upward from front to rear, providing a daylight front for the lower floor. The other version, Plan H-2107-1 (at right), is more suitable for a lot that slopes from side to side.

Either way, this moderately sized home has a number of interesting and imaginative features. Of these, the passive sun room will provoke the most comment. Spanning two floors between recreation and living rooms, this glass-enclosed space serves the practical purpose of collecting, storing and redistributing the sun's natural heat, while acting as a conservatory for exotic plants, an exercise room, or any number of other uses. A link between the formal atmosphere of the living room and the carefree activities of the recreation area is created by this two-story solarium by way of an open balcony railing. Living, dining, and entry blend together in one huge space made to seem even larger by the vaulted ceiling spanning the entire complex of rooms.

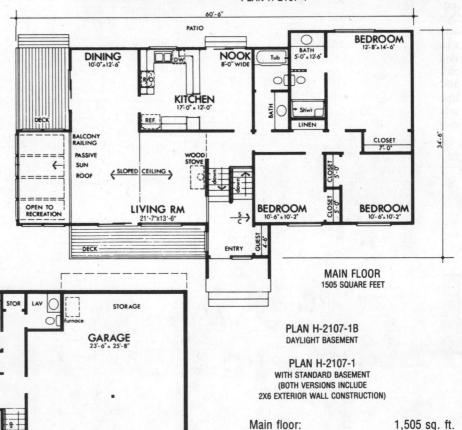

MAIN FLOOR
1505 SQUARE FEET

PLAN H-2107-1B
DAYLIGHT BASEMENT

PLAN H-2107-1
WITH STANDARD BASEMENT
(BOTH VERSIONS INCLUDE
2X6 EXTERIOR WALL CONSTRUCTION)

Main floor:	1,505 sq. ft.
Lower level:	779 sq. ft.
Total living area: (Not counting garage)	2,284 sq. ft.

LOWER LEVEL
779 SQUARE FEET

TO ORDER THIS BLUEPRINT,
CALL TOLL-FREE 1-800-547-5570

220 (prices and details on pp. 12-15.)

Blueprint Price Code C

Plans H-2107-1 & H-2107-1B

Dramatic Western Contemporary

- Dramatic and functional building features contribute to the comfort and desire of this family home.
- Master suite offers a spacious private bath and luxurious hydro spa.
- Open, efficient kitchen accommodates modern appliances, a large pantry, and a snack bar.
- Skylights shed light on the entryway, open staircase, and balcony.
- Upper level balcony area has private covered deck, and may be used as a guest room or den.

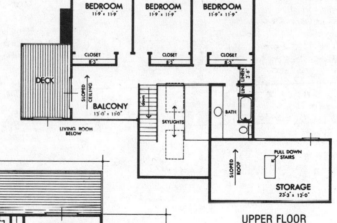

UPPER FLOOR

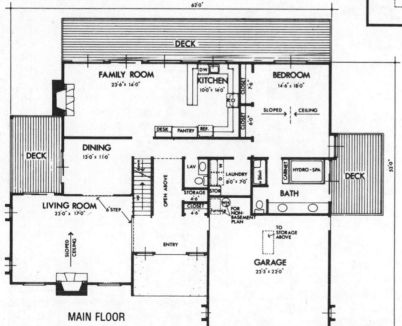

MAIN FLOOR

Plans H-3708-1 & -1A

Bedrooms: 4	Baths: 2½
Space:	
Upper floor:	893 sq. ft.
Main floor:	2,006 sq. ft.
Total living area:	**2,899 sq. ft.**
Basement:	approx. 2,006 sq. ft.
Garage:	512 sq. ft.
Exterior Wall Framing:	2x6

Foundation options:
Daylight basement (Plan H-3708-1).
Crawlspace (Plan H-3708-1A).
(Foundation & framing conversion diagram available — see order form.)

Blueprint Price Code:	D

Plans H-3708-1 & -1A

TO ORDER THIS BLUEPRINT, CALL TOLL-FREE 1-800-547-5570
(prices and details on pp. 12-15.) **221**

PLAN H-2114-1B REAR VIEW

Designed for Outdoor Living

- Dining room, living room, and spa are oriented toward the full-width deck extending across the rear of the home.
- Floor-to-ceiling windows, vaulted ceilings, and a fireplace are featured in the living room.
- Spa room has tile floor, operable skylights, and private access through connecting master suite.
- Upper level offers two bedrooms, spacious bathroom, and a balcony view of the living room and scenery beyond.

MAIN FLOOR

70'-2"

DECK

LIVING ROOM
23/0 x 13/10

DINING
14/0 x 14/0

SPA ROOM
13/6 x 10/0

SPA

SKYLIGHTS ABOVE

up / down

PANTRY

STORAGE

BATH

KITCHEN
11/0 x 11/0

NOOK
12/0 x 11/0

ENTRY

GUEST

LAV

Shr

LINEN

REF

WALK-IN CLOSET
8/0 x 7/6

GARAGE
23/4 x 21/4

BEDROOM
13/6 x 20/6

SEAT

STORAGE

LAUNDRY ROOM FOR PLAN W/O BSMT.

W   D

PLAN H-2114-1A
WITHOUT BASEMENT

PLAN H-2114-1B
WITH DAYLIGHT BASEMENT

RECREATION ROOM
23/0 x 12/0

BEDROOM
13/0 x 11/6

STORAGE
13/0 x 9/6

furnace

up

CLOSET
4/6

CLOSET
4/6

STORAGE

LINEN

BENCH

LAUNDRY

BATH

W

Shr

SAUNA

BENCH

GAME ROOM
13/0 x 20/0

UPPER FLOOR

OPEN TO LIVING ROOM

CLOSET
6/6

CLOSET
6/6

RAIL

down

BATH

LINEN

STOR

tub w/

CLOSET
8/0

BEDROOM
13/6 x 16/0

BEDROOM
12/0 x 11/0

Plans H-2114-1A & -1B

Bedrooms: 3-4	Baths: 2½-3½
Space:	
Upper floor:	732 sq. ft.
Main floor:	1,682 sq. ft.
Spa room:	147 sq. ft.
Total living area:	**2,561 sq. ft.**
Basement:	approx. 1,386 sq. ft.
Garage:	547 sq. ft.
Exterior Wall Framing:	**2x6**

Foundation options:
Daylight basement (Plan H-2114-1B).
Crawlspace (Plan H-2114-1A).
(Foundation & framing conversion diagram available — see order form.)

Blueprint Price Code:

Without basement:	D
With basement:	F

Plans H-2114-1A & -1B

Dramatic Contemporary Takes Advantage of Slope

- Popular plan puts problem building site to work by taking advantage of the slope to create a dramatic and pleasant home.
- Spacious vaulted living/dining area is bathed in natural light from cathedral windows facing the front and clerestory windows at the peak.
- Big kitchen includes pantry and abundant counter space.
- Three main-level bedrooms are isolated for more peace and quiet.
- Lower level includes large recreation room, a fourth bedroom, third bath, laundry area and extra space for a multitude of other uses.

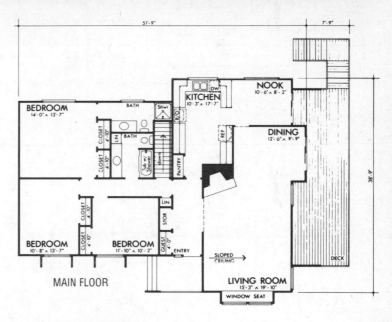

Photo by Kevin Robinson

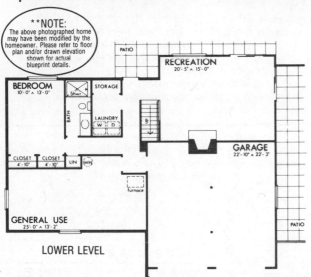

Plan H-2045-5

Bedrooms: 4	Baths: 3
Space:	
Main floor:	1,602 sq. ft.
Lower floor:	1,133 sq. ft.
Total living area:	2,735 sq. ft.
Garage:	508 sq. ft.
Exterior Wall Framing:	2x4

Foundation options:
Daylight basement only.
(Foundation & framing conversion diagram available — see order form.)

Blueprint Price Code:	D

Plans H-2045-5

TO ORDER THIS BLUEPRINT,
CALL TOLL-FREE 1-800-547-5570
(prices and details on pp. 12-15.)

Photo by Kevin Haslip

Convenience and Luxury

- Large roof planes and a modest exterior enclose a thoroughly modern, open floor plan.
- Entry hall, living/dining area and family room all have vaulted ceilings.
- Living room has floor-to-ceiling windows, fireplace and wall-length stone hearth.

- A sun room next to the spacious, angular kitchen offers passive solar heating and a bright look to the area.
- Main floor master suite includes a raised tub and separate shower, plus a large walk-in wardrobe.
- Upstairs, a bridge hallway overlooks the rooms below.
- The daylight basement version includes another 2,025 square feet of versatile space.

**NOTE:
The above photographed home may have been modified by the homeowner. Please refer to floor plan and/or drawn elevation shown for actual blueprint details.

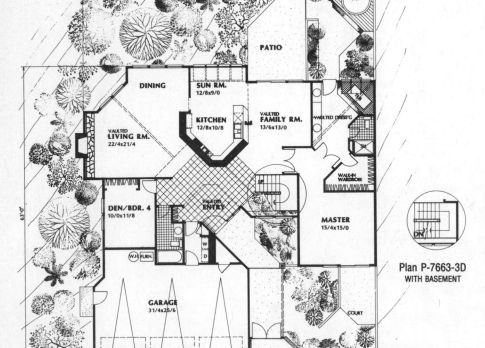

BEDRM. 2
11/6x11/6

OPEN TO BELOW

OPEN TO BELOW

BEDRM. 3
10/0x11/8

OPEN TO BELOW

DOWN

RAIL

UPPER FLOOR

60'-0"

63'-0"

PATIO

SPA

DINING

SUN RM.
12/8x9/0

VAULTED
LIVING RM.
22/4x21/4

KITCHEN
12/8x10/8

VAULTED
FAMILY RM.
13/6x13/0

VAULTED DRESS'G

WALK-IN
WARDROBE

DEN/BDR. 4
10/0x11/8

VAULTED
ENTRY

MASTER
15/4x15/0

W.H. FURN.

W
D

GARAGE
31/4x25/6

COURT

Plan P-7663-3D
WITH BASEMENT

DN

Plan P-7663-3A
WITHOUT BASEMENT
(CRAWLSPACE FOUNDATION)

MAIN FLOOR

Plans P-7663-3A & -3D

Bedrooms: 3-4	**Baths:** 3

Space:

Upper floor:	470 sq. ft.
Main floor:	2,025 sq. ft.
Total living area:	**2,495 sq. ft.**
Basement:	2,025 sq. ft.
Garage:	799 sq. ft.

Exterior Wall Framing:	2x4

Foundation options:
Daylight basement (Plan P-7663-3D).
Crawlspace (Plan P-7663-3A).
(Foundation & framing conversion diagram available — see order form.)

Blueprint Price Code:	C

TO ORDER THIS BLUEPRINT,
CALL TOLL-FREE 1-800-547-5570

Plans P-7663-3A & -3D